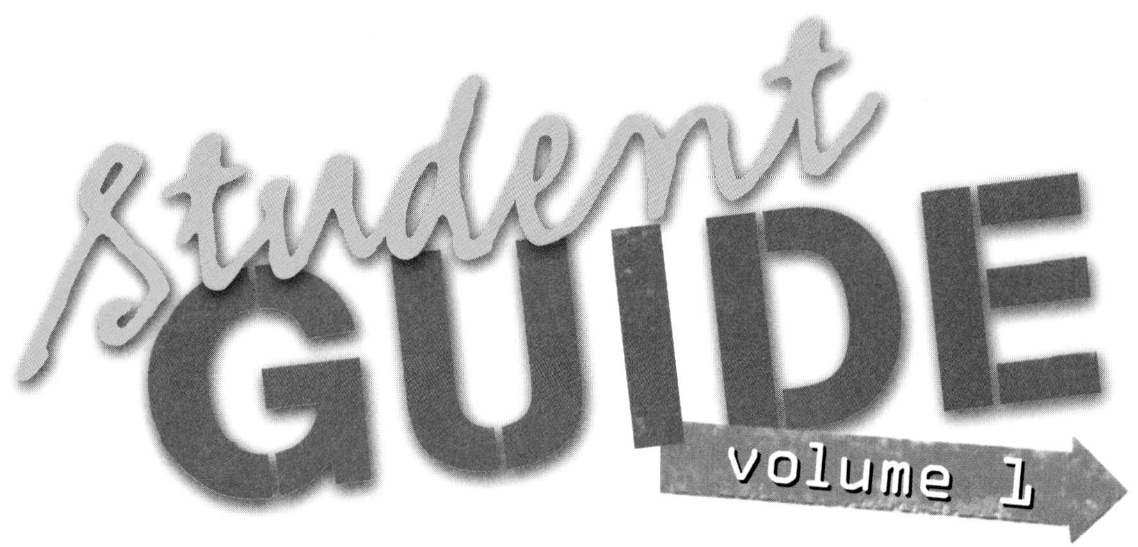


**Program Consultant**

**William F. Tate**

Edward Mallinckrodt Distinguished University Professor
Washington University, St. Louis

Image credits can be found on page 262.



ISBN-13: 978-0-7854-6619-2
ISBN-10: 0-7854-6619-3
2 3 4 5 6 7 8 9 10 12 11 10 09

1-800-992-0244
www.pearson.com

# CONTENTS

## UNIT 1

### Tools for Solving Math Problems



## UNIT 2

### Proportionality

# UNIT 3

## Rational Numbers and Linear Equations



# UNIT 4

## Systems of Linear Equations

# UNIT 1
# Tools for Solving Math Problems

## MATH STRATEGIES

Learn **PROBLEM-SOLVING STRATEGIES** and how to apply them to solve real-world problems.

The Four-Step Problem-Solving Plan

1. Read
2. Plan
3. Solve
4. Check

## VOCABULARY

PROBLEM-SOLVING WORDS:
Know them!
Use them!
Learn all about them!

# The Four-Step Problem-Solving Plan

| Step 1: Read | Step 2: Plan | Step 3: Solve | Step 4: Check |
|---|---|---|---|
| Make sure you understand what the problem is asking. | Decide how you will solve the problem. | Solve the problem using your plan. | Check to make sure your answer is correct. |

When you are given a problem to solve, having a plan makes the task easier.
The Four-Step Problem-Solving Plan is a useful tool to help you solve math problems.

## Step 1: Read

It is very important to read the problem carefully. Try to answer the following questions once you have read the problem.

- What do you know about the problem?
- What is the question in the problem?
- What facts are given in the problem?

If you do not understand some of the words in the problem, you can look them up in a dictionary or the glossary of your textbook.

Read the problem below. Restate the problem in your own words on the lines below. Underline the question and circle any facts that could help you answer it.

1. Emily earns $5.50 per hour babysitting. The table shows her summer babysitting schedule. How much does Emily earn each week she babysits?

______________________________

______________________________

| Emily's Schedule | |
|---|---|
| Monday | 10 AM – 3 PM |
| Tuesday | 2 PM – 7 PM |
| Wednesday | 10 AM – 1 PM |
| Thursday | 2 PM – 8 PM |
| Friday | 10 AM – 5 PM |

## Step 2: Plan

Once you know what the problem is asking, you need to plan how to solve it. Ask:

- Have you solved a similar problem before?
- What problem-solving strategies can you use?

Problem-solving strategies are ways you can set up and solve a problem. In this example, you might want to look for clue words that can tell you what operation to use.

2. Write a plan for solving the problem on the lines below. Explain the steps you will take to get your answer.

______________________________

______________________________

______________________________

______________________________

## Step 3: Solve

To solve the problem, follow the plan you made in Step 2. As you solve, ask:

- Are you following each step of your plan?
- Do you need to change your plan?
- Do you need to try another problem-solving strategy?

It is okay to change your plan if it does not solve the problem.

Make sure to keep a record of everything you did as you solved the problem. This is also known as showing your work. It can help you identify what you did wrong and what you did right as you move on to the next step.

**3.** Show your work in the space below. Circle your final answer.

## Step 4: Check

After you have solved the problem, check your answer. Think about the following questions while you check your answer.

- Have you answered the right question?
- Did you make any mistakes as you followed the steps of your plan?
- Does your answer make sense? Is it reasonable?
- Can you solve it another way and get the same answer?

Reviewing your work once you have finished can help catch any simple mistakes you may have made.

**4.** As you check your answer, write your thoughts on the lines below. Also write down any questions you may have about the Four-Step Problem-Solving Plan. Discuss these questions with a classmate or your teacher.

________________________________________

________________________________________

Use the Four-Step Problem-Solving Plan to solve the problem below. Follow the steps in this lesson. Write your plan on a separate sheet of paper. Write your answer below.

**5.** At the school carnival, students won play money called "Carnival Cash" to spend on prizes. Colleen carried an egg on a spoon for 12 yards. The sign shows how much Carnival Cash someone could win carrying the egg. How much Carnival Cash did Colleen win?

________________________________________

________________________________________

________________________________________

Win Carnival Cash
$2.00 for every foot over 25 feet

# Draw a Picture or Use a Model

A **strategy** is a plan or a way of doing something. Problem-solving strategies help you organize the information you need to solve a problem. A useful strategy is **Draw a Picture or Use a Model.**

Drawing a picture can help you better understand the problem. For example, drawing out the following problem can help you "see" all the games.

## VOCABULARY

**expression:** a mathematical statement including numbers and symbols

**physical model:** a real-life representation of an object

**strategy:** a plan or way of doing something

**Read:** Joseph and Wes went to Kelso's house to play computer games. Altogether they played seven football games and 12 basketball games. How many games did they play?

*What do you know?* They played 7 football games and 12 basketball games.

*What do you need to find out?* How many total games did they play?

**Plan:** Draw a picture to show the games. Count the games.

**Solve:** There are 19 games.

**Check:** $7 + 12 = 19$

This drawing also shows the **expression** $7 + 12$.

1. **Read:** Pat had a Web page with 12 photographs of her dog. Then she posted 6 more dog photos. How many dog photos are on Pat's Web page now? Use the Draw a Picture strategy to solve this problem.

*What do you know?* ______________________________

______________________________

*What do you need to find out?* ______________________________

**Plan:** ______________________________

**Solve:** ______________________________

**Check:** ______________________________

The Use a Model strategy can either refer to a **physical model** or a model on paper. One example of a physical model is base ten blocks. Base ten blocks come in single blocks, rods of 10, and flats of 100.

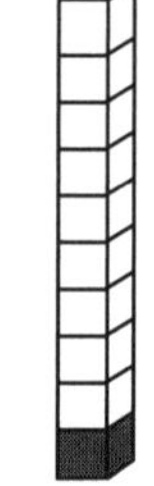

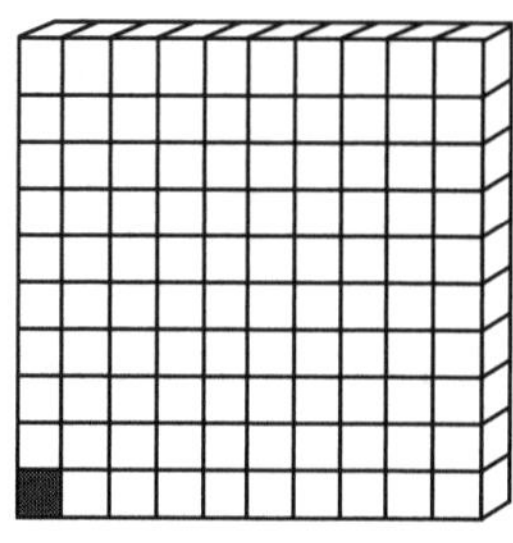

1 single block    one rod of 10 blocks    one flat of 100 blocks

**2. Read:** Junji had 400 songs on his MP3 player. He deleted 215 songs. How many songs were still on the player? Use a physical model to help solve this problem.

*What do you know?* ______________________________

*What do you need to find out?* ______________________________

**Plan:** ______________________________

______________________________

**Solve:** ______________________________

**Check:** ______________________________

**3.** When is it useful to use the Draw a Picture or Use a Model strategy?

______________________________

______________________________

______________________________

**4.** Is there anything you do not understand when using this strategy?

______________________________

______________________________

______________________________

# Find a Pattern

### VOCABULARY

**pattern:** objects, designs, or numbers that change in a specific way

**rule:** a description of the way a pattern works

**Patterns** are objects, designs, or numbers that repeat or change in a certain way. The **Find a Pattern** strategy can help you solve problems where the answer can be found by filling in the pattern.

You need to look at the pattern carefully and decide how it was created. This is the **rule** of the pattern, which describes how the pattern works. With numbers, the rule might be "subtract 3" or "divide by 2." With shapes, the rule might describe a repeating pattern of shapes, such as "triangle, square, then circle." To understand the pattern, you must find the rule.

**Read:** Fill in the missing number in the pattern below.

0.496, 0.796, ________, 1.396, 1.696

*What do you know?* There are four numbers given in a pattern: 0.496, 0.796, 1.396, and 1.696.

*What do you need to find out?* Find the missing number in the pattern.

**Plan:** I should look for a pattern by seeing how the numbers change. I can use this pattern to fill in the missing number.

**Solve:** $0.796 - 0.496 = 0.300$, so the numbers increase by 0.300.
The missing number is $0.796 + 0.300 = 1.096$.

**Check:** 1.096 is 0.300 more than 0.796. 1.396 is 0.300 more than 1.096, so the number fits the pattern.

**1. Read:** Fill in the missing number in the pattern below. Explain what the pattern is.

0.012, 0.032, ________, 0.072, 0.092

*What do you know?* ____________________

*What do you need to find out?* ____________________

**Plan:** ____________________

____________________

**Solve:** ____________________

____________________

**Check:** ____________________

Patterns can also be found in pictures or a series of shapes. For example, the shapes can repeat in a certain order or change the number of sides. You must look carefully to find how the shapes repeat or change.

**2.** What are the next three times the dot will be in the same position as it is in the first shape?

________________

________________

________________

________________

**3.** What are the next three times the dot will be in the same position as it is in the fourth shape?

________________

________________

**4.** Find the number of triangles that will be in the fourth figure if the pattern continues. Draw the fourth figure in the pattern.

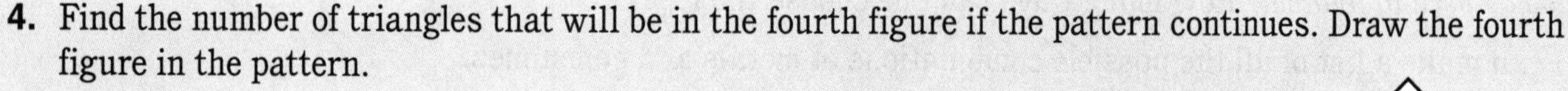

Number of triangles: ________

**5.** Draw a pattern using numbers or shapes. One number or shape should be missing. Then exchange your pattern with a partner who will find and complete the pattern.

# Make a List

When reading, lists are an excellent tool to help you understand the text. In math, the **Make a List** strategy helps you see information in an organized way. For example, lists help you keep track of the possible **combinations** of items. Lists can also help you keep track of possible outcomes. See the example below for one way to use a list.

## VOCABULARY

**combination:** a group of objects in which order does not matter

**tree diagram:** a diagram that shows possible combinations branching off each other

**Read:** Lee's grandpa is giving her a ring for her birthday. Lee can choose the metal and gemstone for her ring. The table shows the metals and stones she can choose. How many different ways can she chose the ring?

*What do you know?* Lee has three metals and five gemstones to choose from.

*What do you need to find out?* How many ways can she choose the ring?

**Plan:** I can make a list of all the possible combinations of metals and gemstones.

**Solve:** Possible combinations:

1. silver, aquamarine
2. silver, opal
3. silver, lapis
4. silver, topaz
5. silver, agate
6. gold, aquamarine
7. gold, opal
8. gold, lapis
9. gold, topaz
10. gold, agate
11. platinum, aquamarine
12. platinum, opal
13. platinum, lapis
14. platinum, topaz
15. platinum, agate

| Metal | Gemstone |
|---|---|
| silver | aquamarine |
| gold | opal |
| platinum | lapis |
| | topaz |
| | agate |

Lee can make a ring 15 different ways.

**Check:** Make sure each gemstone is matched with each kind of metal.

1. **Read:** Mikal has a choice of three toppings to put on his pizza: mushrooms, onions, and green peppers. He can choose thin or deep-dish crust. How many different combinations can he have if he chooses one topping?

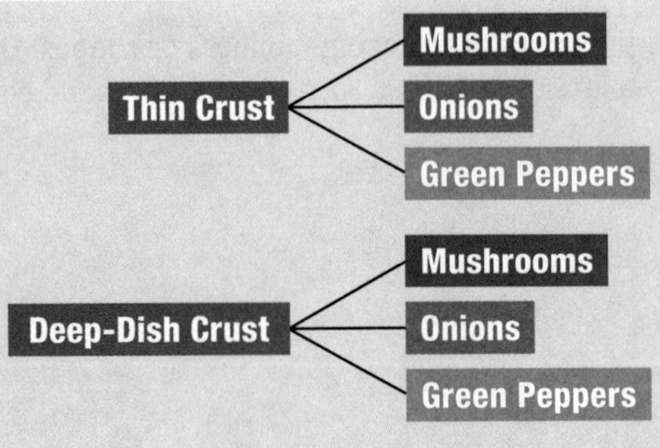


One way to help create a list is to make a **tree diagram.** This diagram shows possible combinations "branching off" like a tree. Here is a tree diagram for this problem.

*What do I know?* ______________________

______________________

*What do you need to find out?* ______________________

**Plan:** ______________________

______________________

**Solve:** ______________________

**Check:** ______________________

**2.** Katie has a red sweatshirt, a blue sweatshirt, a green sweatshirt, and a yellow sweatshirt. She also has a pair of khakis and a pair of jeans. How many outfits can she make?

*What do you know?* ________________

*What do you need to find out?* ________________

**Plan:** ________________

**Solve:** ________________

________________

**Check:** ________________

**3.** Morgan wants to mix two colors of paint to make a new color. He can choose from white, red, blue, and yellow paint. How many different combinations of colors can he choose? Show your work.

White Red Blue Yellow

________________

________________

**4.** Kyra, Sean, Janine, Danni, and Chris are finalists in a drawing for a trip to a carnival. Two of them will be selected to go. How many different pairs could be selected to go to the carnival? Show your work.

________________

________________

**5.** When would you use the Make a List strategy to solve a problem?

________________

________________

________________

**6.** Write a word problem that you must make a list to solve. Then let a partner solve it.

________________

________________

________________

# Graphic Organizers

Graphic organizers are used to arrange information in a way that makes it easy to understand. You can use a graphic organizer to display information from an article or a word problem.

## VOCABULARY

**concept map:** a graphic organizer showing a main topic and related ideas

**flowchart:** a diagram that can be used to show the steps in a process

**three-column chart:** a chart that can be used to take notes or organize ideas

**Venn diagram:** overlapping circles used to compare and contrast ideas

A **Venn diagram** is used to compare and contrast items or ideas. Draw two circles that partly overlap. These circles represent what you want to compare. List the characteristics of one in the left circle. List the characteristics of the other in the right circle. List the characteristics they share in the area where the circles overlap.

**Addition**
combining numbers to find their sum

**Both**
mathematical operations

**Subtraction**
finding the difference between two numbers

Use a **concept map** when recording supporting details of a main topic. The topic is written in a center box or circle. The supporting details are written in circles or boxes connected to the topic.

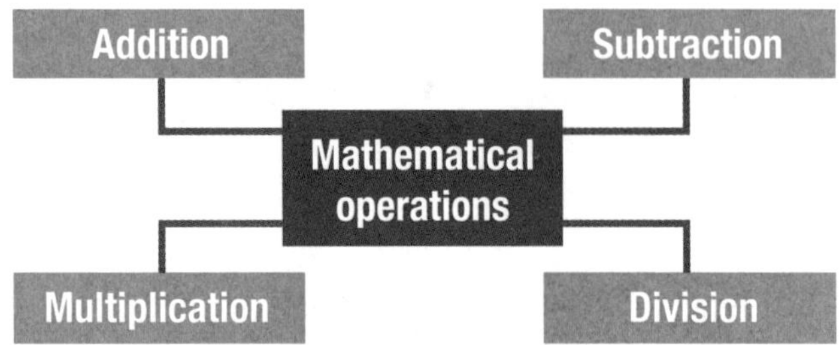


For sequencing, writing steps, or creating a timeline, the **flowchart** is an excellent organizer. The arrows show how the boxes "flow" from one to the next.

| | |
|---|---|
| Step 1: Read | Make sure you understand what the problem is asking. |
| Step 2: Plan | Decide how you will solve the problem. |
| Step 3: Solve | Solve the problem using your plan. |
| Step 4: Check | Check to make sure your answer is correct. |

A **three-column chart** is a good way to organize your thoughts about a new topic. In the first column, list what you know about the topic. In the second column, list the things you want to know about the topic. In the third column, list what you learned from the reading.

| What I know | What I want to know | What I learned |
|---|---|---|
| | | |

**Use graphic organizers to answer the following questions.**

1. On a separate sheet of paper, write the first ten multiples of eight and nine. Then show these multiples in a Venn diagram.

   ______________________________

2. Find a short article that interests you in a magazine or newspaper. On a separate sheet of paper, draw a three-column chart similar to the one shown on page 10. In the first column of the chart, list what you know about the topic of the article. In the second column, list what you want to know about the topic. Then read the article and list what you learned in the third column.

   ______________________________

   ______________________________

   ______________________________

   ______________________________

3. On a sheet of paper, draw a concept map of the article you read for question 2. The concept map should show the main topic and supporting details.

4. The steps below describe the Make a List strategy. Number the steps in order from one to four. Then, on a separate sheet of paper, draw a flowchart of these steps.

   ________ Identify the items to be counted.

   ________ Read the problem.

   ________ Repeat the steps until all the combinations are found. Make sure you do not repeat combinations.

   ________ Choose one item and list all the combinations using that item.

# Try a Simpler Form of the Problem

What you already know about a topic can help you understand what you read. Math is like that, too. Often in problem solving you are asked a difficult question. It becomes easier to answer when you think about what you already know about part of it. You can solve a simpler part of the problem and use that answer to help you solve the rest.

**Read:** A factory makes computers. One out of every 200 computers comes with free game software. If the factory makes 6,000 computers in a day, how many will come with the free software?

*What do you know?* One out of every 200 computers comes with free game software. Every day, the factory makes 6,000 computers.

*What do you need to find out?* How many of the 6,000 computers come with free game software?

**Plan:** I can solve a simpler form of the problem by finding how many computers out of 1,000 have free game software. Then I can multiply the number by 6 to find how many computers out of 6,000 are shipped with free game software.

**Solve:** There are five groups of 200 in 1,000, so there are five computers with free game software out of every 1,000. Out of 6,000, there are $5 \times 6 = 30$ computers with free game software.

**Check:** $30 \div 6 = 5$

**1. Read:** Mindy's store sells sandwiches. About 20 out of every 50 sandwiches are turkey sandwiches. If Mindy's store sells 400 sandwiches a week, about how many are turkey sandwiches?

*What do you know?* ______________________________

______________________________

*What do you need to find out?* ______________________________

**Plan:** ______________________________

______________________________

______________________________

**Solve:** ______________________________

______________________________

**Check:** ______________________________

**2.** A doctor has a list of 209 patients. He sees four patients every hour. If he works eight hours every day for five days, can he see all 209 patients?

**3.** Asha's Cafe has 20 square tables. The side of each table measures 2.7 feet. What is the combined length of all the sides of all the tables? Remember that a square has four sides of equal length.

**4.** The lockers at a public swimming pool are numbered from 1 to 300. On how many lockers does the digit "8" appear at least once? Explain your answer.

**5.** When would you use the Try a Simpler Form of the Problem strategy?

# Make a Table or a Chart

A chart is a way of organizing and displaying information. Different types of charts include flow charts, graphs, and tables.

A table is made up of information such as words and numbers organized into rows and columns. Rows run across a table and columns run up and down. The heading or label of each column helps explain how the information is organized. The title explains what information is in the table.

**Title** Students Enrolled in Crestview Middle School Athletic Programs

**Columns**

**Rows**

| School Year | 2004–2005 | 2005–2006 | 2006–2007 | 2007–2008 | 2008–2009 |
|---|---|---|---|---|---|
| Number of Students | 139 | 139 + 18 = 157 | 157 + 18 = 175 | 175 + 18 = 193 | 193 + 18 = 211 |

In this table, the number of students enrolled in athletic programs at Crestview High School increases by 18 students each year. You can make the table larger to continue the pattern.

**Read:** Each year, the number of students enrolling in athletic programs at Crestview High School increases by 18 students. If this pattern continues, how many students will be enrolled in athletic programs by 2012?

*What do you know?* The number of students enrolled in athletic programs increases by 18 students a year.

*What do you need to find out?* How many students will be enrolled in athletic programs in 2012?

**Plan:** I can make a table to display the number of students enrolled in athletics from 2009 to 2012.

**Solve:** Total students enrolled after each school year:

| School Year | 2009–2010 | 2010–2011 | 2011–2012 |
|---|---|---|---|
| Number of Students | 211 + 18 = 229 | 229 + 18 = 247 | 247 + 18 = 265 |

There will be 265 students enrolled in 2012.

**Check:** 265 − 18 = 247, 247 − 18 = 229, 229 − 18 = 211

1. Lorraine read about 150 words per minute in her first half-hour of reading. She read about 200 words per minute during the second, third, and fourth half-hours of reading. Make a table or a chart in the space below to display the total number of words read after each passing half-hour.

2. Tina likes to do gymnastics. If she does 5 cartwheels every 5 minutes, how many cartwheels can she do in 25 minutes? In the space below, make a table or a chart to find the answer.

3. Michael worked over the summer to make money. He mowed 13 lawns, washed 4 cars, and walked dogs 7 times. He earned $20 for each lawn he mowed, $15 for each car he washed, and $7 for each dog he walked. How much money did he earn in all? In the space below, make a table or a chart to find the answer.

Tables can also be used to display the information you collect in a survey. Use what you have learned about tables to solve the problem below.

4. Take a survey. Ask at least 10 of your friends what their favorite season is: summer, spring, winter, or fall. Then show the results of your survey in a table or a chart on a separate sheet of paper. Make sure your table has a title, and label the columns and rows correctly.

5. When is the Make a Table or a Chart strategy useful?

______________________________________________

______________________________________________

______________________________________________

# Guess, Check, and Revise

**VOCABULARY**

**perimeter:** the distance around the outside of a shape

When you guess what might happen next in a story, you are predicting. If your prediction is incorrect, you can change it and try a new one until you find one that works. The **Guess, Check, and Revise** problem-solving strategy works the same way. You guess a possible answer. Then you try it to see if it is the correct choice. If it is not the correct choice, you can change it and try again.

**Read:** Jerry goes to a store with the money he earned over the summer. He sees the items listed in the table. He buys three items for exactly \$162 before tax. What three items did he buy?

| Item | Cost |
|---|---|
| Encyclopedia Set | \$45 |
| Jeans | \$28 |
| Book | \$12 |
| Shirt | \$22 |
| MP3 Player | \$89 |

*What do you know?* Jerry spent \$162 on three items.

*What do you need to find out?* What three items did he buy?

**Plan:** I can guess and check. If my guess is incorrect, I can guess again.

**Solve:** I guess that Jerry buys the encyclopedia set, jeans, and MP3 player: $\$45 + \$28 + \$89 = \$162$.

**Check:** $\$162 - \$45 - \$28 - \$89 = \$0$

1. **Read:** Julian and Anya spent exactly \$14 on snacks at the movies. What snacks did they buy?

| Movie Snacks | Price |
|---|---|
| Popcorn | \$6 |
| Pretzel | \$3 |
| Nachos | \$5 |
| Drink | \$4 |

*What do you know?* ____________________

*What do you need to find out?* ____________________

**Plan:** ____________________

**Solve:** ____________________

**Check:** ____________________

**2.** There are two ways to use the digits 7, 6, 5, 4, 3, 2, and 1 and subtraction from 100 to make a difference of zero. Here is one way: 100 – 56 – 34 – 7 – 2 – 1 = 0. Find the other way.

______________________________

______________________________

______________________________

One type of problem that often uses the Guess, Check, and Revise strategy is a **perimeter** problem. Perimeter is the distance around the outside of a shape. The perimeter of a rectangle is the sum of its sides. A rectangle has two sides that are one length and two sides that are another length. A square has four sides that are all the same length.

**3. Read:** The computer room at Nadia's school is shaped like a rectangle. The length is 6 feet longer than the width. The perimeter is 116 feet. What are the length and width of the computer room?

*What do you know?* ______________________________

*What do you need to find out?* ______________________________

**Plan:** ______________________________

**Solve:** ______________________________

______________________________

**Check:** ______________________________

**4.** A large rectangular table has a perimeter of 26 feet. The length is 3 feet longer than the width. What is the width of the table?

______________________________

**5.** What other strategy could you use to answer problems 3 and 4?

______________________________

______________________________

**6.** What is one disadvantage of the Guess, Check, and Revise strategy?

______________________________

______________________________

______________________________

# Graphic Organizers

Math graphic organizers can help you compare information.

## VOCABULARY

**bar graph:** a way of comparing information using rectangular bars

**circle graph:** a graph shaped like a circle that shows a whole broken into parts

**coordinate grid:** a grid showing ordered pairs

**ordered pair:** a pair of numbers that names one point on a coordinate grid

**plot:** to find and mark the point named by an ordered pair

**scale:** numbers that are the units used on a bar graph

A **bar graph** uses rectangular bars to compare information. The length or height of each bar represents an amount. The **scale** on the side of the graph gives an amount for each height or length.

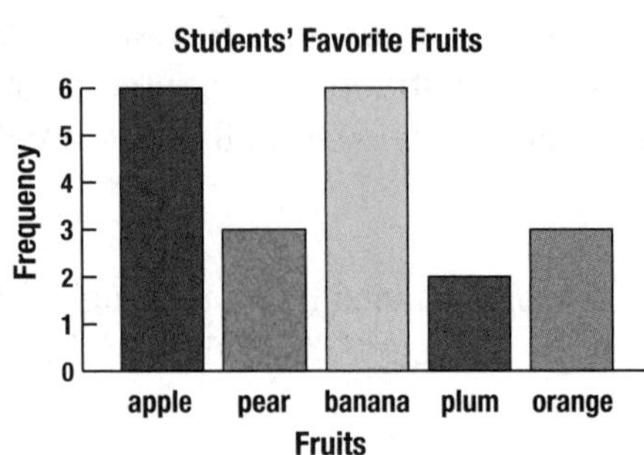


**Circle graphs** are used to show parts of a whole. Each piece in a circle graph is a different part of the whole. Think of a pizza that is cut into eight slices. Each piece is one-eighth of the whole pizza. When pieces of a circle graph are different sizes, they show different amounts.

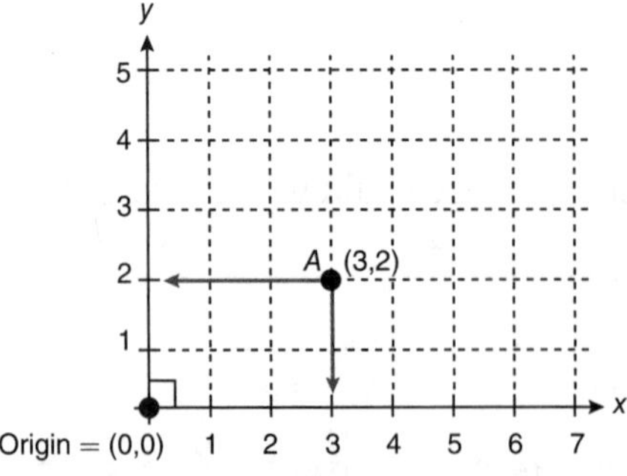

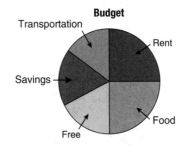


**Coordinate grids** are used to display pairs of numbers called **ordered pairs.** Each ordered pair names one point on the coordinate grid. Marking a point on a coordinate grid is also known as **plotting** the point. The points you plot can represent lines, shapes, or general information.



**Use graphic organizers to organize information and solve the following problems.**

1. Jill made a bar graph of the number of members of different clubs at school. How many more students are in Band than Math Club?

_______________________________________

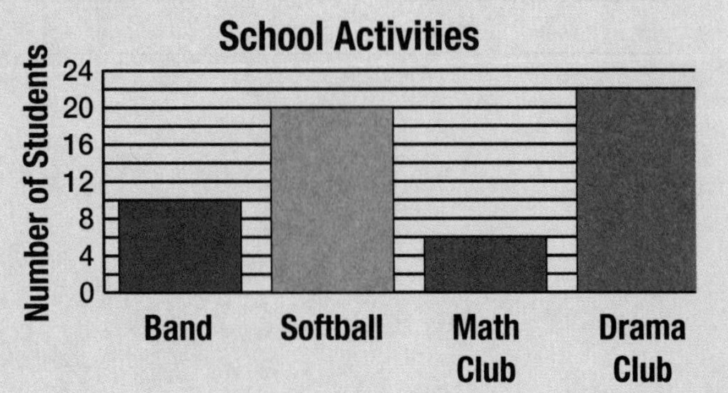

**2.** Fawn surveyed her classmates to find their favorite color. They could choose only one color from purple, blue, or green. She displayed the information in a circle graph. Which color did most students pick?

_______________

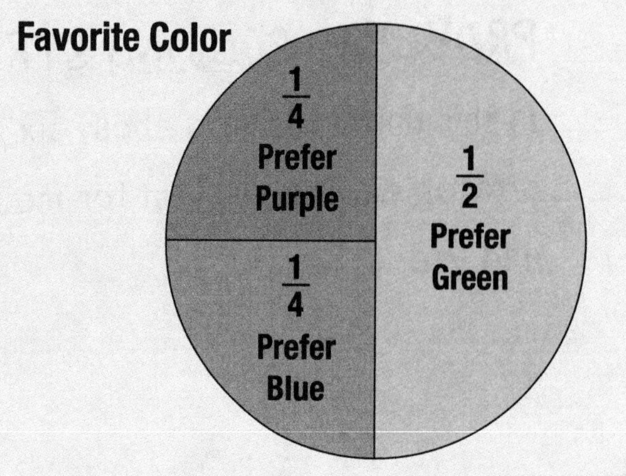


**3.** Look at the coordinate grid. Write the ordered pairs of the points shown.

*A* ________

*B* ________

*C* ________

*D* ________

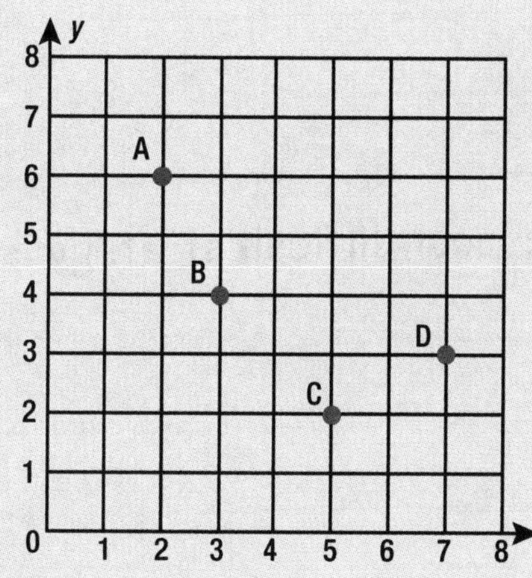


**4.** When you take a survey, which graphic organizer is best to use? Why?

_______________

_______________

_______________

**5.** If you wanted to graph how much money you spent on each ride at a carnival, which organizer should you use? Why?

_______________

_______________

_______________

# Unit 1 Reflection

## Review and Record What You Learned

Unit 1

### PROBLEM-SOLVING STRATEGIES

In this unit, I learned about six problem-solving strategies. The easiest for me to remember and use is

The most difficult strategy is

I do not understand

# UNIT 2
# Proportionality

## MATH SKILLS & STRATEGIES

After you learn the basic **SKILLS**, the real test is knowing when to use each **STRATEGY.**

## READING STRATEGY

Learn the steps to good Summarizing.

## AMP LINK MAGAZINE

**You Do the Math and Math Projects:** After you read each magazine article, apply what you know in real-world problems.

**Fluency:** Make your reading smooth and accurate, one tip at a time.

## VOCABULARY

MATH WORDS:
Know them!
Use them!
Learn all about them!

## CONNECTIONS

You own the math when you make your own connections.

# Reading Comprehension Strategy: Summarizing

## How to Summarize

| Step 1: | Step 2: | Step 3: | Step 4: |
|---|---|---|---|
| Identify the **topic:** Ask, *Who or what is this about?* | Identify the **main idea:** Ask, *What is the main thing the writer is saying about the topic?* | Identify the **important details:** Ask, *What details are needed to understand the main idea?* | Use the main idea and important details to **summarize.** |

## Step 1: Identify the Topic

When you summarize, you identify the most important things in the section you are reading. First, look for the topic. The **topic** is a word or phrase that answers the question, *Who or what is this about?* Good summaries do not include a lot of extra facts. What is the topic of the paragraph below?

**Invaders!**
**Plants and Animals That Don't Belong**

Plants make our world beautiful and improve the air and soil. Animals have their useful and interesting roles on our planet as well. Sometimes, however, some plants and animals end up somewhere they do not belong. These plants and animals are called invasive species. They are species, or kinds of living things, that move from one area to another. They invade a new habitat.

**1.** Who or what is this paragraph about?

________________________________________

________________________________________

________________________________________

________________________________________

## Step 2: Identify the Main Idea

Knowing the topic can help you find the **main idea,** or what the writer wants to tell you about the topic. Any summary should include the author's main idea. Sometimes, the main idea is in the first or second sentence. Sometimes, it is in the last sentence. Sometimes, the main idea is not stated, and you have to figure it out. Find the main idea in the paragraph below.

**Why Are Invasive Species Harmful?**

Species that move into new habitats may not damage them. But if a species has no predators in a habitat—nothing that eats it—then trouble can start. Invasive plants overgrow the native plants that were already in the habitat. They compete for water and sunlight, choking other plants out. Invasive animals may eat up all of a certain kind of plant or animal in the area. If nothing eats the new species, then it will drive out native plants and animals.

**2.** Main idea:

________________________________________

________________________________________

________________________________________

________________________________________

________________________________________

## Step 3: Identify Important Details

Once you have identified the topic and the main idea, look for **important details.** Details explain something or add information about the main idea. When you look for important details, ask yourself, *Does this detail help me understand the main idea? Is it important?* Focusing on only the important details will help you understand and remember what you have read.

### Why Is Hawaii in Trouble?

One place that has been invaded by harmful species is Hawaii. Hawaii is a chain of islands. Species that make it to Hawaii often have no way of leaving. Several species are damaging Hawaii's habitat. Coqui frogs are a good example. Nothing in Hawaii eats them. The problem is that they eat many spiders and insects. This means Hawaii's native birds cannot get enough to eat. The Hawaiian government is training people to recognize the frogs. They hope to slow the spread of the frogs by capturing them.

3. What are important details in this paragraph?

______________________________

______________________________

______________________________

______________________________

______________________________

## Step 4: Summarize

When you **summarize,** you briefly state the main idea of a paragraph or passage in your own words. You also include the important details. Think to yourself, *What would I tell a friend about what I just read?*

Below is a passage with two paragraphs. The main idea of the first paragraph is *how species enter new habitats.* A good summary of this paragraph is: *People often bring new species into a habitat, not knowing the harmful effects.*

### Why Must People Be Careful About Moving Species?

Invasive species can get into new habitats in numerous ways. Usually, people bring them in, hoping to solve a problem. People brought mongooses to Hawaii to eat rats that gnaw sugar cane. However, the mongooses hunt during the day, and the rats are active at night. So, instead of eating rats, the mongooses eat ground birds. Hawaii's nene goose population is suffering because of mongooses.

It is very hard to know how a species will thrive in a new environment. It is also difficult to know what side effects will come from introducing a new species to a given habitat. People must be careful not to bring in species that may harm native plants and animals—sooner or later.

4. Read the second paragraph of the passage. Write the main idea.

______________________________

______________________________

______________________________

5. Write a summary of the second paragraph.

______________________________

______________________________

______________________________

6. Write a brief summary of the whole article (all five paragraphs) by combining the information you have read on these two pages.

______________________________________________________________

______________________________________________________________

7. How might summarizing apply to a math problem?

______________________________________________________________

# Ratios and Proportionality

## Learn the SKILL

When using fertilizers you might see mixing instructions that say, "Mix two gallons of fertilizer mix with three gallons of water." This is an example of a **ratio** and can be written as 2:3. How can you use ratios to find how much water and mix you need to make 10 gallons of fertilizer?

### VOCABULARY

Watch for the words you are learning about.

**cross product:** the products of numbers or expressions diagonally across from each other in a proportion; in $\frac{a}{b} = \frac{c}{d}$, the products of '*ad*' and '*bc*' are equal

**proportion:** an equation stating that two ratios are equal

**ratio:** a comparison of two numbers by division

| SKILL | EXAMPLE | WRITE AN EXAMPLE |
|---|---|---|
| Ratios are used to make a comparison of two or more things. | Two gallons of fertilizer mix and 3 gallons of water make the mix for 5 gallons of fertilizer. This is a ratio of 2:3. To find the amount of each part we need for 10 gallons of fertilizer, we can double the ratio to 4:6. That uses 4 gallons of fertilizer mix and 6 gallons of water. | Create an example of a ratio.<br>__________<br>__________<br>__________ |
| A **proportion** is a statement that two ratios are equal. A proportion can be used to simplify or create larger, equivalent ratios. | A bag of grass seed contains 15 pounds of bent grass and 5 pounds of bluegrass. The ratio is 15:5. A proportion can be used to find the number of pounds of bent grass if a new mixture contains 2 pounds of bluegrass.<br>Using **cross products:**<br>$\frac{15}{5} = \frac{x}{2}$<br>$15 \times 2 = 5x \quad 30 = 5x$<br>$x = 6$ | Write a problem where you need to use a proportion to solve.<br>__________<br>__________<br>__________ |
| Inverse proportions are related inversely. That means that as one number goes up, the other number goes down. | Scott is painting his room. By himself, it will take 8 hours. If he gets a friend to help and they work at the same speed, how long will it take?<br>To solve, we set up an equation: $ax = 8$, where $a$ = the number of people working and $x$ = the time. We know $a = 2$, so we solve for $x$.<br>So, $2x = 8$, $x = 4$. It will take 4 hours. | Write a problem where you need an inverse proportion to solve.<br>__________<br>__________<br>__________<br>__________ |

# YOUR TURN



## Choose the Right Word

ratio  proportion  cross product

**Fill in each blank with the correct word or phrase from the box.**

1. The equation $ad = bc$ for proportion $\frac{a}{b} = \frac{c}{d}$ uses a ________________.
2. A ________________ is used to make a comparison between two things.
3. A ________________ is used to compare two different ratios.

## Yes or No?

**Answer these questions and be ready to explain your answers.**

4. If a bag reads, "This product contains 2 pounds of grass seed for every 3 pounds of dirt," is this definitely a 5-pound bag? ________
5. Is 6:3 an example of a proportion? ________
6. Could the equation $ad = bc$ be an example of a cross product? ________

## Show That You Know

**Complete the table below for $x \times y = 60$.**

| | $x$ | $y$ |
|---|---|---|
| 7. | 2 | |
| 8. | 3 | |
| 9. | | 12 |
| 10. | 6 | |
| 11. | | 5 |
| 12. | 15 | |
| 13. | | 1 |

**Complete the table below for $\frac{2}{3} = \frac{x}{y}$.**

| | $x$ | $y$ |
|---|---|---|
| 14. | 2 | |
| 15. | 4 | |
| 16. | | 15 |
| 17. | 12 | |
| 18. | | 30 |
| 19. | 40 | |
| 20. | | 300 |

# SOLVE on Your Own

## Skills Practice

You can use cross products and then divide to solve for x.


**Solve for x.**

1. $\frac{4}{5} = \frac{x}{15}$ ________

2. $\frac{7}{6} = \frac{x}{18}$ ________

3. $\frac{10}{7} = \frac{x}{63}$ ________

4. $\frac{12}{13} = \frac{x}{13}$ ________

5. $\frac{2}{22} = \frac{x}{11}$ ________

6. $\frac{17}{5} = \frac{x}{75}$ ________

7. $\frac{42}{7} = \frac{x}{1}$ ________

8. $\frac{12}{4} = \frac{x}{3}$ ________

9. $\frac{12}{9} = \frac{x}{6}$ ________

10. $\frac{8}{32} = \frac{x}{12}$ ________

11. $\frac{14}{7} = \frac{x}{15}$ ________

12. $\frac{15}{6} = \frac{x}{20}$ ________

# Ratios and Proportionality

## Strategies

### Try a Simpler Form of the Problem, Find a Pattern

**Step 1: Read** In England, the Industrial Revolution was a time of new machines that created more pollution. Sometimes, pollution helped animals survive. For example, peppered moths come in two types: light or dark. Pollution coated trees with soot and made it easier for dark peppered moths to hide. The table below shows samples of the different moths before and after the Industrial Revolution.

| | Dark peppered moths | Light peppered moths |
|---|---|---|
| Before | 2 | 98 |
| After | 95 | 5 |

If a random sample of 1,000 peppered moths was taken after the Industrial Revolution, how many dark moths would you expect to find?

| STRATEGY | SOLUTION |
|---|---|

**Try a Simpler Form of a Problem**

Look at the problem differently. Do not think of it as many ratios, but as parts of a whole.

**Step 2: Plan** Each pair of numbers adds to 100, so change the ratios to fractions with a denominator of 100. Then find an equivalent fraction with a denominator of 1,000.

**Step 3: Solve** The ratio can be written as a fraction. The left side of the ratio 95:5 is the same as $\frac{95}{100}$. The equivalent fraction is $\frac{950}{1{,}000}$. So, one would expect 950 dark moths in a sample of 1,000 moths.

**Step 4: Check** Change the fractions back into a ratio and simplify. For example, $\frac{950}{1{,}000}$ is the same as the left side of 950:50, which simplifies to 95:5. The answer checks.

**Find a Pattern**

Solve the problem by finding smaller solutions to help see the pattern in the numbers.

**Step 2: Plan** We can find a pattern for every 100 moths by filling in a table with the correct number of dark and light peppered moths.

**Step 3: Solve**

| Dark peppered moths | Light peppered moths | Total |
|---|---|---|
| 95 | 5 | 100 |
| 190 | 10 | 200 |
| 285 | 15 | 300 |
| 380 | 20 | 400 |

The pattern for each 100 added is that the dark moths increase by 95 and the light moths increase by 5. The result after 9 increases of 100 should be 950 dark moths.

**Step 4: Check** Subtract the column 2 value from the column 3 value: $1{,}000 - 50 = 950$. The answer checks.

Choose a Strategy

# YOUR TURN

## Choose the Right Word

ratio  proportion  cross products

**Fill in each blank with the correct word or phrase from the box.**

1. You can use ________________ to find the value of a variable in a pair of equivalent ratios.
2. An equation that states two ratios are equal is called ________________.
3. A ________________ will compare two numbers.

## Yes or No?

**Answer these questions and be ready to explain your answers.**

4. Is 6:3 an example of a ratio? ________
5. Is $\frac{2}{10} = \frac{1}{5}$ an example of a proportion? ________
6. Can you use cross products to solve for $y$ in $19 - y = 3$? ________

## Show That You Know

**Complete the table below for $y \times x = 48$.**

| | $x$ | $y$ |
|---|---|---|
| 7. | 1 | |
| 8. | 3 | |
| 9. | 4 | |
| 10. | 8 | |
| 11. | 12 | |
| 12. | 16 | |
| 13. | 24 | |

**Complete the table below for $\frac{5}{3} = \frac{x}{y}$.**

| | $x$ | $y$ |
|---|---|---|
| 14. | 10 | |
| 15. | 15 | |
| 16. | 25 | |
| 17. | 45 | |
| 18. | 70 | |
| 19. | 105 | |
| 20. | 345 | |

# READ on Your Own

## Reading Comprehension Strategy: Summarizing

## Diseases and Invasive Species, *pages 3–4*

### Before You Read

How can a disease be thought of as an invasion?

### As You Read

**Read "Weeds and Seeds," page 3.** 

Write the topic below.

Topic:

______________________________________________

______________________________________________

**Read "Sickness Spreading," page 4.** 

Write the topic below.

Topic:

______________________________________________

______________________________________________

### After You Read

When someone in a city has a highly contagious disease, the person is sometimes put in isolation, or separated from other people. Why do you think this is done?

______________________________________________

______________________________________________

______________________________________________

### VOCABULARY

Watch for the words you are learning about.

**invasion:** when one group enters a zone that belongs to another group

**microscope:** instrument used to study objects too small to see with the unaided eye

**species:** a group of organisms that have similar traits and genes

**symptoms:** signs that a disease is present

### Fluency Tip

As you read and reread, choose a pace that helps you understand what you read.

# SOLVE on Your Own

## Diseases and Invasive Species, *page 5*

### Organize the Information

**Read the magazine. Then fill in the following table with how much knapweed seed is in the shipment.**

**Formula: Percent ×** ________________ × ________________ × ________________

| Amount of Shipment | Knapweed Seeds |
|---|---|
| $\frac{1}{2}$ of shipment | |
| $\frac{3}{4}$ of shipment | |
| Whole shipment | |

### You Do the Math

Use the information in the table to answer these questions. Write your answers in the space provided.

There are many ways to find the correct answer. Unfortunately, there are even more ways to find a wrong answer!


1. What is the total number of seeds in the 20 bags? How can you use this to find the value of one square in the decimal model? Explain.

_______________________________________________

_______________________________________________

2. What does one-half of a square in the decimal model represent? How does this relate to the number of knapweed seeds?

_______________________________________________

_______________________________________________

### After You Solve

Have you or members of your family ever had the flu? Create a ratio you think would be representative of the amount of people who have caught the flu in their lives, versus the amount of people who have not. On what do you base your answer?

_______________________________________________

_______________________________________________

# Proportionality and Percents

## Learn the SKILL

Heart disease is the number one cause of death in the world. In fact, statistics from the Center for Disease Control suggests that about 13 **percent** of people visiting a hospital are there because of heart disease. In a given sample of people, how can you find what percentage or how many people will likely have heart disease?

### VOCABULARY

Watch for the words you are learning about.

**percent:** a ratio that compares a number to 100; the symbol for percent is %

**percent decrease:** percent less than an original number

**percent increase:** percent more than an original number

| SKILL | EXAMPLE | WRITE AN EXAMPLE |
|---|---|---|
| A percent is a ratio that compares a number to 100. So, 13% would be 13 out of 100. | If a random sample of 600 people is surveyed, then $600 \times 0.13 = 78$ people. This is how many people will likely have heart disease. | Multiply a sample by a percentage.<br>____________________ |
| A **percent increase** is used when you have a given percentage and then you increase it. | A hospital had a staff of 270 people last year. This year the staff increased 10%.<br>The staff now is at $270 \times (1 + 0.1) =$<br>$270 \times 1.1 = 297$ people. | Multiply a sample by one plus the decimal form of the percentage.<br>____________________ |
| A **percent decrease** is used when you have a given percentage and then you decrease it. | In a given region, 70 people are doctors. In the same region this year there was a 10 percent decrease.<br>There are now $70 \times (1 - 0.1) =$<br>$70 \times (0.9) = 63$ doctors. | Multiply a sample by one minus the decimal form of the percentage.<br>____________________ |

Learn the Skill

# YOUR TURN

## Choose the Right Word

percent    percent decrease
percent increase

**Fill in each blank with the correct word or phrase from the box.**

1. If you have a given percent of an amount that is less than the original amount, you have a _______________.
2. If you have a given percent of an amount that is greater than the original amount, you have a _______________.
3. A _______________ is a ratio comparing a number to 100.

## Yes or No?

**Answer these questions and be ready to explain your answers.**

4. Is a percent of a sample one minus the decimal form of the percentage? ________
5. To find a percent increase, should you add 1 to the decimal form of the percent being increased? ________
6. Is 100% of a sample the same number as the sample? ________

## Show That You Know

**Find the percent of the number.**

7. 80% of 95
8. 45% of 42
9. 60% of 50
10. 12% of 67

**Write whether each example is a percent increase or percent decrease.**

11. 97 × 1.25
12. 701 × 0.87
13. 202 × 1.01

# SOLVE on Your Own

## Skills Practice

Remember that
"of" means to
multiply by.

**Find each percent, percent increase, or percent decrease. Write your answer on the line.**

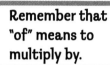

1. 15% of 45 ________
2. 17% of 80 ________
3. 22% of 918 ________
4. 98% of 1,200 ________
5. 42% of 221 ________
6. 67% of 670 ________
7. 35% increase of 72 ________
8. 12% increase of 901 ________
9. 49% decrease of 405 ________
10. 168% increase of 12 ________
11. 99% decrease of 8,912 ________
12. 23% decrease of 812 ________

# Proportionality and Percents

## Strategies

### Try a Simpler Form of the Problem, Make a Table or a Chart

**Step 1: Read** Recently, all the seventh graders at Archer School went on a field trip to the planetarium. On the same day, the entire eighth grade class went to the Museum of Natural History. The seventh grade class had a total of 420 students. Of these, 35% saw a movie about exploring Mars. The eighth grade students had the option of touring the dinosaur exhibit or seeing a movie about the last Ice Age. A total of 286 eighth graders, or 55.9%, saw the movie. What percentage of the total number of students in seventh and eighth grade saw a movie on their field trip?

| STRATEGY | SOLUTION |
|---|---|

#### Try a Simpler Form of the Problem

Start at the end of the problem and break it down into pieces. Ask yourself what you need to find to answer each part of the problem.

**Step 2: Plan** Find the total number of students that went to a movie in each grade and the total that went on the field trips. Then use division to find the percentage of the total that saw a movie.

**Step 3: Solve** To find the total number of seventh graders who saw the movie, multiply 420 by 35%, or 0.35: $420 \times 0.35 = 147$

Now find the total number of eighth graders, $e$, who went on the field trip:

$286 = 0.559 \times e$

$e = 286 \div 0.559 = 511.6$, or 512 eighth grade students

There were a total of $420 + 512 = 932$ students on field trips. The percentage who saw a movie were $433 \div 932 =$ about 46%.

**Step 4: Check** Estimate the number who saw a movie: $0.50 \times 932 = 466$. The estimate is fairly close, so the answer is reasonable.

#### Make a Table or a Chart

With some problems, it helps to use a table to find a hidden question.

**Step 2: Plan** Make a table of everything you can find right now. Identify the hidden question, and then divide to solve.

**Step 3: Solve**

| | Seventh Grade | Eighth Grade | Both |
|---|---|---|---|
| **Total Students** | 420 | can find | can find |
| **Total Who Saw a Movie** | can find | 286 | can find |
| **Percent Who Saw a Movie** | 35 | 55.9 | need to find |

The hidden question is: what is the percentage of the students in both grades who saw a movie? As shown above, 433 of 932 students saw a movie, so the percent is $433 \div 932 =$ about 46%.

**Step 4: Check** Estimate a different way. Round 433 to 400 and 932 to 900 and divide. $400 \div 900 =$ about 0.444, or 44.4%. The answer is reasonable.

# YOUR TURN

Choose a Strategy

## Choose the Right Word

percent    percent increase
percent decrease

**Fill in each blank with the correct word or phrase from the box.**

1. The symbol % means you are dealing with a ________________.
2. A ________________ is when you add to a number and compare it to the original.
3. A ________________ is when you subtract from a number and compare it to the original.

## Yes or No?

**Answer these questions and be ready to explain your answers.**

4. Can you have more than 100% of something? ________
5. If 19 out of 87 people are sick, would 19% of people be sick? ________
6. If you take a decimal form of a percent and add it to 1, are you about to perform a percent decrease? ________

## Show That You Know

**Find the percentage of the whole below.**

7. 22% of 104
8. 96% of 400
9. 1% of 188
10. 33% of 303

**Increase or decrease each number.**

11. 5% increase from 30
12. 45% decrease from 202
13. 11% decrease from 99
14. 100% increase from 50

# READ on Your Own

## Reading Comprehension Strategy: Summarizing

## Diseases and Invasive Species, *pages 6–7*

### Before You Read

Before you read the last article, "Invisible Invasions," what did you think it would be about?

### As You Read

**Read "Pericles' Plan," page 6.** 
Fill in that part of the chart below.

**Read "Mystery at Piraeus," page 7.** 
Fill in that part of the chart below.

**Read "Epidemic!", page 7.** 
Fill in that part of the chart below.

| Pericles' Plan | Mystery at Piraeus | Epidemic |
|---|---|---|
| Topic: | Topic: | Topic: |
| Main Idea: | Main Idea: | Main Idea: |

### After You Read

What did you find most interesting about the plague of Athens?

### VOCABULARY

Watch for the words you are learning about.

**epidemic:** an outbreak of disease that affects an unusually large number of people

**microorganisms:** living things that are so small they are only visible through a microscope

**plague:** a disease that spreads quickly and has a high death rate

**survive:** to continue to live; to avoid death

### Fluency Tip

Read the text more than once. You will read more smoothly and you will be more likely to remember what you read.

# SOLVE on Your Own

## Diseases and Invasive Species, *page 8*

### Organize the Information

**Read You Do the Math in the magazine. Then fill in the blanks in the report below.**

Sir, it is my suggestion that we _____________________. As you know, our army has typhus. After a 12-month campaign we will have lost ________ percent of our army, leaving us with ________ percent of our original force of 60,000, or ________ soldiers. After 18 months we should have ________ soldiers. This means ________________________________________.

### You Do the Math

Use the information in the report above to answer these questions. Write your answers in the space provided.

**If you look at a rate for a whole year, and you want to apply it to a half-year, you can use half the rate.**

1. How can you break up your solution into four or more steps? (Hint: First break up the solution into two steps. Then break up one or both of those steps into smaller pieces.)

_______________________________________________

_______________________________________________

_______________________________________________

_______________________________________________

2. How would you advise the king? Support your answer with calculations.

_______________________________________________

_______________________________________________

_______________________________________________

_______________________________________________

### After You Solve

What are some instances where you think you will use percentages in the future?

_______________________________________________

_______________________________________________

Application

## The Four-Step Problem-Solving Plan

| Step 1: Read | Step 2: Plan | Step 3: Solve | Step 4: Check |
| --- | --- | --- | --- |
| Make sure you understand what the problem is asking. | Decide how you will solve the problem. | Solve the problem using your plan. | Check to make sure your answer is correct. |

**Read the article below. Then answer the questions.**

### The Plague Today

In the 1300s, about half of the population of Europe died of a disease called the plague. At that time, nobody knew what caused the plague or how it spread. It was not until the 1900s that scientists found answers.

Despite scientific advances, the plague is not just an ancient disease. The last major outbreak, or pandemic, began in China around 1855 and has still not been fully controlled. According to the World Health Organization, about 1,000 to 3,000 cases of plague occur each year. Most of these cases occur in countries in Asia and Africa. The exact number is not known because many cases are not identified or reported correctly.

The last outbreak of the plague in the United States occurred from 1924–1925 in Los Angeles. However, about 10 to 15 cases of the plague are still reported each year. Most of these cases occur in western states, including New Mexico, Arizona, Colorado, and Utah. The reason for this is that these states have large numbers of squirrels and other rodents that carry fleas infected with *Yersinia pestis*, the bacterium that causes the plague.

1. Bill says that people do not have to worry about the plague today because it only affected people in the past. Do you agree with Bill? Why or why not?

2. About how many cases of the plague occurred in the United States in the 1990s?

# YOUR TURN

Application

**Read the article below. Then answer the questions.**

## Types of Plague

There are three types of the plague: bubonic, septicemic, and pneumonic. All three types can be treated with antibiotics if the treatment is started early.

Bubonic plague occurs when the bacteria *Yersinia pestis* infects the lymph glands. The glands swell, producing the "buboes" that are typical of the disease. About 40%–60% of people with bubonic plague will die if not treated and about 1%–15% still die after they are treated.

Septicemic plague infects the blood. Anyone with septicemic plague who is not treated will die. About 40% of people with septicemic plague die even after they receive treatment.

Pneumonic plague infects the lungs. Because people can release particles containing *Yersinia pestis* bacteria when they cough, pneumonic plague is the only form of plague that is easily spread from person to person. Anyone with pneumonic plague who is not treated within 24 hours of being infected will die.

1. What is the disease bubonic plague named for?

______________________________

______________________________

2. About what percentage of people with bubonic plague will survive if treated?

______________________________

______________________________

3. If 50 people with septicemic plague are treated with antibiotics, about how many will survive?

______________________________

______________________________

4. Which type of plague is the most likely to cause an epidemic? Explain your answer.

______________________________

______________________________

______________________________

### Fluency Tip

Read with expression. Use expression in your reading of expository text as well as narrative text. Emphasize unusual facts and details.

# READ on Your Own

## Reading Comprehension Strategy: Summarizing

## Diseases and Invasive Species, *pages 9–11*

### Before You Read

In "The Plague of Athens," you read about Pericles. How did the living conditions he set up in Athens help spread disease?

### As You Read

**Read "Dark Days of the Dark Ages," pages 9–11.** 

Then complete the cause-and-effect chart below. Think about the effect of each cause listed. Give two effects for each cause.

| | | |
|---|---|---|
| **Cause:** Rats carry plague bacteria. | **Cause:** People live in unsanitary conditions. | **Cause:** People get sick with plague. |
| ↓ | ↓ | ↓ |
| **Effect:** Ticks and ______ pick up plague bacteria. | **Effect:** | **Effect:** |
| ↓ | ↓ | ↓ |
| **Effect:** Rats are carried to new areas aboard ______________. | **Effect:** | **Effect:** |

### VOCABULARY

Watch for the words you are learning about.

**bacteria:** single-celled living things that do not have a nucleus

**genes:** part of the DNA in all cells; used by cells as codes for carrying every kind of activity in the cell

**infected:** having a disease or the ability to pass on a disease

**pandemic:** a disease that crosses borders

**vector:** method, such as an insect or animal bite, by which a disease is passed along

### Fluency Tip

Preview the text to make sure you can pronounce all names and difficult words.

### After You Read

Why is it important to cover your mouth or nose when you cough or sneeze?

______________________________________________________________

______________________________________________________________

# SOLVE on Your Own

## Diseases and Invasive Species, *page 12*

### Organize the Information

**Complete the list and table below to organize the information you find in the Math Project on magazine page 12.**

Number of Fleas per Rat = ________

Number of Rats per Ship = ________

Number of Ships per Day = ________

Number of Days per Week = ________

Number of Days per Month = ________

It pays to check your answers several times during a long chain of calculations.

| Days | Ships | Total Rats | Total Fleas |
|---|---|---|---|
| 1 | | | |
| | | | |
| | | | |

### Math Project

Use the information in the list and table above to answer these questions. Write your answers in the spaces provided.

1. How can you calculate the number of fleas per ship?

______________________________

2. How can you calculate the number of ships the harbormaster inspects every week?

______________________________

3. Not all months have the same number of days. How could you simplify your calculation of the number of fleas per month and still get a reasonable answer? Explain.

______________________________

### After You Solve

How could you express some of the same information in the table by drawing a picture?

______________________________

______________________________

# Solving Problems with Proportionality

## Learn the SKILL

To attract customers, stores will often use **discounts.** You can often see advertisements that say, "Now 20% off!" Many businesses do this to draw in customers and make a sale. Even banks offer attractive **interest rates** so that you will loan your money to them. However, if you borrow money from a bank they expect you to pay the interest rate. Also, most businesses tend to have charges such as **sales tax** or tips.

A store is selling a pair of $75 shoes for 20% off the price. If there is a 10% sales tax, how much do the shoes cost?

### VOCABULARY

Watch for the words you are learning about.

**discount:** the difference between the original price and the sale price of an item

**interest rate:** the percentage of the balance that an account or investment earns in a fixed period of time

**sales tax:** a tax that is a percentage of the price of an item

| SKILL | EXAMPLE | WRITE AN EXAMPLE |
|---|---|---|
| Discounts or taxes are percentages, which make them proportions. A discount is a percent decrease; a tax is a percent increase. | The price ($75) of an item at a store is 20% off the original price, but there is a state sales tax of 10%. The actual price of the item is:<br>$75(1 - 0.20)(1 + 0.10)$<br>$75(.8)(1.1) = \$66$ | Write a discount problem.<br>____________________<br>Write a sales tax problem.<br>____________________ |
| A tip or gratuity is a charge for service; it is a proportion of the cost of service. | A common tip is 18%. The expected tip for a meal costing $22.50 would be<br>$\$22.50 \times 0.18 = \$4.05$. | Write a tip problem.<br>____________________ |
| When you save money in a bank you receive interest on the amount of money in your account. Likewise, if you borrow money you pay an interest rate. Both of these are percent increases. | You deposit $200 in a savings account. If a bank is offering an annual interest rate of 5%, the amount of money in your account after 1 year is:<br>$\$200 \times 1.05 = \$210$ | Write an interest rate problem.<br>____________________ |

## Choose the Right Word

discount   interest rate   sales tax

**Fill in each blank with the correct word or phrase from the box.**

1. If a store is offering an item for a(n) ________________ it means there is a percent decrease.
2. A(n) ________________ is a percent increase and is applied on most items that you buy in a store.
3. On a loan you would have to pay a(n) ________________.

## Yes or No?

**Answer these questions and be ready to explain your answers.**

4. Could you also think of a tip as a percent increase? ________
5. Is the price of an item the same if you calculate a discount before or after the sales tax? ________
6. If you wanted to find the amount of an item including sales tax, would you treat it as a percent decrease? ________

## Show That You Know

**What is amount of the tip and the total cost of the meal for:**

7. an 18% tip on a $25 meal?
8. a 19% tip on a $42 meal?
9. a 22% tip on a $17 meal?
10. a 21% tip on a $98 meal?

**Adjust a $45 bill for the following:**

11. a 20% discount
12. 5% sales tax
13. a 12% discount
14. 7% sales tax

# SOLVE on Your Own

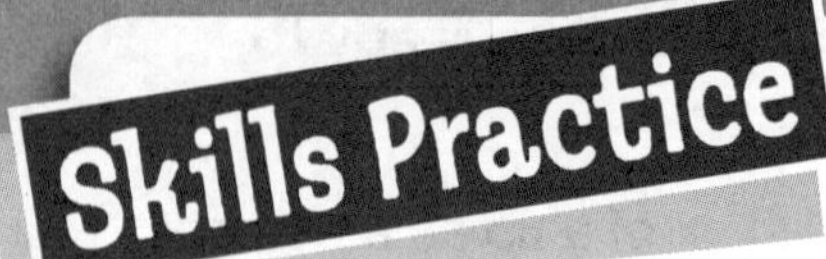

Remember, interest is the same as a percent increase.


**A bank is offering a yearly interest rate of 6.5%. What is the total interest and how much money do you have after 1 year if you open an account with:**

1. $4,500? ____________________
2. $820? ____________________
3. $11,050? ____________________
4. $998? ____________________
5. $1,210? ____________________
6. $8,712? ____________________

**A store is offering sales on different items. If the sales tax is 9%, what is the cost of each item to the nearest penny?**

7. 15% discount on an item costing $400 __________
8. 45% discount on an item costing $16 __________
9. 25% discount on an item costing $875 __________
10. 7% discount on an item costing $1,200 __________
11. 9% discount on an item costing $712 __________
12. 23% discount on an item costing $1,818 __________

# Solving Problems with Proportionality

## Strategies

### Guess, Check, and Revise; Make a Table or a Chart

**Step 1: Read** Today, about 1,500,000 live in Philadelphia. Manhattan has about 1,600,000 people. The current population of Chicago is about 3,000,000 and Los Angeles has about 4,000,000 people. If 60% of a given population has to be vaccinated in order to prevent an epidemic, and if you have 500,000 vaccines, which of these populations could be protected against an outbreak?

| STRATEGY | SOLUTION |
|---|---|

#### Guess, Check, and Revise

Start with a simple mental math problem as a first guess to see if you need to completely solve the problem for all of the cities.

**Step 2: Plan** Start with a simple percentage, such as 50%. Use it with each population. If 50% is greater than 500,000 vaccines for a population, then you know you will not have enough vaccines.

**Step 3: Solve** Find 50% of each population:

| | |
|---|---|
| Philadelphia | 750,000 |
| Manhattan | 800,000 |
| Chicago | 1,500,000 |
| Los Angeles | 2,000,000 |

None of the cities could be protected.

**Step 4: Check** Find half of each population. This is always greater than 500,000, so none of the populations would be protected.

#### Make a Table or a Chart

A table can help organize the calculations needed to solve a complex problem.

**Step 2: Plan** Make a table with the locations and populations. Find 60% of each population and subtract 500,000 from it to find how many more vaccines are needed.

**Step 3: Solve** You have already calculated 50%. Find 10% and add it to 50% to find 60%. Then subtract 500,000 from each.

| Location | Pop. | 50% | 10% | 60% | Amount Needed |
|---|---|---|---|---|---|
| Philadelphia | 1,500,000 | 750,000 | 150,000 | 900,000 | 400,000 |
| Manhattan | 1,600,000 | 800,000 | 160,000 | 960,000 | 460,000 |
| Chicago | 3,000,000 | 1,500,000 | 300,000 | 1,800,000 | 1,300,000 |
| Los Angeles | 4,000,000 | 2,000,000 | 400,000 | 2,400,000 | 1,900,000 |

**Step 4: Check** Work backwards: add the amount needed to 500,000. This should give you 60% of the population. For Philadelphia, $400{,}000 + 500{,}000 = 900{,}000$, which is 60% of 1,500,000. The answer checks.

Choose a Strategy

# YOUR TURN

## Choose the Right Word

discount    interest rate    sales tax

**Fill in each blank with the correct word or phrase from the box.**

1. A(n) ________________ on an item means that there is a percent decrease.
2. The ________________ on a personal loan is a percent increase.
3. A tax added to the cost of an item that is a percent increase is called a(n) ________________.

## Yes or No?

**Answer these questions and be ready to explain your answers.**

4. If you have 50% of a set of cards, does this mean you have half the set? ________
5. If an item is on sale for 30% off, does this mean it is more than half off the original price? ________
6. If you have 0% of pie, does this mean you do not have any pie? ________

## Show That You Know

**Find the discount and the total cost.**

7. 15% discount on $150
8. additional 10% delivery fee for a $350 purchase
9. 25% mark-up on $70
10. less 15% on $599
11. 20% off on $199.95

**Find the amount of sales tax and the total cost. Round to the nearest penny.**

12. 7% on $50.00
13. $8\frac{1}{2}$% on $3,250.00
14. 6% on $798.00
15. 1.5% on $10,000.00
16. 5% on $99.99

# READ on Your Own

## Reading Comprehension Strategy: Summarizing

## Diseases and Invasive Species, *pages 13–15*

### Before You Read

In "Dark Days of the Dark Ages," you read about epidemics and pandemics. What is the difference between the two?

### As You Read

**Read "Flight from Philly," pages 13–14.** 

Fill in that part of the chart below.

**Read "Virus," page 14.** 

Fill in that part of the chart below.

**Read "Vector: Mosquitoes," page 15.** 

Fill in that part of the chart below.

| Flight from Philly | Virus | Vector |
|---|---|---|
| Main Idea: | Main Idea: | Main Idea: |
| Important Details: | Important Details: | Important Details: |
| Summary: | Summary: | Summary: |

### VOCABULARY

Watch for the words you are learning about.

**bloodletting:** a medical treatment in which blood is taken from a person who is ill

**virus:** a cause of disease which itself is not alive; it can reproduce only inside a host cell

### Fluency Tip

Read the text more than once. You will read more smoothly and you'll be more likely to remember what you read.

### After You Read

What can you do to get rid of the breeding grounds of mosquitoes?

# SOLVE on Your Own

## Diseases and Invasive Species, *page 15*

### Organize the Information

**Read the magazine and complete the table below to show how many New Yorkers might die from a yellow fever outbreak.**

| Number of New Yorkers Who Might Die from a Yellow Fever Outbreak | | |
|---|---|---|
| | Philadelphia | New York |
| 1793 Population | | |
| Died from Yellow Fever | | |

### You Do the Math

You can check your answer using a proportion.

Use the information in the table above to answer these questions. Write your answers in the space provided.

1. What information do you need to calculate before finding by how much the population might decrease in New York?

_______________

2. What is the percent decrease of population in Philadelphia?

_______________

3. Use the space below to make a double-bar graph of the data above.

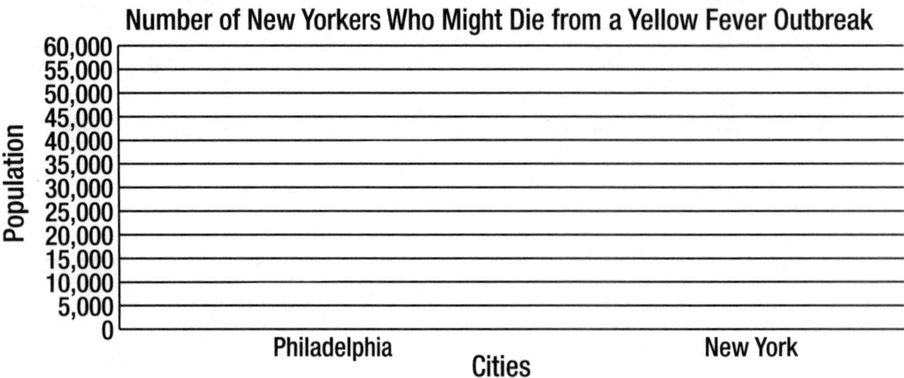


### After You Solve

What precautions can you take to prevent the spread of diseases?

_______________

## The Four-Step Problem-Solving Plan

| Step 1: Read | Step 2: Plan | Step 3: Solve | Step 4: Check |
|---|---|---|---|
| Make sure you understand what the problem is asking. | Decide how you will solve the problem. | Solve the problem using your plan. | Check to make sure your answer is correct. |

**Read the article below. Then answer the questions.**

### Smallpox

Smallpox is caused by a virus called *Variola major.* Viruses are particles that contain some structures similar to those of cells. Viruses, however, are smaller than cells and cannot reproduce on their own. For this reason, many biologists do not consider viruses to be alive.

Smallpox is a very old disease, originating thousands of years ago. The body of Egyptian Pharaoh Ramses V, who died in 1157 BC, has scars that scientists think were caused by smallpox. The disease eventually spread to Europe and was carried to the Americas by European explorers and settlers.

In the late 1700s, when Edward Jenner lived, smallpox killed more people than anything else. It was responsible for about 10% of deaths overall, but 20% in towns and cities. The reason for the higher rate in towns and cities was that people lived closer together, allowing the disease to spread more easily.

Due to worldwide vaccination campaigns, the last reported case of smallpox occurred in 1977. The disease is now considered to have been eliminated, except for a few samples stored in scientific laboratories.

1. Out of 35 people living in London, England, in 1780, how many would be expected to die of smallpox?

______________________________

______________________________

______________________________

2. During the 1700s, it was common for wealthier people to move out of cities temporarily during smallpox outbreaks. Why do you think they did this?

______________________________

______________________________

______________________________

3. Do you think the general public is still vaccinated against smallpox today? Why or why not?

______________________________

______________________________

______________________________

Application

# YOUR TURN

**Read the article below. Then answer the questions.**

## Smallpox Stages

When a person is exposed to smallpox, the disease passes through stages. The first stage is incubation. It lasts 7 to 17 days and the person is not contagious.

During the prodrome stage, the person experiences the first symptoms, which can include high fever and aching head and body. This stage lasts 2 to 4 days and the person may be contagious.

The early rash stage lasts about 4 days and is most contagious. A rash begins in the mouth and spreads over the skin as red spots that later turn into raised bumps.

The next stage is the pustular rash. The bumps change into pustules, which feel like a solid pellet under the skin. This stage lasts about 5 days and the person is still contagious.

In the next stage the pustules scab over. This stage also lasts about 5 days and the person is still contagious.

Finally, the scabs fall off and scars form. This stage lasts about 6 days and the person is still contagious. Once all of the scabs have fallen off, the person is no longer contagious.

### Fluency Tip

Read at an even pace. Slow down for complicated instructions or explanations to be sure each direction or step is understood.

1. During what stage or stages do you think a person with smallpox would be most likely to infect others? Explain your answer.

___________________________

___________________________

___________________________

___________________________

2. What is the least amount of time all of the stages of smallpox could take?

___________________________

3. What is the greatest amount of time all of the stages of smallpox could take?

___________________________

4. When is a person infected with smallpox not contagious?

___________________________

___________________________

# READ on Your Own

## Reading Comprehension Strategy: Summarizing

## Diseases and Invasive Species, *pages 16–19*

### VOCABULARY

Watch for the words you are learning about.

**vaccination:** treatment with infected cells to give a person a mild form of a disease, which then prevents the person from getting a serious form of the disease

### Fluency Tip

Take your time when reading complex material so you can make sense of difficult ideas.

### Before You Read

When you read "What Could Scare Off George Washington?" did you think Washington was right to run away from a fight with yellow fever? Why?

### As You Read

**Read "The First Vaccine," pages 16–18.** 

Then fill in the blanks in the sentences below to create a summary of the reading.

Edward ________________ noticed that people who had already had ________________ did not get ________________. People traditionally had put pus from a person with mild smallpox into a cut on their own bodies. However, they sometimes got full-blown ________________. Jenner deliberately infected a boy with ________________, then exposed him to ________________ to see if he would get sick. He did not, meaning that he had been successfully ________________.

### After You Read

What might happen if you did not get one of the vaccines a doctor would normally give you?

______________________________________________________________________

______________________________________________________________________

# SOLVE on Your Own

## Diseases and Invasive Species, *page 19*

### Organize the Information

**Use a table like the one below to organize the information you find in the Math Project on magazine page 19.**

| Number of People in Village | Number of People at Risk |
|---|---|
| 1,000 | |
| 10,000 | |
| 20,000 | |

### Math Project

Keep in mind that percentages often will add up to 100%.


Use the information in the table above to answer these questions. Write your answers in the spaces provided.

1. How can you calculate the failure rate of the vaccine?

_______________

2. How can you calculate the number of people in the first village who are still at potential risk?

_______________

_______________

3. How can you calculate the number of people in the other villages who are still at risk?

_______________

### After You Solve

How could you express some of the same information in the table using another graphic organizer?

_______________

_______________

# Put It Together

## Proportions, Predictions, and Probability

You have learned how to write and solve equations with proportions. For example, suppose a company packages 15 items into a box. You might ask how many items there are in 20 boxes. You can solve the question by writing the proportion $\frac{1}{15} = \frac{20}{x}$. The answer to the question is 300. You can be confident there are a total of 300 items in 15 boxes.

Sometimes proportions are used to make predictions. You might want to predict the number of students that will be absent from school on a day in January. You have records that show the average daily absence during January for the last three years has been 4% ($\frac{4}{100}$) of the students. If there are 850 students in the school, how many students do you predict will be absent? Write and solve the proportion $\frac{4}{100} = \frac{x}{850}$.
Your prediction is 34 students. Will there really be 34 students absent? This is a mathematical computation based on information from previous years. The exact number of students absent may not be 34.

If you know the probability of something occurring, you can use that information to help make better predictions. Remember, if 4% ($\frac{4}{100}$) of students are absent, then 96% ($\frac{96}{100}$) are not absent.

## Practicing Proportions

**Solve the proportions for x.**

1. $\frac{7}{12} = \frac{63}{x}$ ________

2. $\frac{9}{13} = \frac{x}{65}$ ________

3. $\frac{x}{56} = \frac{11}{7}$ ________

4. $\frac{156}{x} = \frac{13}{12}$ ________

5. $\frac{1}{4.2} = \frac{5}{x}$ ________

6. $\frac{8}{15} = \frac{4}{x}$ ________

7. $\frac{4.5}{7.2} = \frac{x}{3.2}$ ________

Connections

# YOUR TURN

## Proportions, Predictions, and Probability

You have learned that proportions and probability can help you make predictions. The probability of an event occurring can be expressed as a fraction, decimal, or percent.

Suppose an article in a newspaper claims 480 of the 800 students in the local high school participate in one or more sports. That same claim could be made in other forms. The article could have said that 6 out of every 10 students participate in one or more sports. You can also state that 60% ($\frac{60}{100}$) of the students participate in one or more sports.

Think about how you would predict the number of students that will participate in one or more sports next year when the school population increases to 850 students.

1. What fraction of the school population does not participate in sports?

______________________________

2. Write a proportion to find the number of students participating in sports next year. Use the present number of students participating in sports, the present number of students, and next year's school population. Do not solve the proportion.

______________________________

3. What is the simplest fractional value that you can use in place of 60%?

______________________________

4. Write a proportion to find the number of students participating in sports next year. Use the percent of students presently participating in sports and next year's school population. Do not solve the proportion.

______________________________

5. Which proportion (Example 2 or 4) is easier to solve? Solve one of the proportions.

______________________________

6. What other method can you use to solve this problem?

______________________________

______________________________

## Show That You Know

**Read the information below. Then answer the questions.**

Can all of these statistics be true?

Daniel found statistics about pandemics and noticed that they were written in a variety of forms. One article reported that $\frac{1}{5}$ of the world population had contracted influenza. Other reports of the same pandemic listed from 20 to 100 million deaths in the world. The world population was estimated at 1.6 billion during that time. Another article reported that $\frac{1}{4}$ of the United States population contracted the disease. Of these, an estimated 2.5%, or 675,000, died.

1. What was $\frac{1}{5}$ of the world population during the influenza pandemic?

2. What does your answer to problem 1 represent?

3. What fraction of the world population was 100 million at the time of the pandemic?

4. What does your answer to problem 3 represent?

5. The fraction $\frac{1}{40}$ can be used to represent 2.5%. What proportion can you write to calculate the number of people in the United States who contracted influenza?

## Show That You Know (continued)

6. According to your calculations, how many people in the United States contracted influenza?

7. What information can you use to calculate the population of the United States at that time?

8. Write the proportion for problem 7 and solve.

## Review What You've Learned

9. What have you learned in this Connections lesson about using proportions to make predictions?

10. What have you learned in this Connections lesson that you did not already know?

11. What have you learned in this lesson about checking the reliability of data with proportions, predictions, and probability?

# Review and Practice

## Skills Review

**Ratios and proportions:**

2 gallons of milk cost \$6, what will 5 gallons cost?

Write a **proportion** to find out:

$\frac{6}{2} = \frac{x}{5}$

Multiply the **cross products** to find $x$.

$6(5) = x(2)$

$30 = 2x, x = \frac{30}{2}, x = \$15$

**Inverse proportions:**

A woman walked 4 miles. If she walked for 2 hours, she would have walked at a speed of 2 mph. If she walked 4 hours, she would have walked at a speed of 1 mph.

As time increased by a factor of 2, speed decreased by the same factor. Speed and time are inversely related for a given constant distance.

**Percent:**

22% is 22 out of 100.

22% can also be shown as a ratio: $\frac{22}{100}$, or a decimal: 0.22.

$140\% = \frac{140}{100}$ or 1.4

**Percent increases and decreases:**

An 11 percent increase of $x$:

$x + (0.11)(x)$

An 11 percent decrease of $x$:

$x - (0.11)(x)$

**Percentages in daily life:**

**Sales tax** and tips are examples of percent increases. **Discounts** are percent decreases.

30% discount of \$15.30:

$(15.30) - (15.30)(0.3) = \$10.71$.

Or: $(1.0 - 0.3)(15.30) = \$10.71$.

**Interest rates:**

Interest rates are percent increases.

A bank gives a 2.3% monthly interest rate, and there is \$600 in an account.

After one month that account will have:

$\$600 + \$600(0.023) = \$613.80$

## Strategy Review

- When you have a ratio problem with large numbers, try to solve a similar problem with smaller numbers first. Then solve the problem with the large numbers.
- If you need to solve a percentage problem described in words, first organize information by making a table or a chart.
- You can also guess, check, and revise with percent problems involving big numbers.

## Skills and Strategies Practice

**Complete the exercises below. Round your answers to the nearest cent or tenth of a percent.**

1. A $45 pair of shoes was on sale for 25% off. What was the new price of the shoes?

   ________

2. 230 students have gym classes on Thursdays. If there are 702 students in the school, what percentage have Thursday gym classes?

   ________

3. In this school, there are enough badminton rackets for 35% of the students. Are there enough rackets for the students who take gym on Thursdays?

   ________

4. Kevin buys a sandwich for $5.60. He wants to tip the server 12 percent. How much money should he leave?

   ________

5. If 3 pairs of socks cost $9.90, what will 2 pairs cost?

   ________

6. Jay's bank account has a monthly interest rate of 1.2%. If he has $400 in his account, what is the total he will have one month later?

   ________

**Estimation is one way to check whether your answers are reasonable. For example, you may be asked to find the amount a person pays at a restaurant if they add a 15% tip to their bill of $107 dollars. To estimate the answer, round $107 to $100. Since 15% of $100 is $15, the final amount paid should be around, but not equal to, $115.**

# Mid-Unit Review

**Circle the letter of the correct answer. Round numbers when necessary.**

**1.** A store offers a jacket for a 22% discount. If the original price was \$60, what is the sale price?

A. \$13.20 C. \$46.80
B. \$15.20 D. \$48.00

**2.** Solve for $x$. $\frac{4}{16} = \frac{x}{20}$

A. 2 C. 5
B. 4 D. 16

**3.** Gina bought a lamp with a price of \$15.40 and paid 6.5% sales tax. What is the total amount?

A. \$25.40 C. \$14.75
B. \$16.40 D. \$17.46

**4.** Erika gets a lamp that was originally \$34 at an 11% discount. She also has to pay 8% sales tax on the sale price. What is the total amount Erika pays?

A. \$33.40 C. \$30.26
B. \$32.68 D. \$33.05

**5.** What is 3.9% of 20?

A. 0.78 C. 8.0
B. 7.8 D. 0.90

**6.** What is 114% of 34?

A. 148 C. 38.67
B. 38.76 D. 47.94

**7.** If 12 identical beads weigh 13 oz, how much do 10 beads weigh?

A. 12.2 oz C. 10 oz
B. 11 oz D. 10.8 oz

**8.** A woman receives a 10% discount on a \$12 tablecloth. What is the discount price?

A. \$10 C. \$11
B. \$10.80 D. \$13.20

**9.** If 5 bananas cost \$2.20, how much do 7 bananas cost?

A. \$2.42 C. \$8.03
B. \$6.40 D. \$3.08

**10.** Georgie takes her friends to dinner and receives a bill for \$103. If she wants to add a 17% tip, how much money will she leave altogether?

A. \$107.51 C. \$120.51
B. \$130.51 D. \$117

**11.** A train goes 0.5 miles in 40 seconds. What is its speed?

A. 0.0125 miles per second
B. 0.125 miles per second
C. 0.0125 miles per hour
D. 0.8 miles per second

**12.** A bus normally goes 50 miles in 1 hour. One day it took 3 hours to go 50 miles. How different was its speed from normal on that day?

A. 3 times as fast C. $\frac{1}{5}$ as fast
B. $\frac{1}{4}$ as fast D. $\frac{1}{3}$ as fast

## Mid-Unit Review

**13.** Salim has $490 dollars in a bank account that has a yearly interest rate of 5%. After one year, how much money will he have?

A. $514.50 C. $735
B. $526.50 D. $492.45

**14.** On Tuesday, 40 students ate lunch in the cafeteria. This number increased by 30% on Wednesday. How many students ate lunch in the cafeteria on Wednesday?

A. 70 C. 46
B. 52 D. 45

**15.** A bakery discounts day-old bread 25%. If the original price for a loaf was $1.80, what is the day-old sale price?

A. $0.25 C. $1.35
B. $0.45 D. $2.25

**16.** What is 82% of 349?

A. 296.64 C. 97.72
B. 300 D. 286.18

**17.** A garden has 100 plants. If the number of plants decreased by 8%, how many plants would be left?

A. 8 C. 108
B. 92 D. 88

**18.** Kip buys a plant that was originally $18 at a 5% discount. He also has to pay 8% sales tax. What is the total amount he pays?

A. $17.10 C. $17.47
B. $18.90 D. $18.47

**19.** Mr. Tripp borrows $1,000 from a bank at 1.1% monthly interest. If he repays the loan after one month, how much will he have to pay?

A. $1,011 C. $1,050
B. $111 D. $1,001.10

**20.** What is 124% of 20?

A. 2.48 C. 28.4
B. 24.8 D. 32.4

**21.** Solve for $m$. $\frac{1}{40} = \frac{m}{30}$

A. 0.75 C. 0.5
B. $\frac{4}{3}$ D. .3

**22.** What is 1% of 500?

A. 50 C. 5
B. 1 D. 0.5

**23.** Ms. Marshall buys a rug at a 17% discount sale. The rug was originally $523. What is the sale price?

A. $88.91 C. $434.09
B. $486.39 D. $514.11

**24.** Solve for $x$. $\frac{5}{30} = \frac{x}{360}$

A. 6 C. 65
B. 60 D. 63

**25.** Solve for $y$. $\frac{7}{21} = \frac{y}{27}$

A. 9 C. 3
B. $\frac{1}{3}$ D. $4\frac{1}{3}$

# Similar Figures and Scale Factors

## Learn the SKILL

Before architects begin construction they are asked to make a scale model or a **scale drawing** of what they want to build. This is simply a small model of a whole. A **scale factor** is used as a ratio or proportion to create a model. A scale factor is also used to create **similar figures**. If a square has a perimeter of 20 inches and a similar figure is made using a scale factor of $\frac{1}{2}$, what is the perimeter of the similar figure?

### VOCABULARY

Watch for the words you are learning about.

**scale drawing:** an enlarged or reduced drawing of an object that is similar to the actual object

**scale factor:** the ratio of the dimensions of the image to the dimensions of the original figure

**similar figures:** two figures are similar if their corresponding angles have the same measure and the lengths of their corresponding sides are proportional; the symbol ~ means "is similar to"

| SKILL | EXAMPLE | WRITE AN EXAMPLE |
|---|---|---|
| A scale factor refers to the reduction of a side of a figure rather than its area or volume. If the scale factor is greater than 1, it is an enlargement. A scale factor that is less than 1 but greater than 0 is a reduction. | If a square has a perimeter of 20 inches, then each side measures 5 inches. To find the measurements of a similar square with a scale factor of $\frac{1}{2}$, you can multiply each side by $\frac{1}{2}$.<br>$5 \times \frac{1}{2} = 2.5$ in.<br>$2.5 \times 4 = 10$ in. | Write a problem increasing the length of a side of a figure from 20 feet.<br>________________<br>Write a problem decreasing the length of a side of a figure from 15 yards.<br>________________ |
| Scale factors can work in reverse. If there are two similar figures, you can find the scale factor between them using division. | Triangle A's sides each measure 6 in. Triangle B's sides each measure 2 in. The scale factor for Triangle A can be found by dividing 6 by 2.<br>$\frac{6}{2} = 3$ The scale factor is 3. | Square A's sides each measure 12 in. Square B's sides each measure 3 in. Show how to find the scale factor of Square A.<br>________________ |
| You can prove two figures are similar by using scale factors. To determine if two polygons are similar, find the scale factors for the sets of corresponding sides. If the scale factors are equal, the shapes are similar. | The length of Rectangle A measures 4 in. The width measures 3 in. The length of Rectangle B measures 8 in. The width measures 7 in. Are the rectangles similar?<br>$\frac{4}{8} = 0.5$ $\frac{3}{7} \approx 0.43$<br>No, the rectangles are not similar. | Draw two similar figures. |

Learn the Skill

# YOUR TURN

## Choose the Right Word

scale drawing   scale factor   similar figures

**Fill in each blank with the correct word or phrase from the box.**

1. A ________________ is a drawing meant to represent a similar object.
2. A ________________ is how much a figure is reduced or enlarged by.
3. Two figures that are related by a scale factor are ________________.

## Yes or No?

**Answer these questions and be ready to explain your answers.**

4. Would you multiply a scale factor by an original figure's perimeter to find the similar figure's perimeter? ________
5. Would you multiply a scale factor by an original figure's area to find the similar figure's area? ________
6. Can a similar figure have a scale factor of zero? ________

## Show That You Know

**What are the two possible scale factors for the similar figures below?**

7. 2    8

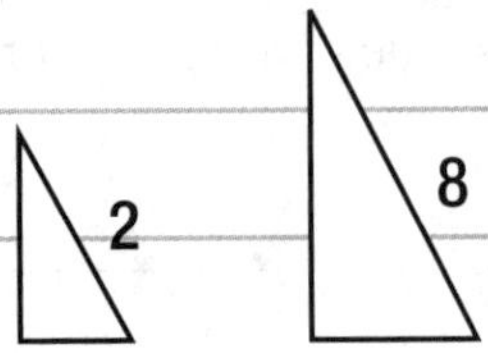

8. 4    7

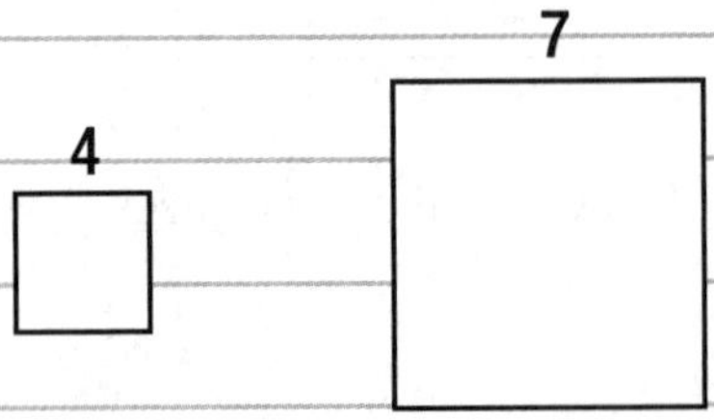

**Find the length of the missing side using the given scale factor.**

9. 7    ?

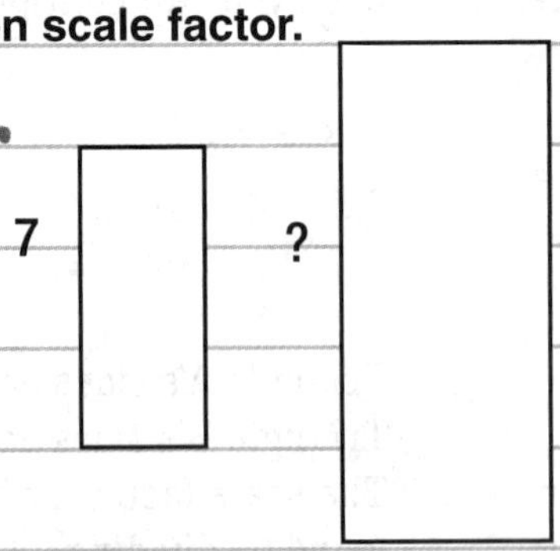

scale factor of 3.2

10. 5.1    ?

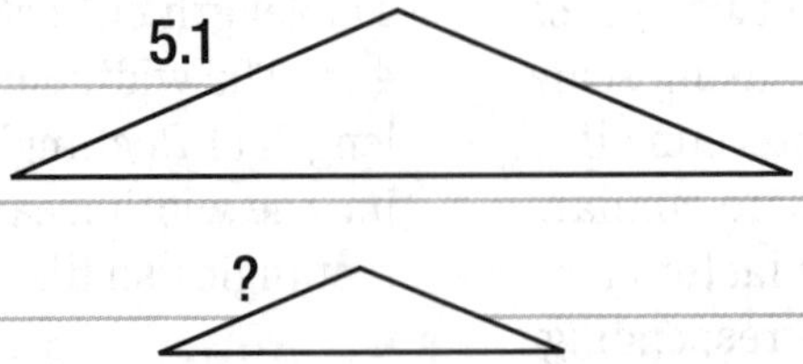

scale factor of $\frac{1}{3}$

# SOLVE on Your Own

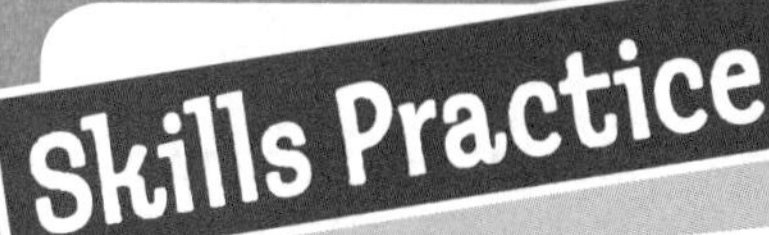


Find the two possible scale factors for the figures.

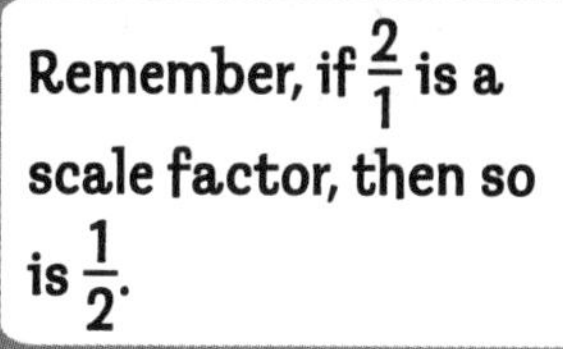

Remember, if $\frac{2}{1}$ is a scale factor, then so is $\frac{1}{2}$.

1. ______________

3 5

2. ______________

7 8

3. ______________

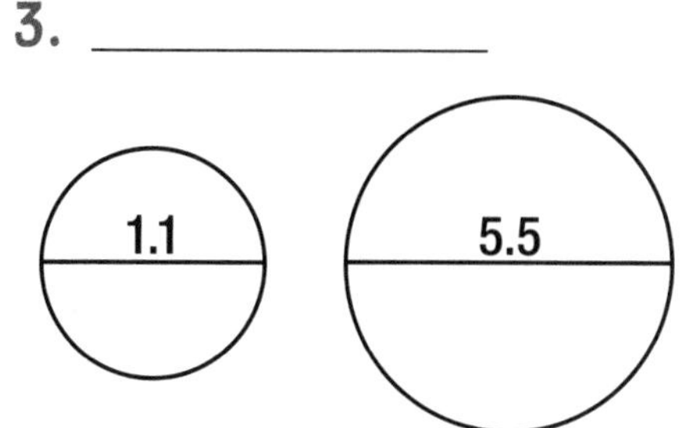


Determine if the figures below are similar.

4. ______________

5. ______________

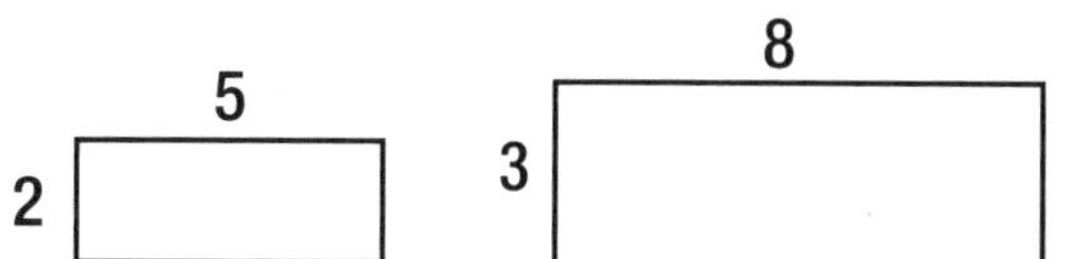


6. ______________

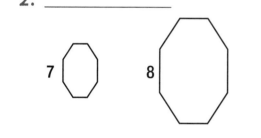

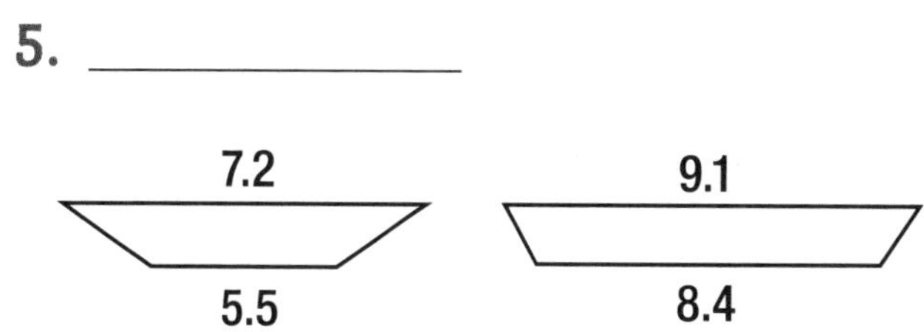

# Similar Figures and Scale Factors

## Strategies

### Guess, Check, and Revise; Find a Pattern

**Step 1: Read** For a hospital, a builder sketches 20 rooms with a total area of 6,000 sq ft. He uses two sizes of rooms that he says are similar rectangles. The small room is 10 ft by 20 ft. Its area is 200 sq ft. Ten of these rooms will be 2,000 sq ft. For the large room, he doubles the length and width to 20 ft × 40 ft. He says 10 of these rooms have an area of 4,000 sq ft, so the total area is 2,000 + 4,000 = 6,000 sq ft. What error did the builder make? Can you find similar rectangles, 10 small ones and 10 large ones, which combine to give an area of 6,000 sq ft?

| STRATEGY | SOLUTION |
|---|---|
| **Guess, Check, and Revise**<br>The rooms are similar rectangles. However, the builder had the wrong area for the 10 large rooms. It should be $10 \times 20$ ft $\times 40$ ft $= 8{,}000$ sq ft. These sizes of rooms do not work; guess other sizes. | **Step 2: Plan** Guess a scale factor of 2. If the small room is $x$ by $y$, the large room is $2x$ by $2y$. Add the areas for 10 rooms of each.<br>**Step 3: Solve** The areas will be $10xy$ and $10(2x)(2y)$. Add:<br>$10xy + 10(2x)(2y) = 10xy + 40xy = 50xy = 6{,}000$ sq ft<br>$xy = 6{,}000 \div 50 = 120$ sq ft<br>So, the small room could be 8 ft × 15 ft and the large room 16 ft × 30 ft. Another answer would be 10 ft × 12 ft and 20 ft × 24 ft .<br>**Step 4: Check** Check the first answer. The area of the small rooms is $10 \times 8 \times 15 = 1{,}200$ sq ft. The area of the large rooms is $10 \times 16 \times 30 = 4{,}800$ sq ft. The total is $1{,}200 + 4{,}800 = 6{,}000$ sq ft. |
| **Find a Pattern**<br>Looking for patterns may be a way to find many answers. Look for scale factors that give room areas that add to numbers that are likely to be factors of 6,000. | **Step 2: Plan** Find the area of one small and one large room for different scale factors. Then see if the sum is a factor of 6,000.<br>**Step 3: Solve** Try a scale factor of 3. The ratio of the areas is 9:1. So, if $a$ is the area of the small room, then the area of both rooms is $a + 9a = 10a$. Ten times this, or $100a$, gives an answer:<br>$100a = 6{,}000$ sq ft, so $a = 60$ sq ft. This will work.<br>If the scale factor is 4, then $a + 16a = 17a$; but 17 is not a factor of 6,000, so this does not work.<br>Try a scale factor of 7. $a + 49a = 50a$; This works:<br>$10 \times 50a = 6{,}000$ sq ft, so $a = 12$ sq ft.<br>If the small room is 2 ft × 6 ft, the large room can be 14 ft × 42 ft.<br>**Step 4: Check** The small room's area is 12 sq ft. The large room's area is $14 \times 42 = 588$ sq ft. This works: $10(12 + 588) = 6{,}000$ sq ft. |

# YOUR TURN

Choose a Strategy

## Choose the Right Word

scale   scale drawing   scale factor

**Fill in each blank with the correct word or phrase from the box.**

1. A ________________ is the ratio that compares a length in a drawing to the corresponding length in the actual object.
2. A ________________ is a ratio of dimensions.
3. A model or drawing of the enlargement or reduction of an object is called a ________________.

## Yes or No?

**Answer these questions and be ready to explain your answers.**

4. If the lengths of the sides of an object have been reduced by a scale factor of $\frac{1}{2}$, has the area been reduced by more than this? ________
5. Can two similar figures have the same areas, but different dimensions? ________
6. Does a scale factor of 0 imply the new figure is the same as the original? ________

## Show That You Know

**The scale of a drawing is $\frac{1}{2}$ inch equals 20 feet. Find the actual length.**

7. 2 in.
8. 1 in.
9. 5.8 in.
10. 7 in.
11. 1.5 in.

**The figures below are similar. Find the scale factor. Then solve for the variables.**

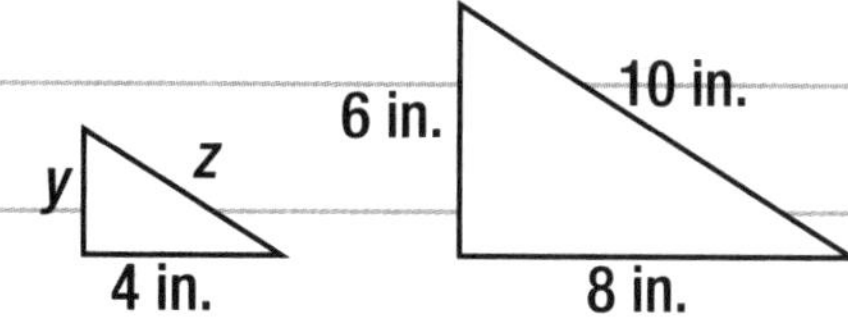


12. $y =$
13. $z =$

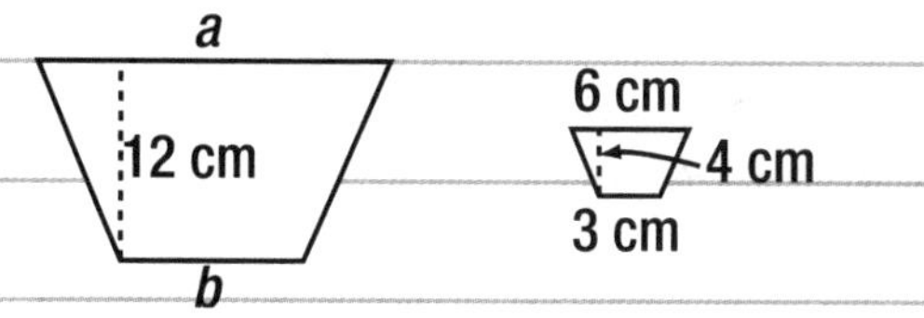


14. $a =$
15. $b =$

# READ on Your Own

## Reading Comprehension Strategy: Summarizing

### VOCABULARY

Watch for the words you are learning about.

**alien:** coming from a foreign area

**ecosystem:** a community of organisms and their surroundings working together as a unit

### Fluency Tip

Before reading, look through sentences for words you do not know. Find out how to pronounce them.

## Diseases and Invasive Species, *pages 20–22*

### Before You Read

You read about Edward Jenner in "The First Vaccine." Do you think that Jenner would be punished if he performed his experiment today? Explain.

### As You Read

**Read "From Another World," pages 20–21.** 

Fill in that part of the chart below.

**Read "Snake Attack," pages 21–22.** 

Fill in that part of the chart below.

| From Another World | Snake Attack |
|---|---|
| **Important Details:** | **Important Details:** |
| **Summary:** | **Summary:** |

### After You Read

What could have been done to protect Guam's native bird population?

# SOLVE on Your Own

## Diseases and Invasive Species, *page 22*

### Organize the Information

**Read You Do the Math in the magazine. Then fill in the blanks below.**

Number of power outages = ________

How many years are there from 1978 to 1997? ________ − ________ = ________

Guess by estimation:

$\frac{1{,}600}{20} \rightarrow \frac{2{,}000}{20} =$ ________

Check: Divide 1,600 by 20.

Is your quotient close to your guess? ________

An average is a rate. It often has units that include "per," such as miles per gallon or outages per year.


### You Do the Math

Use the information in the list to answer these questions. Write your answers in the space provided.

1. How will you find the average number of power outages per year?

________________________________________

________________________________________

2. If the time you were looking at were 1996 to 1997, what difference would you find if you subtract? Is this the correct difference to use for the elapsed time from the start of 1996 to the end of 1997? Explain.

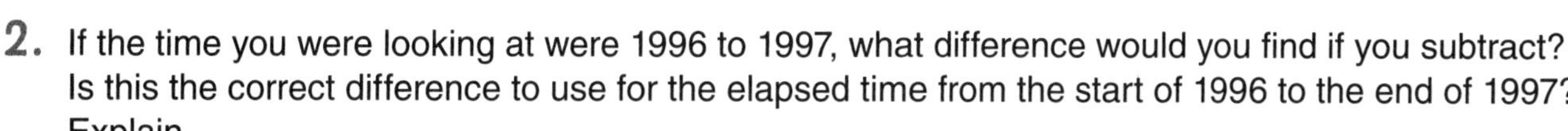

________________________________________

________________________________________

3. What was the average number of power outages per year in Guam from 1978 to 1997?

________________________________________

________________________________________

### After You Solve

What are some times where you had trouble counting a difference?

________________________________________

________________________________________

# Proportionality and Graphing

## Learn the SKILL

A **graph** is a way to visually see the solutions to a problem. For instance, if you know a pound of oranges costs $1.89 you could use multiplication to find the cost of 3 pounds, 4 pounds, and so on. You can also use graphing to see all possible solutions at once. Not all graphs are simple and straightforward, so take samples of the graph to either represent the whole or to compare to the whole.

The graph to the right compares the cost of chicken and fish per pound. What is the slope of each line? What is the rate of the cost of chicken and fish?

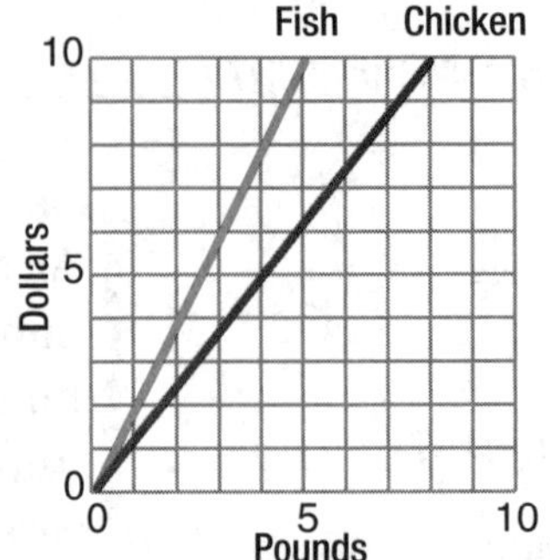


### VOCABULARY

Watch for the words you are learning about.

**graph:** a visual display that shows data in different ways

**rate:** a ratio that compares two quantities measured in different units

**slope:** a ratio that describes the tilt of a line

***x*-axis:** the horizontal axis of the coordinate plane

***y*-axis:** the vertical axis of the coordinate plane

| SKILL | EXAMPLE | WRITE AN EXAMPLE |
|---|---|---|
| A line **slope** is a ratio that describes a line's tilt (how steep or flat it is) in a graph. To find slope ($m$), divide the change in the value of $y$ by the change in the value of $x$.<br>$m = \frac{\text{change in } y\text{-value}}{\text{change in } x\text{-value}}$<br>Comparing any two points on the same line will give the slope. | To find the slope of the "Chicken" line above, we must first find 2 points on the line. Look for points where the line crosses exactly over whole numbers to make it easier. We will choose (4, 5) and (8, 10).<br>$m = \frac{\text{change in } y\text{-value}}{\text{change in } x\text{-value}} = \frac{(5-10)}{(4-8)} = \frac{-5}{-4} = \frac{5}{4}.$<br>Two negatives make a positive, so the slope ($m$) of this line is $\frac{5}{4}$. | Look at the "Fish" line above. Write an equation to find the slope.<br>____________________<br>____________________ |
| A **rate** is a ratio that compares two amounts measured in different units. Statements such as "a car traveling 60 miles per hour" or "gas is $3 per gallon" are examples of rates. | To find the rate of the "Fish" line above, find a point on the line and compare $x$ with $y$. The value of $x$, 1, is the quantity of pounds and the value of $y$, 2, is the quantity of dollars. Therefore, fish costs $2 per pound. | Calculate the rate of the "Chicken" line using the graph above. |
| A graph can be made by drawing a picture of data collected. Determine what each segment of the $x$-axis and the $y$-axis represents. | If you are graphing something with a constant rate then you need information on only two data points. | Draw a graph. |

# YOUR TURN



## Choose the Right Word

slope  rate  *y*-axis

**Fill in each blank with the correct word or phrase from the box.**

1. A ________________ is a ratio that describes the tilt of a line.
2. A ________________ is a ratio that compares two different units.
3. The ________________ is the vertical axis on a coordinate plane.

## Yes or No?

**Answer these questions and be ready to explain your answers.**

4. Can you determine a rate without a graph? ________
5. Can you determine the slope of two points if they are not plotted on a graph? ________
6. Are the *x*-axis and the *y*-axis interchangeable? ________

## Show That You Know

**Determine the rate of each.**

7. 5 pounds of beef cost $12
8. 6 grapefruits cost $10.56
9. 7 gallons of milk cost $17.43
10. A car travels 85 miles in 2.5 hours
11. A person runs 18.3 miles in 3 hours

**These ordered pairs show the locations of points. Use them to find the slope of a line that crosses the points.**

12. (0, 0) (2, 3)
13. (3, 3) (6, 9)
14. (2, 5) (18, 5)
15. (6, 7) (10, 10)
16. (4, 1) (3, 0)

# SOLVE on Your Own

## Skills Practice

**Below is a graph of a trip. Use the graph to answer questions 1–5.**

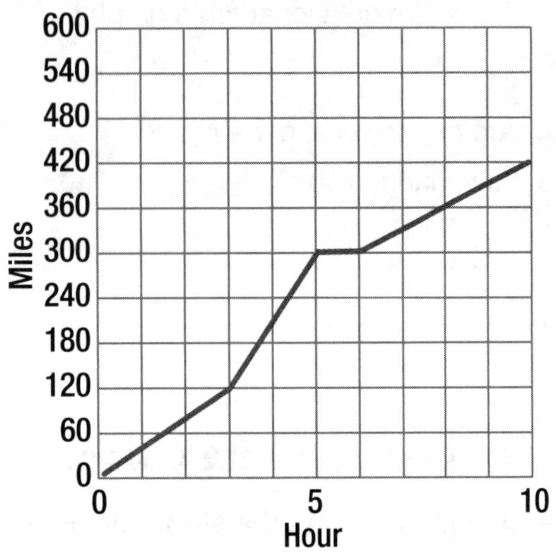

Remember, the slope is the change in the y-value (output) over the change in the x-value (input).


1. Between the fifth and sixth hours, what is the rate of speed of the car? ________________

2. What is the slope between the sixth and eighth hours? ________________

3. What is the rate of the speed of the car from the third hour to the fifth hour? ________________

4. What is the slope between the fifth and sixth hours? ________________

5. What is the slope between the eighth and tenth hours? ________________

6. It costs $48 dollars to rent a car for 2 days. Draw a graph to determine the cost after 7 days.

________________________________________________________________

________________________________________________________________

# Proportionality and Graphing

## Strategies

### Make a Table or a Chart, Draw a Picture or Use a Model

**Step 1: Read** A one-year-old Empress tree and a one-year-old Ameri-Willow tree are planted at the same time. Five years later, the Ameri-Willow tree is 12 feet taller than the Empress tree. The Ameri-Willow tree grows at a rate of 8 feet per year. What could be the growth rate for the Empress tree?

| STRATEGY | SOLUTION |
|---|---|

#### Make a Table or a Chart

Making a table of the data points can help you find many solutions. For each number of years, you can look for a difference of 12 ft in the table values.

**Step 2: Plan** List the known data points for the Ameri-Willow tree (shaded gray). List possible data points for the Empress tree. In year six, look for a distance of 12 feet.

**Step 3: Solve** Make a table.

| | Growth Rate (Feet Per Year) | | | | | | |
|---|---|---|---|---|---|---|---|
| **Years** | **2** | **3** | **4** | **5** | **6** | **7** | **8** |
| **1** | 2 | 3 | 4 | 5 | 6 | 7 | 8 |
| **2** | 4 | 6 | 8 | 10 | 12 | 14 | 16 |
| **3** | 6 | 9 | 12 | 15 | 18 | 21 | 24 |
| **4** | 8 | 12 | 16 | 20 | 24 | 28 | 32 |
| **5** | 10 | 15 | 20 | 25 | 30 | 35 | 40 |
| **6** | 12 | 18 | 24 | 30 | 36 | 42 | 48 |

**Step 4: Check** After 6 years and a growth rate of 6 feet per year, the difference is 48 ft – 36 ft = 12 ft.

#### Draw a Picture or Use a Model

You can use a graph to solve a proportion problem. In this problem, you look for two proportions in which the vertical distance between the graphs is 12 ft at six years.

**Step 2: Plan** Graph for the Ameri-Willow tree using a growth rate of 8 ft per year. Draw graphs for the possible growth rates of the Empress tree. At six years, look for a data point that is 12 less than the value on the Ameri-Willow tree graph.

**Step 3: Solve** Draw the graph.

**Step 4: Check** For 6 years, and a growth rate of 6 feet per year, the difference is 48 ft – 36 ft = 12 ft.

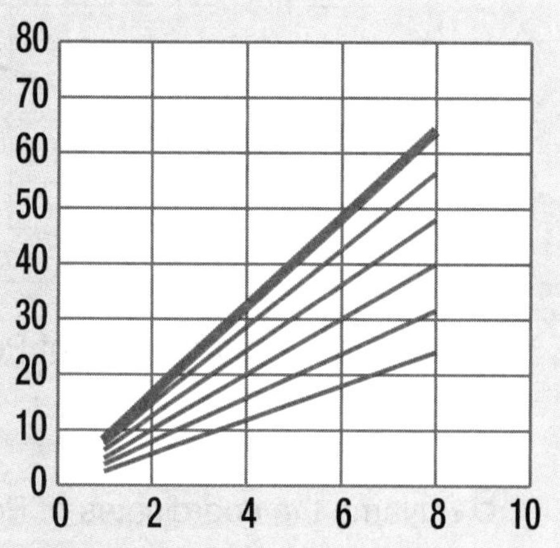

Choose a Strategy

# YOUR TURN

## Choose the Right Word

slope graph *x*-axis

**Fill in each blank with the correct word or phrase from the box.**

1. A ________________ is a visual display that shows data in different ways.
2. A tilt of a line is known as the ________________ of the line.
3. The ________________ is the horizontal axis on a coordinate plane.

## Yes or No?

**Answer these questions and be ready to explain your answers.**

4. Can you determine the slope of a graph by looking at only 1 point? ________
5. Can you determine the slope of the graph by looking at 2 points? ________
6. If you know all the values of *x* can you determine the slope of a graph? ________

## Show That You Know

**Use the graph below to find the slope of the line.**

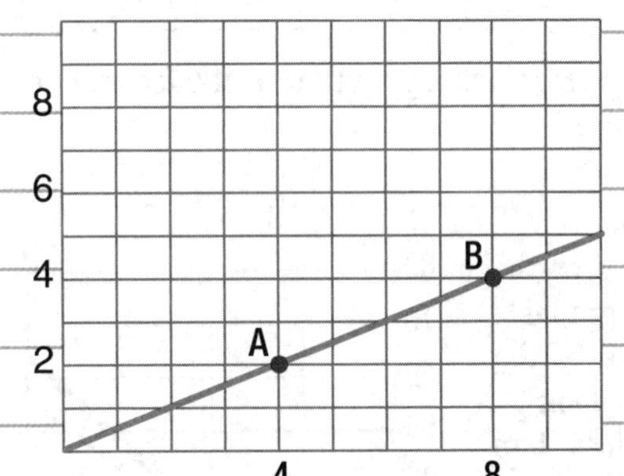


7. Name the coordinates of Point *A*.
8. Name the coordinates of Point *B*.
9. What is the slope of line *AB*?

**Use these ordered pairs to find the slope of a line.**

10. (5, 2) and (9, 3)
11. (4, 6) and (5, 9)
12. (10, 3) and (1, 1)
13. (13, 18) and (9, 2)

# READ on Your Own

## Reading Comprehension Strategy: Summarizing

## Diseases and Invasive Species, *pages 23–24*

**VOCABULARY**

Watch for the words you are learning about.

**invasive species:** a species that moves or is transported to an ecosystem and competes with local species

**Fluency Tip**

Reread sentences that you find difficult. Change our expression as you read.

### Before You Read

In reading "In the Way," you learned about the mistakes humans make in spreading invasive species. How could these mistakes be prevented?

### As You Read

**Read "Spinning Out of Control," pages 23–24.** 

Fill in that part of the chart below.

**Read "Fighting Back," page 24.** 

Fill in that part of the chart below.

| Spinning Out of Control | Fighting Back |
|---|---|
| **Important Details:** | **Important Details:** |
| **Summary:** | **Summary:** |

### After You Read

Can an invasive species be beneficial? Explain.

# SOLVE on Your Own

## Diseases and Invasive Species, *page 25*

### Organize the Information

**Read You Do the Math in the magazine. Then fill in the table below.**

1 km = 3,280 ft

50 km = ______________ ft

A simple relationship may be simple to apply, as long as you do not confuse x with y!

| Year, $x$ | 1 | 5 | 10 | |
|---|---|---|---|---|
| Distance, $y$ | 60 | | | 164,000 |

### You Do the Math

Use the information in the table above to answer these questions. Write your answers in the space provided.

1. Write an equation or rule to show the relationship of $x$ and $y$.

______________________________

2. What do $x$ and $y$ in the equation stand for?

______________________________

______________________________

3. How long would it take the kudzu plant to grow 1 kilometer? Show your work using an equation.

______________________________

4. How long would it take the kudzu plant to grow 50 kilometers? Explain.

______________________________

______________________________

### After You Solve

What other climbing or trailing plants do you know?

______________________________

## The Four-Step Problem-Solving Plan

| Step 1: Read | Step 2: Plan | Step 3: Solve | Step 4: Check |
|---|---|---|---|
| Make sure you understand what the problem is asking. | Decide how you will solve the problem. | Solve the problem using your plan. | Check to make sure your answer is correct. |

**Read the article below. Then answer the questions.**

### Zebra mussels

Zebra mussels are a type of freshwater shellfish. Shellfish are not actually fish; they are invertebrates—animals without a backbone. Clams and oysters are also examples of shellfish.

The scientific name of the zebra mussel is *Dreissena polymorpha*. They were given their common name because they often have stripes on their shells like a zebra. The *polymorpha* in their scientific name means "many forms" and refers to the fact that not all zebra mussels have stripes. Some have shells that are all dark or light colored.

Adult zebra mussels are very small, about the size of a fingernail. This is one reason they can be carried from one body of water to another on ships without anyone noticing. Even worse, their larvae, or young, are so small that they are nearly invisible. These larvae, called veligers, can swim freely, unlike adult zebra mussels that attach themselves to surfaces such as rock or wood.

Zebra mussels reproduce very quickly. Every year, an adult female zebra mussel can make between 30,000 and 100,000 eggs. Each egg takes a year to develop first into a veliger, and then into an adult that can reproduce again.

1. Why might zebra mussels be easily carried on ships without anyone noticing?

_______________

_______________

_______________

_______________

2. Suppose one female zebra mussel is introduced into a lake. She produces 40,000 eggs, $\frac{1}{20}$ of which develop into female zebra mussels. Assuming the same rate of egg production, how many eggs will the next generation of zebra mussels produce?

_______________

_______________

_______________

_______________

Application

# YOUR TURN

**Read the article below. Then answer the questions.**

## Spread of Zebra Mussels

Zebra mussels are native to southern Russia. The construction of canals in Europe in the 1700s and 1800s allowed the mussels to spread throughout Europe's major rivers. They arrived in Britain in 1824 and are now found throughout Europe.

The first report that zebra mussels had reached North America came from Lake St. Clair, on the U.S.-Canada border, in 1988. Lake St. Clair connects Lake Huron and Lake Erie, parts of the Great Lakes system. By 1990—only two years later—zebra mussels had spread throughout the Great Lakes.

From the Great Lakes, zebra mussels moved into nearby rivers, eventually reaching the Mississippi River. The Mississippi River runs over 1.2 million square miles through much of the central United States. By 1994, zebra mussels had been reported in waters in or next to 19 states all over the eastern and central United States. Since then, they have reached Connecticut, Virginia, Nebraska, and North Dakota. They continue to spread, recently as far as Nevada.

### Fluency Tip

Be careful to read every word without skipping or substituting words. If a sentence or paragraph does not make sense, reread every word.

1. How did zebra mussels spread throughout Europe's major rivers?

 ______________________________

2. Where did zebra mussels first appear in North America?

 ______________________________

3. About what percentage of states in the United States have zebra mussels?

 ______________________________

 ______________________________

4. Suppose zebra mussels are now found in 100,000 square miles of the Mississippi River and double their range every 3 years. Over what area will they be found in 6 years?

 ______________________________

 ______________________________

 ______________________________

# READ on Your Own

## Reading Comprehension Strategy: Summarizing

## Diseases and Invasive Species, *pages 26–28*

### Before You Read

You read about kudzu in "An Unstoppable Vine." Why do you think kudzu grows better in the American South than it had in Japan?

### As You Read

**Read "Who Is Invading Whom?", pages 26–28.** 

Rewrite the following sentences in the correct order.

Zebra mussels are carried onboard ships across the Atlantic.

Zebra mussels spread out from the Great Lakes.

Ships dump out water carrying zebra mussels.

Ships take on water carrying zebra mussels.

1. ______________________________

2. ______________________________

3. ______________________________

4. ______________________________

### After You Read

Why are people who move fishing boats from lake to lake often required to clean them thoroughly?

______________________________

### VOCABULARY

Watch for the words you are learning about.

**aquatic:** living in water or related to water

**larvae:** early form of a living thing that hatches from an egg; it is unlike its parent but will change as it grows (singular: larva)

### Fluency Tip

Read complex material at a natural pace but slowly enough to make sense of difficult concepts.

# SOLVE on Your Own

## Diseases and Invasive Species, *page 29*

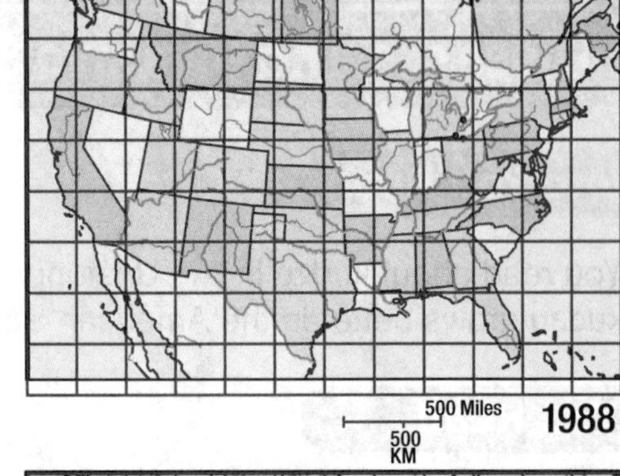


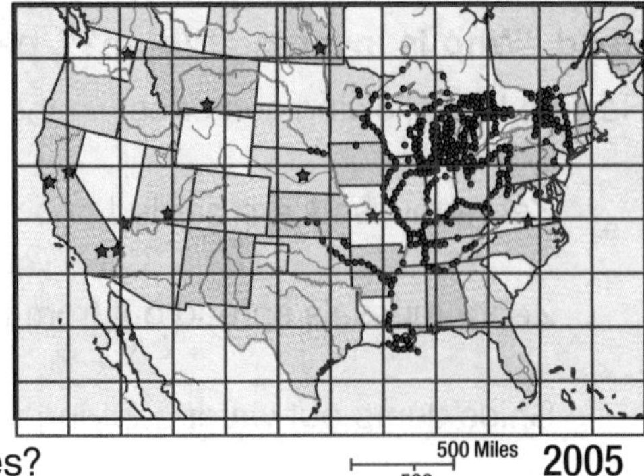


### Organize the Information

**Use a list like the one below to organize the information you find in the Math Project on magazine page 29.**

| |
|---|
| Number of square units on the map: ________ square units |
| Estimated area of the United States: ________ square units |
| Area of the mussel range in 1988: ________ square units |
| Area of the mussel range in 2005: ________ square units |

### Math Project

Use the information in the list above to answer these questions. Write your answers in the spaces provided.

1. How could you use the grid on the map to estimate the areas of the zebra mussel range and the whole United States?

_______________

_______________

2. How could you express the range of zebra mussels as a percentage of the area of the whole United States?

_______________

3. Count the areas you determine do not have units of measurement such as square miles. Does this figure matter for the purpose of this exercise? Explain your answer.

_______________

_______________

### After You Solve

How could you express some of the same information in the list by drawing a picture?

_______________

_______________

# Percentages, Histograms, and Circle Graphs

## Learn the SKILL

To determine the interests and characteristics of a population, politicians often hire people to take opinion polls. However, after they collect their **data** they face the issue of how to display their data. A simple way to do this is to list the percent totals. However, a more visually pleasing way is to use graphs like **histograms** or circle graphs. Which one of these methods would you use to represent a survey of people's favorite drinks?

### VOCABULARY

Watch for the words you are learning about.

**data:** information gathered from surveys or experiments

**histogram:** a graph that shows how many items occur between two numbers; used to display large amounts of data

| SKILL | EXAMPLE | WRITE AN EXAMPLE |
|---|---|---|
| Percents are ratios that compare a number to 100. | To find a percentage you need to take a part of the whole and divide it by the whole. In a survey, all percentages must add up to 100%. | Sixty out of 80 people said they preferred orange juice to apple juice. Use this data to show how to find a percentage. ______ |
| Histograms are similar to bar graphs because they both show data using bars. A histogram's data, though, is in a set range, like ages 0–10, not tied to one specific number. A histogram's bars have no space between them. | A histogram can display a large amount of data. 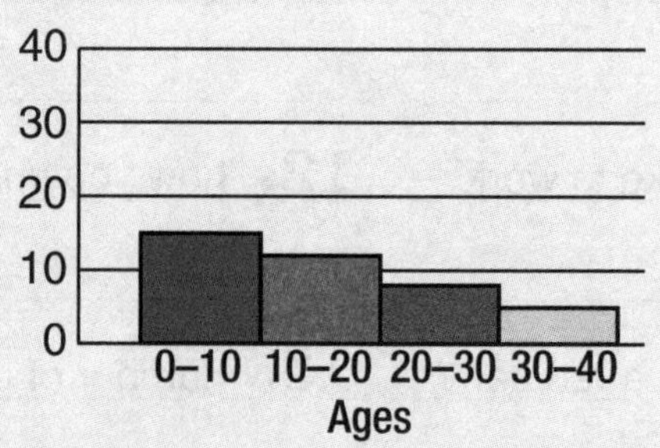  | Create a histogram of ages in your class. |
| Circle graphs are based on percentage. The circle represents 100% of a whole group. Each piece is part of that 100%. | Together, the pieces of a circle graph total 100%. 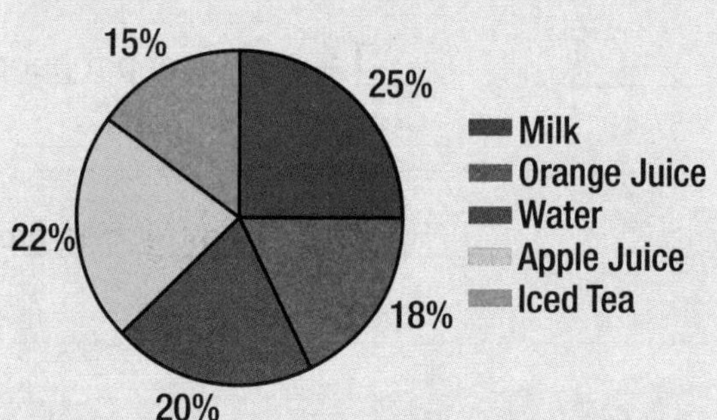  | Create a circle graph of favorite drinks in your class. |

Learn the Skill

# YOUR TURN

## Choose the Right Word

data histogram circle graph

**Fill in each blank with the correct word or phrase from the box.**

1. During a survey, ________________ is collected.

2. A ________________ is a bar graph in which there is no space between the bars.

3. A ________________ uses percentages to show data.

## Yes or No?

**Answer these questions and be ready to explain your answers.**

4. Can a circle graph show more or less than 100%? ________

5. Would a survey about hair color be best put into a histogram? ________

6. Can you find a percentage if you know how many people are in a group and how many people were surveyed? ________

## Show That You Know

**Find the percentage. Round if necessary.**

7. 40 people are surveyed; 12 choose apples as their favorite fruit

8. 200 people are surveyed; 15 bike to work

9. 67 people are surveyed; 17 own a red car

10. 414 people are surveyed; 214 will vote for your candidate

**Choose the best way to display the data: a circle graph or a histogram.**

11. a survey of people's ages

12. how you spend your allowance

13. number of glasses of water people drink per day for different age groups

14. type of pet people own

15. number and types of books a person owns

# SOLVE on Your Own

## Skills Practice

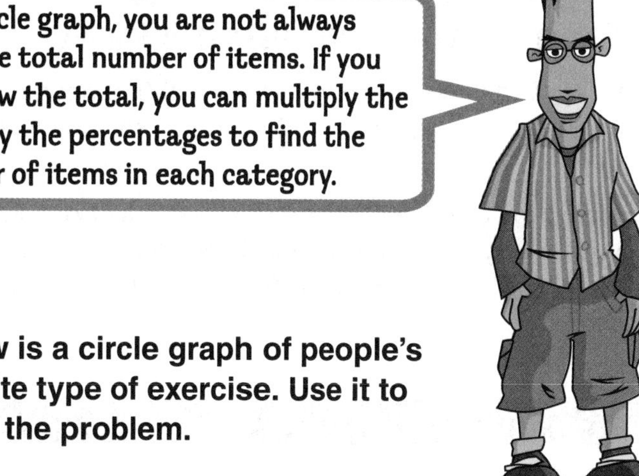

In a circle graph, you are not always told the total number of items. If you do know the total, you can multiply the total by the percentages to find the number of items in each category.


**Solve.**

1. What is 17% of 218? ________

2. 18 is 10% of what? ________

3. 50 is what percent of 400? ________

4. 9 is what percent of 60? ________

5. What is 4% of 1,012? ________

**Below is a circle graph of people's favorite type of exercise. Use it to solve the problem.**

6. If 400 people were surveyed, how many people like each form of exercise?

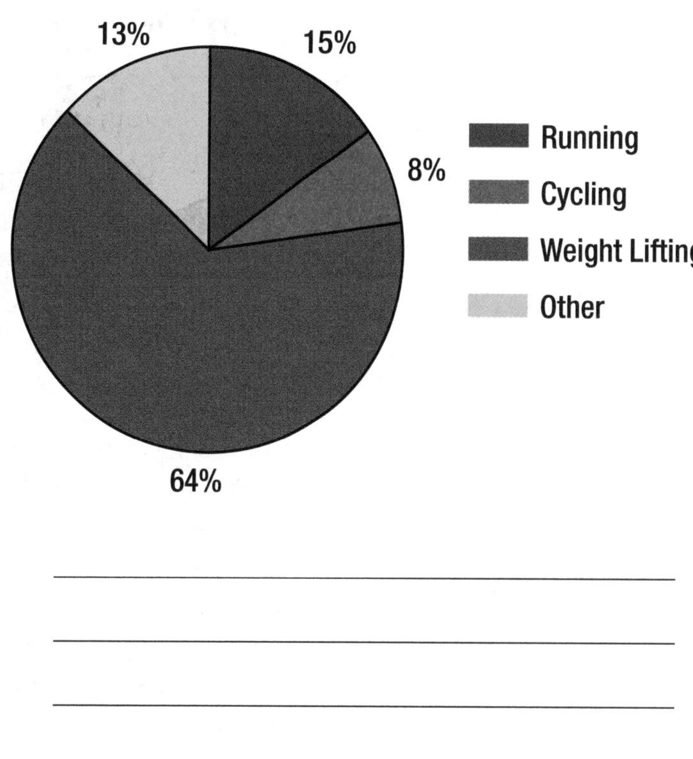


______________________________________

______________________________________

______________________________________

______________________________________

Choose a Strategy

# Percentages, Histograms, and Circle Graphs

## Strategy

### Draw a Picture or Use a Model

**Step 1: Read** Suppose you survey 10,000 people in a city to see if you want to market a product there. You collect the data on the right.

Your company produces two products. Product A sells best to people 20–40 years old. Product B sells best to a people aged 40–60. Which product would you recommend your company sell in this city?

| Age | Number of people |
|---|---|
| 0–10 | 988 |
| 11–20 | 1,201 |
| 21–30 | 2,017 |
| 31–40 | 2,228 |
| 41–50 | 1,718 |
| 51–60 | 1,090 |
| 61+ | 758 |

**STRATEGY**

**Draw a Picture or Use a Model**

You can find out which product is more marketable using a circle graph or a histogram. It may help to circle or shade the age ranges in which each product sells best.

**SOLUTION**

**Step 2: Plan** To make a histogram, use the ranges and the values in the table. To make a circle graph, find the percentage of each category by dividing the number in the category by the total, 10,000. Then use the percentages to make the circle graph. Finally, look at each graph and decide the best argument to make with that graph.

**Step 3: Solve** The graphs look like this:

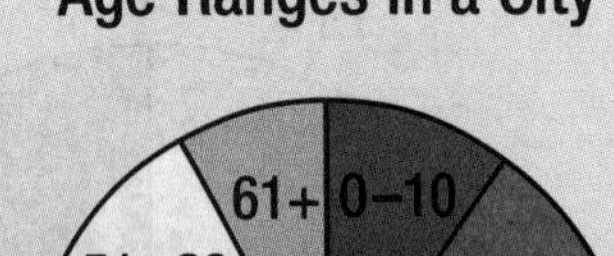
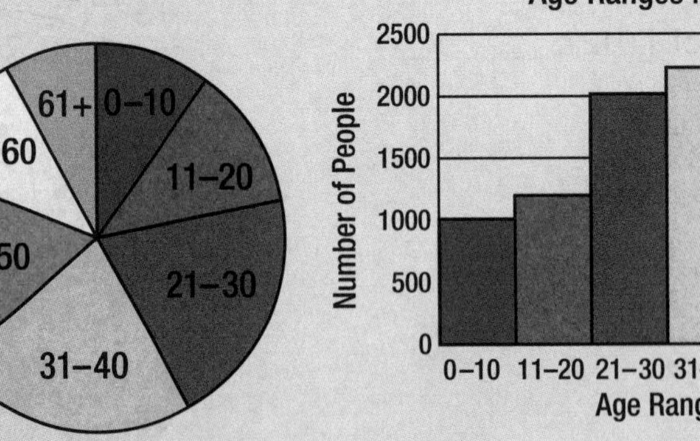

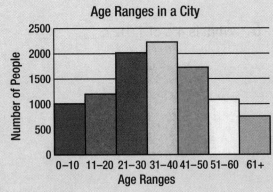


What can you tell from the histogram? You can argue that the peak of the population is in the 21–40 year-old range.

What story can tell with the circle graph? By itself, the 31–40 year-old range almost equals the entire 41–60 year-old range. So the difference is the area in yellow, the 21–30 year-olds. That is a large slice of the pie!

**Step 4: Check** You can check the graphs against each other to make sure they are accurate. For example, the largest bar should be the same as the largest section of the circle graph. In both, it is the 31–40 year-old range.

# YOUR TURN

Choose a Strategy

## Choose the Right Word

histogram circle graph bar graph

**Fill in each blank with the correct word or phrase from the box.**

1. A ________________ is data that is shown in separated bars.
2. A ________________ is a graph that shows how many items are between two numbers.
3. A ________________ shows percentages based on 100.

## Yes or No?

**Answer these questions and be ready to explain your answers.**

4. Could you use a survey about how much television different age groups watch on a histogram? ________
5. Would a circle graph be a good way to show how many roses the local flower shop sells every weekend? ________
6. Does a histogram display data within a certain range, rather than of a specific number? ________

## Show That You Know

**The table below shows the favorite movie genres of Melissa's class. Make a circle graph of the data.**

7.

| Comedy | Horror | Action | Romance | Drama |
|---|---|---|---|---|
| 8 | 4 | 7 | 3 | 5 |

**The players on Ryan's basketball team recorded the number of free throws they can make in 30 seconds. Make a histogram from the table below.**

8.

| Player | 1 | 2 | 3 | 4 | 5 | 6 | 7 | 8 | 9 |
|---|---|---|---|---|---|---|---|---|---|
| Free throws | 4 | 1 | 5 | 2 | 7 | 3 | 6 | 10 | 12 |

| Player | 10 | 11 | 12 | 13 | 14 | 15 | 16 | 17 | 18 |
|---|---|---|---|---|---|---|---|---|---|
| Free throws | 14 | 0 | 2 | 8 | 9 | 4 | 9 | 4 | 12 |

# READ on Your Own

## Reading Comprehension Strategy: Summarizing

## Diseases and Invasive Species, *pages 30–31*

### VOCABULARY

Watch for the words you are learning about.

**influenza:** a virus that causes diseases commonly known as the "flu"

**mutate:** to change from one form into another; the change is passed on to offspring

### Fluency Tip

If you find yourself reading so quickly that you are missing the meaning, slow down.

### Before You Read

You read about zebra mussels in "Who Is Invading Whom?" How are invasive species introduced?

### As You Read

**Read "Worldwide Invasion," pages 30–31.** 

Fill in that part of the chart below.

**Read "Avian Flu," page 31.** 

Fill in that part of the chart below.

| Worldwide Invasion | Avian Flu |
|---|---|
| **Important Details:** ___ ___ ___ | **Important Details:** ___ ___ ___ |
| **Summary:** ___ ___ ___ ___ | **Summary:** ___ ___ ___ ___ |

### After You Read

How can we prevent a worldwide pandemic from happening again?

___

___

# SOLVE on Your Own

## Diseases and Invasive Species, *page 32*

### Organize the Information

**Read the magazine. Then fill in the chart below.**

**Find 30,000, 32,500, or 35,000 divided by 10,000,000. Since these numbers are large, try changing the numbers to smaller numbers. You can do this by dropping three zeros from both dividend and divisor.**

| 30 divided by 10,000 | |
|---|---|
| 32.5 divided by 10,000 | |
| 35 divided by 10,000 | |

The value of a fraction remains the same if you divide the numerator and denominator by the same number.


### You Do the Math

Use the information in the table above to answer these questions. Write your answers in the space provided.

1. Why were three zeros dropped from both dividend and divisors?

_______________

_______________

2. Since the answer would be the same if the three zeros were dropped for both divisor and dividends, fill in the blanks below.

| 30,000 divided by 10,000,000 | |
|---|---|
| 32,500 divided by 10,000,000 | |
| 35,000 divided by 10,000,000 | |

3. Convert the second column to percents. What is the average?

_______________

### After You Solve

The chart above shows that 0.3% to 0.4% of the population died from Spanish flu in New York in 1918. Why would you not express these numbers as fractions?

_______________

## The Four-Step Problem-Solving Plan

| Step 1: Read | Step 2: Plan | Step 3: Solve | Step 4: Check |
|---|---|---|---|
| Make sure you understand what the problem is asking. | Decide how you will solve the problem. | Solve the problem using your plan. | Check to make sure your answer is correct. |

**Read the article below. Then answer the questions.**

### The AIDS Epidemic

Scientists think that the AIDS epidemic began around 1950 in West Africa. Most likely the virus was originally transmitted to humans from chimpanzees at around that time. The oldest blood sample containing HIV—the virus that causes AIDS—was collected in 1959 from a man in the Democratic Republic of Congo.

HIV reached the United States some time in the 1970s. Around 1980 doctors began reporting cases of unusual diseases that people with healthy immune systems would not normally get. The HIV virus itself was discovered in 1983.

According to the World Health Organization, about 39.5 million people worldwide today are living with HIV. About 1 million of these people live in the United States. In 2006 there were 4.3 million new HIV infections. About 2.8 million of these infections occurred in sub-Saharan Africa. The same year, 2.9 million people died as a result of AIDS. Despite advances in prevention and treatment of AIDS, there is still no cure for the disease, and the epidemic continues to grow.

1. Why is HIV/AIDS considered a relatively new disease?

_______________

_______________

2. After reading the article, how do you think that AIDS attacks the human body?

_______________

_______________

3. Out of all the new AIDS infections in 2006, what percentage occurred in sub-Saharan Africa?

_______________

4. How many more people were living with HIV at the end of 2006 compared with the beginning of the year?

_______________

_______________

# YOUR TURN

Application

Read the article below. Then answer the questions.

## Invasive Species in Canada

Like the United States, Canada also has many invasive species that cause many problems. About 5% of animal species and 27% of vascular plant species are not native to Canada.

You read earlier about the zebra mussel. This animal, originally from Russia, now lives throughout the Great Lakes system. There it competes with native mussels for food and damages boats, harbors, and water pipes. The damage caused by the zebra mussel is projected to cost the United States and Canada as much as $5 billion over the next 10 years.

An example of an invasive plant is purple loosestrife. This plant was deliberately brought to Canada from Europe in the early 1800s to plant in gardens. However, it has since spread to wetlands all over eastern North America. There, it takes over, affecting the whole balance of the wetland ecosystem.

Even species native to Canada can sometimes be considered to be invasive. For example, the moose had never lived on the island of Newfoundland until it was brought there by people. The moose population must now be carefully managed to avoid excessive grazing on trees, which would affect both the forestry industry and other animals that live in the forests.

1. About what percentage of vascular plant species in Canada are native to Canada?

______________________________

______________________________

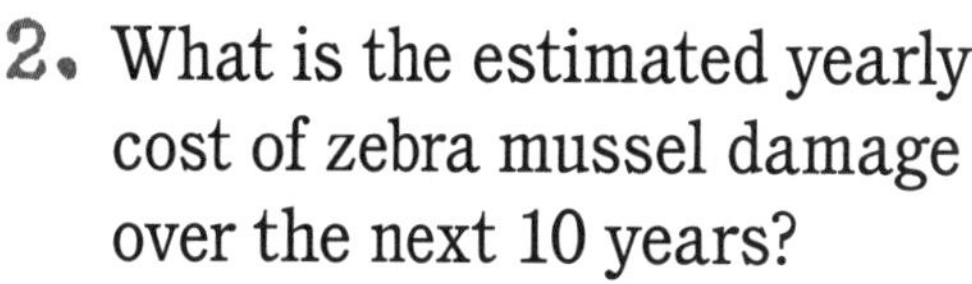

2. What is the estimated yearly cost of zebra mussel damage over the next 10 years?

______________________________

3. How does purple loosestrife harm wetlands?

______________________________

______________________________

4. How can an animal native to a country still become invasive?

______________________________

______________________________

______________________________

### Fluency Tip

Pay attention to punctuation, and pause between phrases and sentences.

# READ on Your Own

## Reading Comprehension Strategy: Summarizing

### Diseases and Invasive Species, *pages 33–35*

**Fluency Tip**

Before reading, look through sentences for words you do not know. Find out how to pronounce them.

### Before You Read

You read about the pandemic of 1918 in "Dangerous Chickens?" How was it possible that the pandemic caused more deaths than the fighting in World War I?

### As You Read

**Read "A Vaccine for Invasions," pages 33–35.** 

Then complete the cause-and-effect chart below. Think about the effect of each cause listed. Give two effects for each cause.

| Cause: HIV Transmitted from Chimpanzees to Humans |
| --- |
| Effect: The virus ________________ into a form that can pass from person to person. |
| Effect: The AIDS ________________ begins. |
| **Cause: New Treatments for AIDS Developed** |
| Effect: ________________ |
| Effect: ________________ |
| **Cause: New Virus Appears That Can Move from Person to Person** |
| Effect: ________________ |
| Effect: ________________ |

### After You Read

What is the most effective way to deal with HIV/AIDS?

________________________________________

# SOLVE on Your Own

## Diseases and Invasive Species, *page 36*

### Organize the Information

Be careful when you do a "chain" of calculations. If you make one small mistake, all the remaining answers will be wrong.

**Use a list like the one below to organize the information you find in the Math Project on magazine page 36.**

Cost per Year to Fight Weed = ______________

Cost of Crops Destroyed by Weed = ______________

Cost of Farms Damaged by Weed = ______________

Cost of Forage Pushed out by Weed = ______________

### Math Project

Use the information in the list above to answer these questions. Write your answers in the spaces provided.

1. How can you calculate the minimum and maximum cost per year to fight the weed?

______________________________________________

______________________________________________

2. How can you find the total annual cost of the damage done by the weed?

______________________________________________

3. When finding out which expense is greater, does it matter if the cost to fight the weed is at its maximum or its minimum? Explain your answer.

______________________________________________

______________________________________________

### After You Solve

How could you express some of the same information in the table by using a model?

______________________________________________

______________________________________________

Connections

# Put It Together

## Introducing Populations and Samples

You have learned how to use proportions to make predictions. How can you make predictions about entire groups of people or objects? The entire group of people or objects you want information about is called the population by statisticians. The most accurate way to gather information from the entire group is to ask or test each member of the group.

Sometimes this is not reasonable. It can be too expensive or take too much time. When it is not possible to ask each person in a population, statisticians use a representative sample that has the same characteristics as the whole group. If the sample is truly representative, then the results can be used to predict the result for the entire population.

Once you have the sample, you can use the result to make your predictions by writing and solving a proportion.

| | |
|---|---|
| Example 1: | Information: 60 respond yes; 100 surveyed; total population = 500<br>Prediction: $\frac{60}{100} = \frac{x}{500}$<br>$x = 300$ people of the population will respond "yes" |
| Example 2: | Information: 77 respond no; 200 surveyed; total population = 750<br>Prediction: $\frac{77}{200} = \frac{x}{750}$<br>$x = 288.75$ people of the population will respond "no" |
| An answer of 289 people makes more sense. Keep in mind that these are predictions. They can be thought of as estimations. An answer of 290 people would also make sense. | |

## Practicing Using Populations and Samples

**Predict the number of people responding "yes" or "no."**

1. 50 say no, 150 surveyed, total population = 600 ________________
2. 80 say yes, 320 surveyed, total population = 1,000 ________________
3. 90 say no, 450 surveyed, total population = 2,700 ________________
4. 38 say yes, 65 surveyed, total population = 382 ________________

## Thinking About Populations and Samples

To make an accurate prediction using population sampling, you must phrase the question so that the response of the people surveyed accurately reflects their opinions or actions. You must also use a sample that is large enough to represent the population.

In a random sample, each person has an equally likely chance of being selected. If these rules are not followed, your survey could produce a biased sample that does not represent the population.

Imagine you are conducting a survey in your school.

1. How would you decide on the number of students to use in your population sample if there were 800 students in the school?

2. How could you select a random sample to answer the question?

3. What problems might there be if you took your entire sample from one class?

4. What do you need to think about when you write your question?

5. Suppose you ask 150 of the 800 students a question with four possible responses, A, B, C, or D. The results were: 25 chose A, 32 chose B, 58 chose C, and the rest chose D. What are your predictions for the number of students in the entire population that should choose A, B, C, and D?

6. Would you expect exactly the same answers if all 800 students were asked the same question? Why?

## Show That You Know

**Read the information below. Use what you read about using proportions to make predictions about populations to answer the questions.**

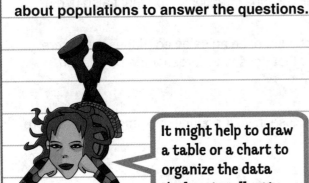

It might help to draw a table or a chart to organize the data Nathan is collecting.


Nathan recently read an article that claimed the number of people with allergies and asthma has dramatically increased and doctors are not sure why. Asthma most frequently starts in childhood, but it can occur at any age. Asthma, the most common chronic disease, is frequently triggered by allergies.

Nathan is planning to survey students in his school of 750 students to estimate the number of students that have allergies, asthma, or both.

1. How many students do you think he should survey for the population sample?

2. What question can he ask that will accurately represent the entire population?

3. Would the school nurse's office be a good place to take the survey? Why or why not?

4. Where would be a good place to take the survey?

## Show That You Know *(continued)*

5. Suppose Nathan completed his survey and 36 of 180 students answered "yes." What simple fraction could Nathan use to explain the results of his survey?

6. What proportion can Nathan write to predict the number of students in the school who have allergies or asthma?

7. What is Nathan's prediction?

## Review What You've Learned

8. What have you learned in this Connections lesson about samples and conducting surveys?

9. What have you learned in this Connections lesson that you did not already know?

10. How will this lesson help you to interpret the results of surveys?

# Review and Practice

## Skills Review

**Scale factors:**

A field is 50 ft long and 200 ft wide. A **scale drawing** of the field is 0.5 ft long and 2 ft wide.

The **scale factor** is 0.01 (or $\frac{1}{100}$).

**Similar figures:**

For figures to be similar, all corresponding sides must be related by the same **scale factor.**

**Lines on a graph:**

Dried apples weigh 2 lb per carton. Shown on a **graph.**

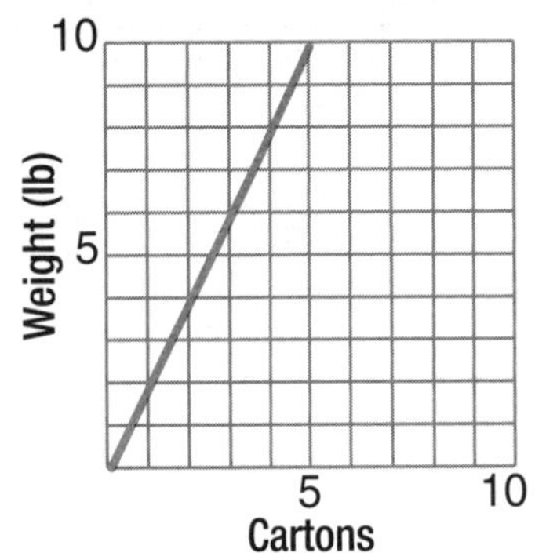


**Rates and slope:**

The **slope** of a line is a rate.

If you did not know a rate, it could be found by using a line on a graph as in the graph on the left.

First, find two points, such as (1, 2) and (5, 10).

**Slope** $= \frac{(10 - 2)}{(5 - 1)} = \frac{8}{4} = \frac{2}{1}$ or 2

The weight per carton is 2 lb.

**Histograms:**

A **histogram** shows how often things in different categories occur. The number of chickens that are in each of 4 groups:

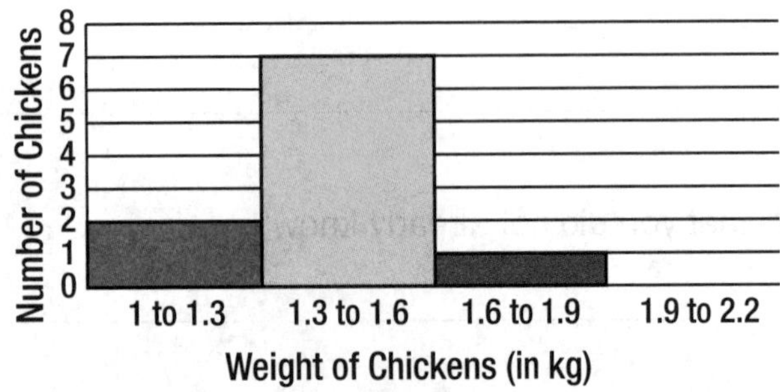


**Circle graphs:**

Percentages are easily shown in **circle graphs.** If a circle graph showed that 5% of people lived in blue houses, this would be represented by a piece of the circle that was 5% of the area of the whole circle.

## Strategy Review

- Make scale drawings for rectangular design plans, such as building plans. Guess, check, and revise the dimensions of the drawing when you know the planned area.
- Make a graph to find rates, such as growth rates of plants, or speed of cars. When making a graph, first list all points that you are going to plot.
- Use graphics like histograms and circle graphs to explain data to others.

## Skills and Strategies Practice

**Complete the exercises below.**

**1.** A square has sides that are 30 cm. A similar square has sides that are 15 cm. What is the scale factor?

______________________

**2.** The points (0, 3) and (1, 7) are on a line on a graph. What is the slope of this line?

______________________

**3.** Which type of graph would be used to show the number of students that fall into each height group: 5 ft–5 ft, 2 in.; 5 ft, 3 in.–5 ft, 5 in.; and 5 ft, 6 in.–5 ft, 8 in.?

______________________

**4.** Why are these not similar figures?

______________________

______________________

______________________

______________________

**5.** What is 37% of 349?

______________________

**6.** If 24 lb of potting soil costs $16, what is the cost per pound?

______________________

**If you have time, compute problems a second time. Then check your original answer. You may understand how to find scale factors for similar figures. However, you could still answer a test question about scale factors incorrectly if you make a simple multiplication or division mistake. Double-checking your answers will help you to correct such mistakes before you turn in the test.**

# Unit Review

**Circle the letter of the correct answer.**

**1.** A scale drawing is made of a city, using a scale factor in inches of $\frac{1}{10,000}$. If a street is 3 in. long on the drawing, how long is the actual street?

A. 13,000 ft C. 2,500 ft
B. 40,000 ft D. 2,000 ft

**2.** Which are similar shapes?

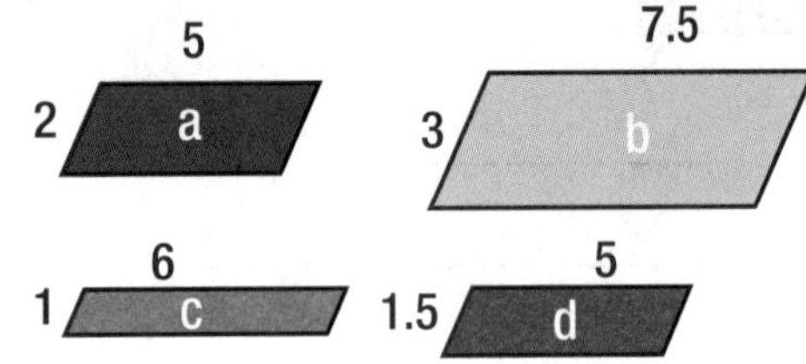


A. b and c C. a and b
B. c and d D. a and d

**3.** What is the scale factor for the similar shapes in question 2?

A. 0.3 or $\frac{10}{3}$ C. $\frac{3}{2}$ or $\frac{2}{3}$
B. 1 D. $\frac{1}{4}$ or 4

**4.** A place mat was made for a dollhouse using a scale factor of $\frac{1}{13}$. If the doll place mat is 1.4 in. long, how long is the real place mat?

A. 16.8 in. C. 13.4 in.
B. 0.94 in. D. 18.2 in.

**5.** If 13 lbs of grass seed costs $2.60, what is the cost per pound?

A. $0.20 C. $5.00
B. $2.00 D. $2.20

**6.** Use these ordered pairs to find the slope of a line: (0, 1) (3, 13)

A. 1 C. 2
B. 4 D. 3

**7.** If 5 ice teas cost $3.75, what do 2 ice teas cost?

A. $1.00 C. $2.25
B. $1.50 D. $0.75

**8.** What is a possible scale factor for these similar figures?

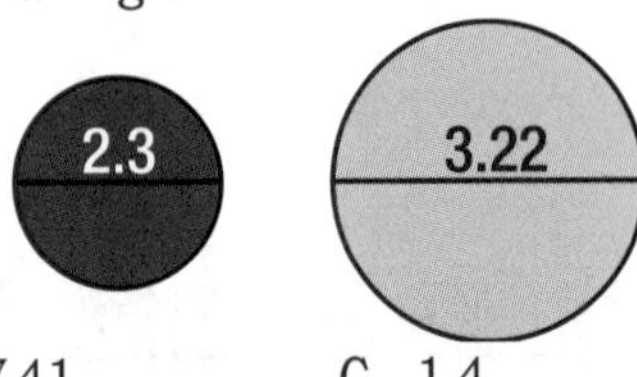


A. 7.41 C. 1.4
B. 0.92 D. 1

**9.** Which type of graph is best used to show the percentages of people who like different types of foods?

A. histogram
B. histogram or circle graph
C. circle graph
D. neither

**10.** What is 10% of 523?

A. 5.23 C. 523
B. 52.3 D. 470.7

**11.** A group of 230 people was surveyed. 13 people own a turtle. What percentage of people own a turtle?

A. 5.7% C. 10%
B. 0.057% D. 0.10

**12.** Ten percent of ________ is 24.3.

A. 2.43 C. 24.3
B. 0.243 D. 243

**13.** These figures are similar figures. What is the scale factor?

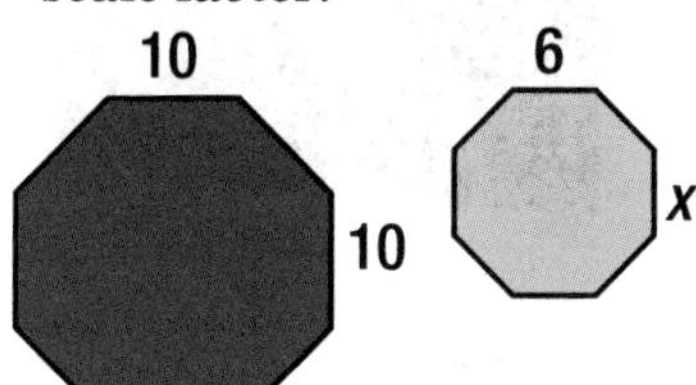


A. $\frac{x}{5}$ C. $\frac{5}{3}$
B. $\frac{2}{5}$ D. $\frac{5}{2}$

**14.** In question 13, what is the value of $x$?

A. 4 C. 10
B. 2 D. 6

**15.** Use these ordered pairs to find the slope of a line: (5,9) (10, 18)

A. $\frac{9}{5}$ C. 2
B. $\frac{5}{9}$ D. $\frac{1}{2}$

**16.** The graph shows the favorite subjects for seventh graders at one school in town. If there are 200 students, how many students said Science was their favorite subject?

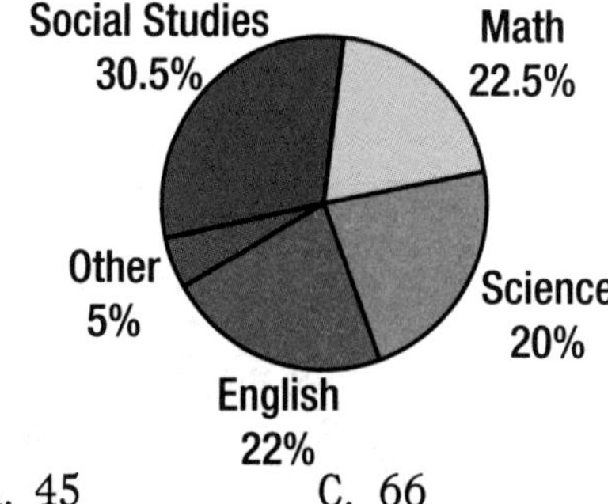


A. 45 C. 66
B. 44 D. 40

**17.** For the graph in 16, how many students said English was their favorite subject?

A. 50 C. 35
B. 67 D. 44

**18.** A $\frac{1}{16}$ model of a statue is 2.3 ft high. How tall is the actual statue?

A. 23 ft C. 36.8 ft
B. 32 ft D. 39.2 ft

**19.** Jill sews 14 patches in a quilt in 35 minutes. How many patches does she sew per minute?

A. 2 C. 2.5
B. 4 D. 0.4

**20.** The graph shows the distance you walked during a normal day. What is the slope between hours 1 and 3?

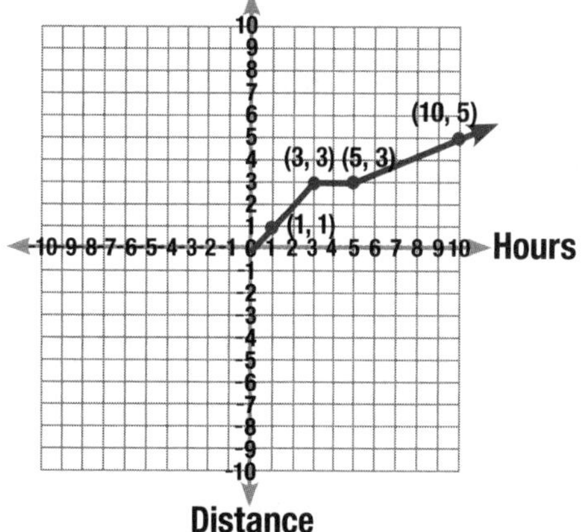


A. 3 C. 2
B. 1 D. 5

**21.** For the graph above, what is the slope between hours 5 and 10?

A. 2 C. 3
B. $\frac{2}{5}$ D. $\frac{5}{2}$

# Unit 2 Reflection

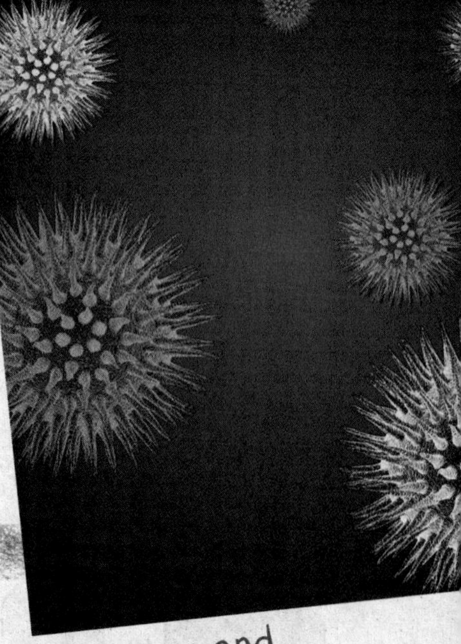

Diseases and Invasive Species

## MATH SKILLS

I can use a ratio to

The difference between a histogram and a bar graph is

## MATH STRATEGIES & CONNECTIONS

When dealing with proportionality, the math strategy that works for me is

Proportions are used to make predictions by

## READING STRATEGIES & COMPREHENSION

The easiest part about summarizing is

One way that summarizing helps me with reading is

The vocabulary words I had trouble with are

## INDEPENDENT READING

One thing I learned about diseases was

I read most fluently when

# UNIT 3
# Rational Numbers and Linear Equations

## MATH SKILLS & STRATEGIES

After you learn the basic **SKILLS**, the real test is knowing when to use each **STRATEGY.**

## AMP LINK MAGAZINE

**You Do the Math and Math Projects:** After you read each magazine article, apply what you know in real-world problems.
**Fluency:** Make your reading smooth and accurate, one tip at a time.

## READING STRATEGY

Learn why **Questioning** helps you understand what you read.

## VOCABULARY

MATH WORDS:
Know them!
Use them!
Learn all about them!

## CONNECTIONS

You own the math when you make your own connections.

# Reading Comprehension Strategy: Questioning

## How to Question

| Goal Setting | Question Words | Between the Lines | Beyond the Text |
|---|---|---|---|
| Ask, *What is my reason for reading this text?* | Ask, *What important details can I find in the text?* | Ask, *What decisions can I make about the facts and details in the text?* | Ask, *What connections can I make between the text and my life?* |

Asking questions helps you get the most out of what you are reading. Questions such as *What do I think this article is about?* and *What will I learn?* will help you set a goal before you read. Once you have set that goal, you are more likely to remember and understand what you read. Look quickly at the text. Scan for titles, headings, pictures, captions, and boldfaced words. Ask a goal-setting question.

**The Stones of Yap**

People have used many different things as money, from cows to coconuts. The people of a small South Pacific island have one of the most unusual types of currency. Huge stones called *rai* (ri) are their traditional form of money.

**1.** What clues will help you ask a good goal-setting question?

______________________________

______________________________

Check as you read to make sure the text is answering your question. You may have to change the question.

At least 500 years ago, some fishermen from Yap got lost. They landed on the nearby island of Palau (pah LOWH). There they saw huge limestone rocks. These stones could not be found on Yap. Because they were rare, they could be valuable. The fishermen brought back some pieces of stone to their leaders. One was shaped like a whale, called *rai* in Yapese. That is how the money stones got their name.

**2.** Was your goal-setting question answered? If you need to change it, ask the new question now.

______________________________

______________________________

Asking questions about the details helps you remember what you are reading. When reading about people, ask *"Who?"* If something important happened, ask *"What?"*, *"Where?"*, *"When?"*, *"Why?"*, and *"How?"*

The leaders on Yap began sending people to Palau to get more stones. The trip was dangerous. Ten men had to row more than 250 miles. Once they reached the island, they dug up stones. These pieces of limestone could be up to 12 feet wide, and many weighed several tons. They took up so much room in a canoe that some rowers had to stay behind. Those who sailed with the stones did not all survive the trip home. As a result, one measure of a *rai's* value is how many lives it cost.

**3.** What questions are answered by details in the passage?

______________________________

______________________________

______________________________

______________________________

While reading, you may think of a question to ask. Using sticky notes can help. Write your question on one and then stick it on the page where you will find the answer. Then you can go back and review all of them after reading the article.

Other things also affect the value of a *rai.* Stones cut with shell tools are worth more than those cut with iron tools. Large stones are generally more valuable than smaller ones. However, a small stone with a beautiful shape might be worth more than some large stones. The story of a stone also affects its worth. One stone has a high value because no one died during the trip to collect it.

**4.** Write two questions you might ask yourself while reading this passage. Then underline the answers in the text.

______

______

Sometimes, you may not find the answer to a question in the text. Instead, you have to think about what you are reading. This kind of questioning is called "reading between the lines." How can you decide on good "between the lines" questions? You put together information found in different places in the text. Why did the author include that information? What is the author trying to say? Then put this information together with what you already know about the topic.

For over 500 years, people on Yap have used *rais* as money. A stone about 25 inches wide might be exchanged for a pig. Larger stones were used when buying land or giving wedding gifts. To save the trouble of moving the big stones, people just left them where they were. So a stone in one village might be owned by someone in another village. As a result, the *rais* are a record of relationships among the Yap.

Stones are not the only form of money on Yap. For less important deals, its people once used shells or coconuts. Now they use U.S. dollars. The *rais* still have value, both as money and as a way to keep Yap's customs alive.

Stones used as money on the island of Yap are called *rais.*

**5.** In which two paragraphs does the author describe what makes a *rai* more or less valuable?

______

**6.** Write a between-the-lines question.

______

______

**7.** What do you know about money? Put that information together with text information.

______

______

**8.** What text information answered the between-the-lines question?

______

______

______

**9.** What is the most useful thing you have learned about questioning?

______

______

**10.** What questions do you have about how to use this strategy?

______

______

# Use the Strategies

**Use the reading comprehension strategies you have learned to answer questions about the article below.**

## The History of Paper Money in America

The American colonies usually traded and used foreign coins to pay for goods and services. When the Revolutionary War started, the United States needed a better way to pay for supplies and help. So in 1776, the national government started printing money. The government printed about $240 million in paper notes called continentals. Each state printed its own money as well. It helped, but only for a while. As the war continued and the governments printed more and more money, the bills were worth less and less. Citizens refused to use them. Paper money turned out so badly that the U.S. government did not print paper money for public use for many years.

The government printed paper money again in the 1860s. To help pay for the costs of the Civil War, the U.S. government printed about $430 million in bills. They were called legal tender notes or United States notes. Most people just called them *greenbacks*. The fronts were printed in black and white, but the backs were printed in green. The Confederate States also printed paper money. It became nearly worthless when the South was defeated.

In 1863 and 1864, the government passed the National Bank Acts. These acts created a group of banks that could print money for the government. The acts also set one standard for money. Eventually, people stopped using the different types of money and used the national standard instead.

Under federal law, only the Department of the Treasury and the Federal Reserve System can print the money we use now. Dollar bills are called *Federal Reserve Notes* (which is printed across the top of the front of every bill). The bills feature historical figures, symbols, and mottoes significant to our nation.

1. When was the first time paper money was printed in the United States?

_______________
_______________
_______________
_______________
_______________

2. Summarize the outcome of the U.S. government's first attempt at using paper money.

_______________
_______________
_______________
_______________
_______________
_______________
_______________
_______________

3. What are *greenbacks* and how did they earn their name?

_______________
_______________
_______________
_______________
_______________
_______________

## Reading Comprehension Strategies: Summarizing, Questioning

**Use the reading comprehension strategies you have learned in this and the previous units to answer the questions below.**

1. Summarize what happened with paper money during the Civil War.

 ______________________________

 ______________________________

2. Why would people want to use paper money instead of gold or trading?

 ______________________________

 ______________________________

3. Why was it important for the government to print paper money at the start of the Revolutionary War?

 ______________________________

 ______________________________

4. Do you think there are any reasons why trading would be better than using paper money?

 ______________________________

 ______________________________

## Problem-Solving Strategies: Draw a Picture or Use a Model, Find a Pattern

**Use these problem-solving strategies to answer the questions below.**

1. Keiko and Jen have many different coins and bills. Keiko has four $1 bills and one $2 bill. Jen has two $1 bills and one $5 bill. If they trade in all their bills for quarters, how many quarters would they have altogether? Draw a picture to help you.

 ______________________________

2. Viktor's dad earned a $200 bonus from his job. His dad says that he will give 5% of it to Viktor. How much money will Viktor get from his dad?

 ______________________________

3. Fill in the missing numbers in the pattern below.

 9.2, 9.7, ________, 10.7, 11.2

4. Rose is running a cash register at a card store. She puts in a $1 bill, a $5 bill, a $10 bill, a $1 bill, a $5 bill, a $10 bill, and a $1 bill. If the pattern continues, what would be the next two bills she puts into the register?

 ______________________________

# Integers and Rational Numbers

## Learn the SKILL

The temperature in Colorado can sometimes change from 30°C to −10°C. By how many degrees can the temperature change?

### VOCABULARY

Watch for the words you are learning about.

**absolute value:** the distance that a number is from zero on a number line

**integers:** the set of positive whole numbers, their opposites, and zero

**rational number:** any number that can be written as a ratio or fraction ($\frac{a}{b}$), where a and b are integers and b is not zero

| SKILL | EXAMPLE | COMPLETE THE EXAMPLE |
|---|---|---|
| The regular counting numbers from zero to infinity are called whole numbers. These whole numbers, zero, and the whole numbers to the left of zero are called **integers.** | 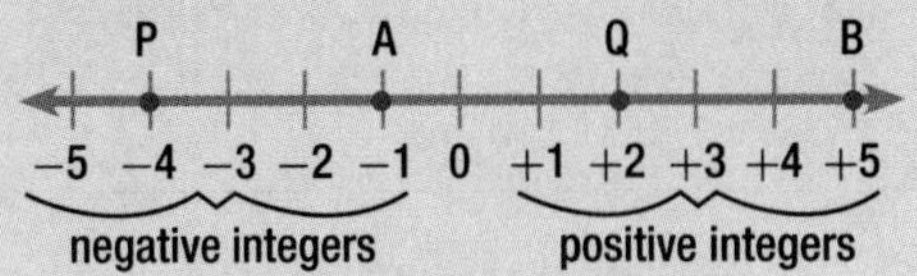 <br>Point $P$ is at −4 (negative 4).<br>Point $Q$ is at +2 (positive 2). | Identify the integer.<br>Point $A$ is at ________.<br>Point $B$ is at ________. |
| Integers have opposites. Opposites are the same distance from zero. | 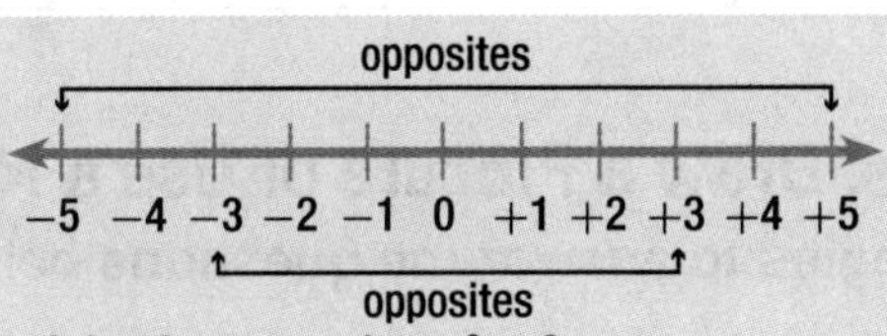 <br>−3 is the opposite of +3. | +21 is the opposite of ________.<br>−18 is the opposite of ________. |
| The distance from zero is called the **absolute value.** Absolute value is shown by placing a bar on both sides of a number. | $\|7\| = 7$<br>Read as: The absolute value of 7 is 7.<br>$\|-8\| = 8$<br>Read as: The absolute value of −8 is 8. | $\|-14\| =$ ________<br>$\|+36\| =$ ________<br>$\|+28\| =$ ________ |
| Any number that is written as a ratio of two numbers is a **rational number.** This means the number can be written as a fraction in which the numerator and the denominator are integers (except for 0 in the denominator). | $1.5 = \frac{3}{2}$<br>$5 = \frac{5}{1}$<br>$0.25 = \frac{1}{4}$ | Write the rational number as a ratio. Remember how to write a fraction.<br>$-6.8 =$ ________<br>$9\frac{1}{3} =$ ________ |
| You can use a number line to find rational numbers between other numbers, including fractions, mixed numbers, and decimals. | Use the number line to find a rational number between −3 and −1, and between 2 and 4.<br>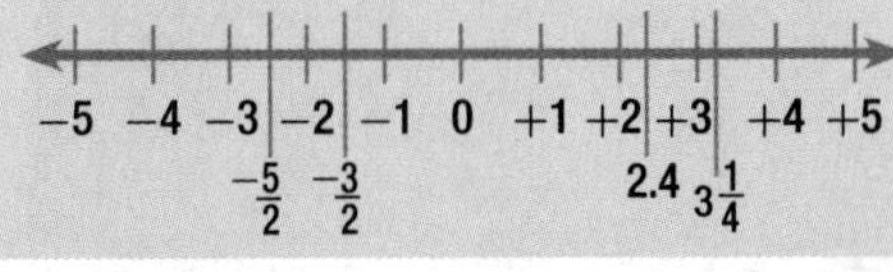  | Find a rational number between the given numbers.<br>1.4 and 1.5 ________<br>$3\frac{1}{4}$ and $4\frac{1}{4}$ ________ |

# YOUR TURN

## Choose the Right Word

rational numbers absolute value
mixed numbers negative numbers integers

**Fill in each blank with the correct word or phrase from the box.**

1. The distance from a number to zero on a number line is its ________________.
2. Both ______________ and ______________ are rational numbers.
3. Numbers that can be written as $\frac{a}{b}$ are ________________.
4. Integers less than zero are ________________.

## Yes or No?

**Answer these questions and be ready to explain your answers.**

5. Is zero an integer? ________
6. Are there any integers between 1 and 2? ________
7. Are there any rational numbers between 1 and 2? ________
8. Can positive numbers also be written without a positive sign? ________

## Show That You Know

**Name an integer for the situation.**

9. a deposit of $50
10. drop of 7 degrees in temperature
11. at sea level
12. increase property value by $1,000
13. $5 discount
14. loss of 9 yards

**Write the opposite integer.**

15. 65
16. –789
17. 524
18. 4,025
19. –798

**Find the absolute value.**

20. $|87|$
21. $|900|$
22. $|-34|$
23. $|2{,}987|$
24. $|-7{,}999|$

# SOLVE on Your Own

## Skills Practice

Plotting positive and negative numbers on a number line will help you to compare and order them.


**Find a rational number between the two given numbers. Use the number line below.**

$-3 \quad -2 \quad -1 \quad 0 \quad +1 \quad +2 \quad +3$

1. 1 and 1.5 ________
2. 1.5 and 2 ________
3. 2 and $2\frac{1}{2}$ ________
4. $2\frac{1}{2}$ and 3 ________

**Write each rational number as a ratio $\frac{a}{b}$.**

5. $1\frac{2}{7} =$ ________
6. $-3.5 =$ ________
7. $2\frac{8}{9} =$ ________
8. $14\frac{1}{4} =$ ________
9. $13.2 =$ ________

**Use >, <, or = to compare.**

10. +4 ________ −5
11. −8 ________ 0
12. |−2,404| ________ 2,404
13. +964 ________ −964

**Put the following integers and rational numbers in order from least to greatest.**

14. 8, −8, 0, −3, 3 ________________
15. −72, 68, −45, 25 ________________
16. $\frac{2}{21}, -3\frac{1}{14}, \frac{21}{7}$ ________________
17. $0.75, \frac{5}{2}, -1\frac{1}{4}, 1.\overline{5}$ ________________

# Integers and Rational Numbers

## Strategy

### Draw a Picture or Use a Model

**Step 1: Read** Members of the school science club pay $1.50 in dues for every meeting. Sometimes people forget to bring their money, and sometimes people pay what they can in advance. The club's treasurer keeps track of how much people have paid using the following table. Put the names of the students in order by what they have paid, from least to greatest. Who owes the most money?

| Student | Amount |
|---|---|
| Albert | +$3.50 |
| Beatriz | –$2.75 |
| Chad | –$5.00 |
| Kiana | +$1.50 |
| Marta | +$2.00 |
| Paul | –$1.50 |

**STRATEGY**

**Draw a Picture or Use a Model**

Drawing a picture can help you visualize a problem about comparisons.

You can draw a number line and plot points on it to compare and order the positive and negative rational numbers.

**SOLUTION**

**Step 2: Plan** Draw a number line from the lowest amount, –$5, up to the highest amount, $3.50. Then plot each amount and write each name in order from left to right.

**Step 3: Solve** Plot each person's amount on the number line.

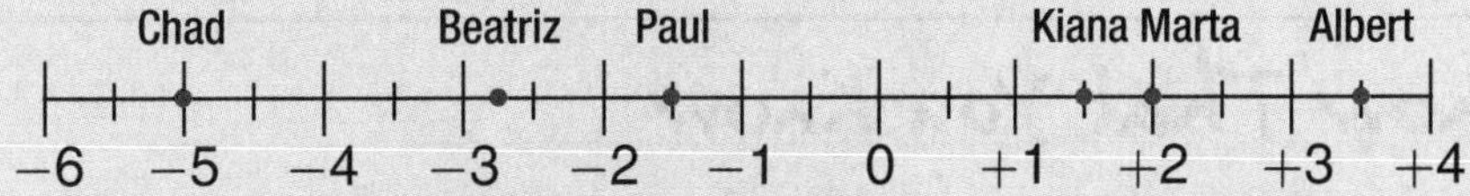


Now you can simply read off the list of names from left to right: Chad, Beatriz, Paul, Kiana, Marta, Albert. Chad is the person who owes the most money.

**Step 4: Check** You can also order the numbers by looking at the signs and the place values of each amount. The numbers with negative signs will all be less than the numbers with positive signs.

Negatives: –$2.75, –$5.00, –$1.50

Positives: +$3.50, +$1.50, +$2.00

Within each of these groups, look at the place values to order the numbers. Just remember that the negative numbers go in reverse order from the positives:

–$5.00, –$2.75, –$1.50, +$1.50, +$2.00, +$3.50

The correct order is Chad, Beatriz, Paul, Kiana, Marta, Albert. Chad is the person who owes the most money.

Choose a Strategy

# YOUR TURN

## Choose the Right Word

integer    positive    negative

**Fill in each blank with the correct word or phrase from the box.**

1. A positive ________________ is a whole number to the right of zero on a number line.
2. Numbers greater than zero are ________________.
3. Integers less than zero are ________________.

## Yes or No?

**Answer these questions and be ready to explain your answers.**

4. Can the absolute value of a negative number be greater than the absolute value of a positive number? ________
5. Is zero a rational number? ________
6. Can a negative number be written without a negative (–) sign? ________
7. Can $5.00 owed to someone be shown as –$5.00? ________

## Show That You Know

**Put each list of integers or rational numbers in order from least to greatest.**

8. 0, –2, 2, 3, 4, –4
9. –15, $\frac{3}{4}$, $\frac{1}{4}$, –0.05
10. 122, 134, 133 $\frac{1}{2}$, –1,000
11. 0.5, 1.5, 1.23, –1.23

**Order the money values from greatest to least.**

12. $5.60, $2.25, $3.25, $4.99
13. $1,000, $100.99, $1,000.99, $599.00
14. –$0.25, $0.25, $0.11, $0.99, –$0.75

# READ on Your Own

## Reading Comprehension Strategy: Questioning

## Money: Earn It, Save It, Spend It, *pages 3–4*

### Before You Read

Have you ever traded something you owned for something that another person owned? What were the items you traded? How did you decide if the trade was fair?

### As You Read

As you read "History of Money," think about what the author is saying and the words the author uses. Ask yourself questions, such as "Why is the author providing this information?" and "Why did the author choose to use these words?"

**Read "History of Money," pages 3–4.** STOP

Read the "between-the-lines" question below. Then write the answer.

| History of Money |
|---|
| **"Between-the-lines" question:**<br>Why does the author start the article by having you think about an ancient market? |
| **Answer:**<br>______________________________<br>______________________________ |

### After You Read

Do you think all the countries of the world should use the same currency? Explain.

____________________________________________

____________________________________________

### VOCABULARY

Watch for the words you are learning about.

**broker:** a person who is trained to buy and sell stocks or commodities

**commodities:** common items with standard values that are used for trade

**currency:** the types of money used by a country

### Fluency Tip

Rereading paragraphs will help you read smoothly. Do not skip or substitute words.

# SOLVE on Your Own

## Money: Earn It, Save It, Spend It, *page 5*

Plotting the positive and negative amounts on a number line will help you compare and order the price changes.


### Organize the Information

**Read the magazine article. Then plot the changes in commodities prices.**

–2 –1 0 1 2 3 4 5 6

### You Do the Math

Use the information you plotted on the number line above to answer these questions. Write your answers in the space provided.

1. How can you use place value to help you compare the numbers?

_______________________________________________

_______________________________________________

2. What sign do numbers have that show an increase? How does this help you to find the three commodities with the greatest increase in price?

_______________________________________________

_______________________________________________

3. What sign do numbers have that show a decrease? How does this help you to find the three commodities with the greatest decrease in price?

_______________________________________________

_______________________________________________

### After You Solve

Do you think you would like to be a futures broker? Why or why not?

_______________________________________________

_______________________________________________

# Adding and Subtracting Negative Numbers

> **VOCABULARY**
>
> Watch for the words you are learning about.
>
> **additive inverse:** the opposite of a number

## Learn the SKILL

In the last football game, Reggie rushed for a loss of 4 yards on the first play. On the second play, Reggie gained 7 yards. How many total yards did Reggie gain or lose in the first two plays? To find the total yards, add $-4$ and 7.

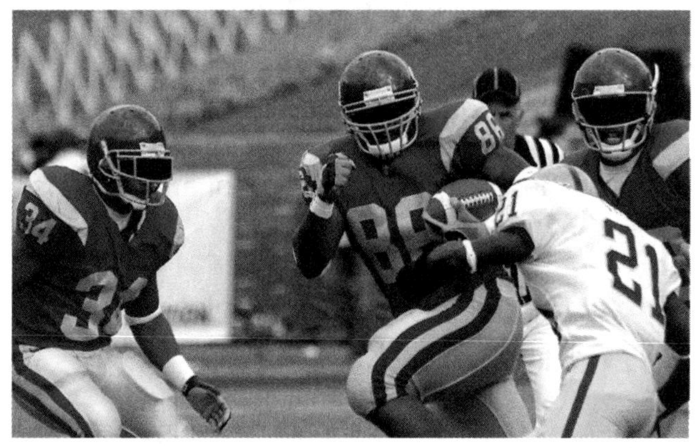


| SKILL | EXAMPLE | COMPLETE THE EXAMPLE |
|---|---|---|
| **Adding with like signs**<br>To add integers with like signs, add their absolute values and use the sign of the addends. | $-1 + (-3) \rightarrow \lvert -1 \rvert + \lvert -3 \rvert = 4 \rightarrow -4$<br>$-23 + (-2) \rightarrow \lvert -23 \rvert + \lvert -2 \rvert = 25 \rightarrow -25$ | Solve.<br>$-4 + (-2) =$ ________<br>$-5 + (-6) =$ ________ |
| **Adding with unlike signs**<br>To add integers with unlike signs, begin at 0 on the number line. Move left if the sign is negative. Move right if the sign is positive. | Start from 0. Move 4 units left and then 7 units right. So, $-4 + 7 = 3$.<br>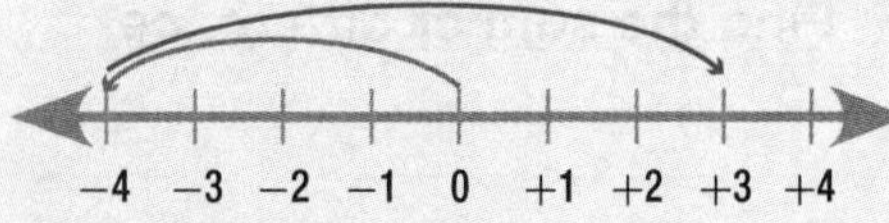<br> | Solve.<br>$5 + (-6) =$ ________<br>$-17 + 19 =$ ________ |
| Another way to add integers with unlike signs is to subtract their absolute values and keep the sign of the integer with the greatest absolute value. | $-8 + 1 \rightarrow \lvert -8 \rvert - \lvert 1 \rvert = 7 \rightarrow -7$<br>$15 + (-9) \rightarrow \lvert 15 \rvert - \lvert -9 \rvert = 6$ | Solve.<br>$-13 + 21 =$ ________<br>$5 + (-6) =$ ________ |
| **Subtracting with unlike signs**<br>To subtract an integer is to add its opposite. | $5 - 6 \rightarrow 5 + -6 = -1$<br>$-17 - (-7) \rightarrow -17 + 7 = -10$<br>$-8 - 19 \rightarrow (-8) + (-19) = -27$ | Solve.<br>$22 - (-8) =$ ________<br>$-56 - 49 =$ ________ |
| When you add an integer and its **additive inverse,** the sum is always zero. | $9 + (-9) = 0$<br>$-7 + 7 = 0$ | Solve.<br>$46 + (-46) =$ ________<br>$-18 + 18 =$ ________ |

Learn the Skill

# YOUR TURN

## Choose the Right Word

absolute values additive inverse
positive negative

**Fill in each blank with the correct word or phrase from the box.**

1. The ________________ of an integer is its opposite.
2. The sign of the sum of two positive integers is ________________.
3. The sign of the sum of two negative integers is ________________.
4. When adding integers with the same signs, you can add the ________________ of the integers.

## Yes or No?

**Answer these questions and be ready to explain your answers.**

5. Is $|9| > |-9|$? ________
6. Is 15 the additive inverse of +15? ________
7. When adding different signs, will the sign of the sum always be whatever the sign of the first addend is? ________
8. In $x - 5 = 9$, is $x = -4$? ________

## Show That You Know

**Write the additive inverse of each number.**

9. 5
10. 8
11. –125
12. 49
13. 7

**Find the sum or difference.**

14. $4 + (-10) =$
15. $|954| + |-100| =$
16. $-4 + 10 =$
17. $-11 + 8 =$
18. $76 - (-56) =$
19. $-37 - 29 =$
20. $-19 - (-22) =$

# SOLVE on Your Own

## Skills Practice

Remember that when you subtract an integer, you actually add its opposite.


**Find the sum.**

1. $-16 + (-12) =$ ________

2. $-400 + (-200) + 15 =$ ________

3. $256 + (-121) =$ ________

4. $345 + (-123) + 14 =$ ________

5. $\begin{array}{r} -198 \\ +\ 68 \\ \hline \end{array}$

6. $\begin{array}{r} 72 \\ +\ -11 \\ \hline \end{array}$

7. $\begin{array}{r} -15 \\ +\ 29 \\ \hline \end{array}$

**Find the difference.**

8. $-140 - (-15) =$ ________

9. $90 - 17 =$ ________

10. $-27 - (-4) =$ ________

11. $-153 + 153 =$ ________

12. $\begin{array}{r} 28 \\ -\ -13 \\ \hline \end{array}$

13. $\begin{array}{r} -39 \\ -\ +8 \\ \hline \end{array}$

14. $\begin{array}{r} -648 \\ -\ 378 \\ \hline \end{array}$

**Evaluate.**

15. $3\frac{1}{2} + (-2\frac{1}{3}) + (-8) - (-6) =$ ________

16. $-23.5 - 78.2 + (-80.4) + 9.1 =$ ________

17. $200 + 315 - (-45) + (-10) =$ ________

# Adding and Subtracting Negative Numbers

## Strategy

### Draw a Picture or Use a Model

**Step 1: Read** The high and low temperatures for several days last winter are shown below.

December 30: High, 20°F; low, −5°F

January 31: High, 15°F; low, −15°F

February 8: High, −5°F; low, −25°F

Which day had the greatest temperature difference?

**STRATEGY**

**Draw a Picture or Use a Model**

You can use a number line to help you add and subtract integers. A number line can also be useful to help you "see" the difference between two numbers or the range of a set.

**SOLUTION**

**Step 2: Plan** Draw a number line ranging from −30 to 30, numbered by fives. Use it as a model to find the differences.

**Step 3: Solve** The temperature differences can be found by counting along on the number line. Remember that to subtract the negative numbers, you add the opposite integer.

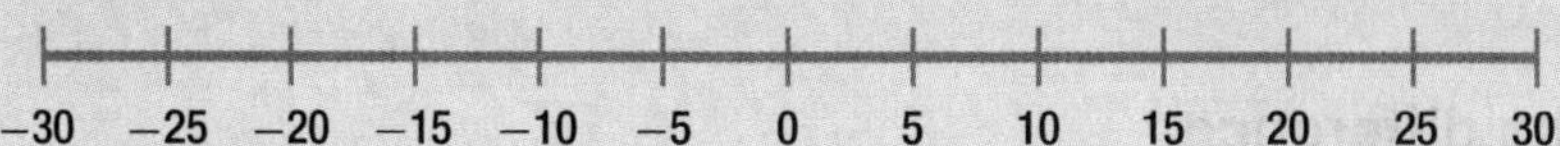


So you have:

December 30: $20 - (-5) = 20 + 5 = 25$

January 31: $15 - (-15) = 15 + 15 = 30$

February 8: $-5 - (-25) = -5 + 25 = 20$

The greatest difference is for January 31. That day had a 30° change in temperature.

**Step 4: Check** Find the location of each temperature for each day on the number line. You can draw a different-colored line to show the temperature change for each day. Then look for the longest line. The longest line is for January 31.

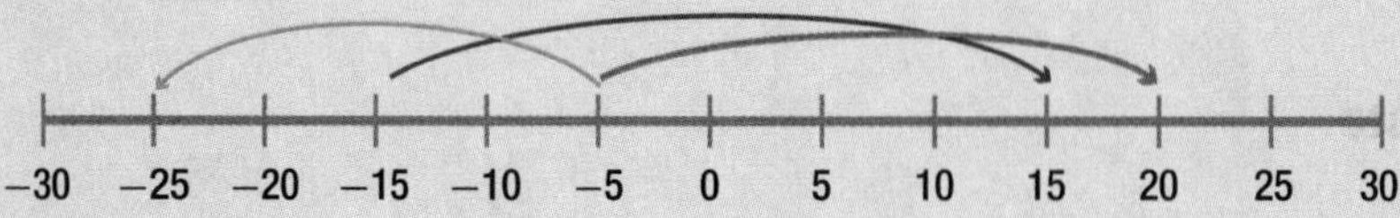

# YOUR TURN

Choose a Strategy

## Choose the Right Word

absolute values negative opposite
positive subtract

**Fill in each blank with the correct word or phrase from the box.**

1. In order to ________________ negative numbers, you add their opposite numbers.
2. The ________________ of a negative number is a ________________ number.
3. A positive number subtracted from a smaller positive number will result in a ________________ number.
4. To add two negative numbers, add the ________________ of the numbers and keep the negative sign.

## Yes or No?

**Answer these questions and be ready to explain your answers.**

5. Can you subtract two negative numbers? ________
6. Can you add a positive number and a negative number? ________
7. Can you add or subtract any two integers? ________
8. Is the absolute value of a negative number always negative? ________
9. Can a number line help you to add and subtract integers? ________
10. Is adding the opposite the same as subtracting? ________

## Show That You Know

**Add or subtract the integers. Draw a number line on a separate sheet of paper to help you.**

11. $3 + (-1) - 2 - 6$
12. $8 - 2 + (-7) - (-5)$
13. $12 + 20 - 45 - (-15)$
14. $-36 + 19 - (-17) - (+25)$

**Solve each problem by adding or subtracting integers. Draw a number line on a separate sheet of paper to help you.**

15. The temperature dropped from 51°F to −2°F just 6 hours later when the cold front rolled in. How much did the temperature change in those 6 hours?
16. The level of the lake decreased from 1 foot below normal to 12 feet below normal by the end of the summer. How much did the level of the lake change?

# READ on Your Own

## Reading Comprehension Strategy: Questioning

## Money: Earn It, Save It, Spend It, *pages 6–7*

### Before You Read

Remember what you read about money in "History of Money." What is the word for common goods with standard values that are used for trade?

### As You Read

To preview, look at headings, pictures, captions, and boldfaced words.

**Preview "The Stock Market," pages 6–7.** 

Write a goal-setting question in the chart below.

**Now read "The Stock Market," pages 6–7.** 

Answer your question in the chart below.

| The Stock Market |
|---|
| **Goal-setting question:** ______ |
| **Answer:** ______ ______ ______ |

### After You Read

Do you think you would make a good stockbroker? Why or why not?

______

______

## VOCABULARY

Watch for the words you are learning about.

**bankruptcy:** a legal process that helps people or businesses repay or get rid of their debt

**dividend:** a small piece of the profits of a company that is paid to the shareholders

**financial:** related to making money by buying and selling business investments

**investors:** people who put their money into a company in the hope of earning more money

**shareholders:** people who buy stock in a company

## Fluency Tip

Remember to read sentences that end in question marks and exclamation points with a different tone than sentences that end with a period.

# SOLVE on Your Own

## Money: Earn It, Save It, Spend It, *page 8*

### Organize the Information

**Read You Do the Math in the magazine. Then complete the table below.**

| | Start Time | Cost of One Share | Cost of 100 Shares | End Time | Selling Price for 100 Shares | Profit or Loss |
|---|---|---|---|---|---|---|
| Stock 1 | | | | | | |
| Stock 2 | | | | | | |
| Stock 3 | | | | | | |

### You Do the Math

Use the information in the table above to answer these questions. Write your answers in the space provided.

Making a table may help you answer the magazine questions.


1. How can you find the value of 100 shares of stock?

2. What parts of the graphs should you look at to determine the company that will make the most money?

3. What happened to the price per share of Stock 2? Explain.

### After You Solve

Which company's stock would you like to buy? Why?

Application

## The Four-Step Problem-Solving Plan

| Step 1: Read | Step 2: Plan | Step 3: Solve | Step 4: Check |
|---|---|---|---|
| Make sure you understand what the problem is asking. | Decide how you will solve the problem. | Solve the problem using your plan. | Check to make sure your answer is correct. |

**Read the article below. Then answer the questions.**

### Credit Incentives

The use of credit cards has become commonplace in our society. Besides the interest fees they charge their card holders, credit-card companies also collect a fee from merchants, or people who own a business, who accept their cards.

Most credit-card companies offer incentives, or something that urges you to buy—not only to apply for one of their cards but to use it for purchasing, or buying, everything from airline tickets to groceries. Such incentives include cash back or rebates. Some cards give 1% back on most purchases and 5% back on purchases made at convenience stores, gas stations, grocery stores, and "member merchants." Rebates may be in the form of a credit on your bill, a gift card, or more dollars. Additional cell phone minutes are also a common incentive as well as discounts on car rentals and insurance.

Companies are aware that unless they can reward their customers in some way, these customers will take their business to a company that will.

1. How are consumers benefiting from different credit-card companies trying to get their business?

______________________________

______________________________

2. Credit-card Company A offers a 5% rebate on airline tickets. If, during the course of the year, you spent $3,500 on airline tickets, how much of a rebate would you receive?

______________________________

______________________________

# YOUR TURN

Application

**Read the article below. Then answer the questions.**

## Incentives Above and Beyond

Consumers have gotten so used to the rebates that they demand more than the usual incentives from their cards. Credit-card companies have responded by offering incentives that are a little more creative than what is usually offered in the industry. Incentives include the following:

**Automatic Payment Plan**—A person is allowed to subtract purchases from their future paychecks and spread payments out over 2 to 6 months, interest-free.

**Profit-Sharing Plan**—A credit card offers stock instead of cash back. Customers can earn as much as 12% back. The money goes into a special fund.

**Dining Out Plan**—This card offers a prepaid credit card that acts like a gift certificate.

The incentives from credit-card companies are limited only by the imaginations of the people who run the companies. For now, consumers are reaping the rewards of such imaginations.

1. How are the newer credit-card incentives different from rebates?

_______________

_______________

2. Ms. Ryan's credit card rewards her with 3% cash back for every dollar spent on groceries and 1% cash back for any other object purchased. This month she spent $150.00 on groceries and $60.00 on other things. How much cash back should she receive?

_______________

_______________

3. Why do credit-card companies keep changing their incentives?

_______________

_______________

### Fluency Tip

Use expression to help listeners understand the meaning of a passage.

# READ on Your Own

## Reading Comprehension Strategy: Questioning

## Money: Earn It, Save It, Spend It, *pages 9–11*

### VOCABULARY

Watch for the words you are learning about.

**transaction:** a transfer of money or other items of value

### Fluency Tip

Read and reread to practice maintaining an even pace throughout the text.

### Before You Read

You read about the Buttonwood Agreement in "The Stock Market." Why would it be an advantage for the 24 brokers to trade only among themselves?

### As You Read

**Read "Buy Now; Pay Later," pages 9–11.** 

Think about "question word" questions that ask *Who? What? Where? When? Why?* and *How?* as you read. Place sticky notes next to the answers. For each section, write one of the question word questions and answer it in the chart below.

Read page 10. Fill in that part of the chart below. Read page 11. Fill in that part of the chart below.

| Page 10 | Page 11 |
|---|---|
| **"Question word" question:** ______ ______ | **"Question word" question:** ______ ______ |
| **Answer:** ______ ______ | **Answer:** ______ ______ |

### After You Read

What do you think life was like before credit cards?

______

______

# SOLVE on Your Own

## Money: Earn It, Save It, Spend It, *page 12*

page 12

### Organize the Information

To quickly estimate a balance, round money to the nearest 10 before adding or subtracting.


**Use a list like the one below to organize the information you find in the Math Project on magazine page 12.**

| Credits | Debits | |
|---|---|---|
| $452.65 | $358.20 | $250.00 |
| $452.65 | $250.00 | $23.00 |
| $452.65 | $58.70 | $28.00 |
| $452.65 | $100.00 | $250.00 |
| | $75.38 | $73.00 |
| | $23.80 | $35.00 |

### Math Project

Use the information in the list above to answer these questions. Write your answers in the space provided.

1. When was the balance the highest? What is this balance?

_______________________________________________

_______________________________________________

2. If this is your regular spending pattern, when would you pay your bill next month? Explain.

_______________________________________________

_______________________________________________

### After You Solve

How could you express the same information in the list by drawing a graph?

_______________________________________________

_______________________________________________

# Multiplying and Dividing Negative Numbers

## Learn the SKILL

During the last year, the houses on Kelly Street have declined in value by $24,000. What is the average decrease per month of the property value on Kelly Street?

| SKILL | EXAMPLE | COMPLETE THE EXAMPLE |
|---|---|---|
| **Multiplying with like signs**<br>If the factors have the same signs, the product is positive. | Find the product.<br>$(-5) \times (-5) = +25$<br>$8 \times 4 = 32$ | Solve.<br>$(-3) \times (-5) =$ ________<br>$9 \times 6 =$ ________ |
| **Multiplying with unlike signs**<br>If the factors have different signs, the product is negative. | Find the product.<br>$+6 \times (-4) = -24$<br>$-7 \times 10 = -70$ | Solve.<br>$-1.5 \times 2 =$ ________<br>$6 \times (-8) =$ ________ |
| **Dividing with like signs**<br>If both numbers have the same signs, the quotient is positive. | Find the quotient.<br>$\frac{-50}{-10} = 5$<br>$\frac{27}{9} = 3$ | Solve.<br>$\frac{-75}{-5} =$ ________<br>$\frac{200}{20} =$ ________ |
| **Dividing with unlike signs**<br>If the numbers have different signs, the quotient is negative. | Find the quotient.<br>$\frac{-16}{2} = -8$<br>$\frac{-\$24{,}000}{12} = -\$2{,}000$ | Solve.<br>$\frac{-72}{8} =$ ________<br>$\frac{150}{-15} =$ ________ |

# YOUR TURN

## Choose the Right Word

positive negative

**Fill in each blank with the correct word from the box. You may use the words more than once.**

1. The quotient of two integers with like signs is ________________.
2. The product of two integers with like signs is ________________.
3. The quotient of two integers with unlike signs is ________________.
4. The product of two integers with unlike signs is ________________.

## Yes or No?

**Answer these questions and be ready to explain your answers.**

5. Is $\frac{|15|}{|-5|} = -3$? ________
6. Can $\frac{+4}{-8}$ be simplified to $-(\frac{1}{2})$? ________
7. Is $(-4)(90) = 360$? ________
8. Is $-\frac{81}{9} \times (-2) = -18$? ________

## Show That You Know

**Find the missing number in each expression.**

9. $+5 \times \quad\quad = -95$
10. $-8 \times \quad\quad = -24$
11. $\frac{\quad}{3} = 24$
12. $\frac{+84}{-6} =$
13. $\frac{144}{\quad} = -12$

**Compute.**

14. $+4 \times (-8) =$
15. $-78 \times 3 =$
16. $50 \times (-33) =$
17. $\frac{-1,680}{-35} =$
18. $\frac{60}{-15} =$
19. $+4 \times (-50) =$

# SOLVE on Your Own

## Skills Practice

Be sure you understand whether numbers you are working with are positive or negative. This will help you to put the correct sign in your answer.

**Find the product.**

1. $-14 \times (-3) =$ ________
2. $-75 \times 5 =$ ________
3. $(8)(-11) =$ ________
4. $1{,}128 \times (-19) =$ ________
5. $(-9)(-4) =$ ________

**Find the quotient.**

6. $\frac{-64}{-8} =$ ________
7. $\frac{404}{-4} =$ ________
8. $\frac{-156}{-2} =$ ________
9. $\frac{-153}{+153} =$ ________
10. $\frac{2{,}225}{-89} =$ ________
11. $\frac{-5{,}928}{13} =$ ________

**Evaluate.**

12. $-0.003 \times -0.002 =$ ________
13. $-1.1\overline{)0.154} =$ ________
14. $\frac{-21}{28} =$ ________
15. $-3 \times (-5) \times 2 \times (-8) =$ ________

# Multiplying and Dividing Negative Numbers

## Strategies

### Make a List, Try a Simpler Form of the Problem

**Step 1: Read** Lenora bought a new pair of shoes that was on sale for 20% off the original price. There was also a sales tax of 7.5% added to the purchase. If she paid a total of \$74.39, how much did the shoes originally cost?

| STRATEGY | SOLUTION |
|---|---|
| **Make a List**<br>Making a list using the values that you know will help you see how to solve the problem. Be sure to put the amounts in the order in which the percentages are taken. Then you can work backward to find each amount. | **Step 2: Plan** Start with letting $x$ be the unknown original price. Then list the original price, price after discount, and price after sales tax.<br>**Step 3: Solve** The original price is $x$. The discount is $-0.20 \times x$, and the discounted amount is $x - 0.2x$, or $0.8x$. Then the total is $0.8x \times 1.075$.<br>List each amount: $x$, $x \times 0.8 =$ ______, ______ $\times$ 1.075, \$74.39.<br>Then you can work backward through the list, dividing to get each previous amount. First, divide the sales tax amount: \$74.39 ÷ 1.075 = \$69.20. Then divide the discount: \$69.20 ÷ 0.80 = \$86.50.<br>So the original price was \$86.50.<br>**Step 4: Check** Multiply the discount by the original amount: \$86.50 × (−0.20) = −\$17.30.<br>Then add that to the original amount: \$86.50 + (−\$17.30) = \$69.20.<br>Now multiply by the sales tax: \$69.20 × 0.075 = \$5.19.<br>Then add that to the discounted amount: \$69.20 + \$5.19 = \$74.39.<br>That is the total amount in the problem, so \$86.50 is the correct original price. |
| **Try a Simpler Form of the Problem**<br>If you do not know how to approach a problem, try it with simpler numbers. | **Step 2: Plan** Suppose the original price was \$100, the discount was 50%, and the sales tax was 10%.<br>**Step 3: Solve** Using these easier numbers, you see that the discounted amount is \$50, and the sales tax on that would be \$5, for a total of \$55. Work backward to check:<br>$\frac{\$55}{1.10} = \$50 \longrightarrow \frac{\$50}{0.5} = \$100$<br>Now work backward using the original numbers:<br>$\frac{\$74.39}{1.075} = \$69.20 \longrightarrow \frac{\$69.20}{0.8} = \$86.50$<br>**Step 4: Check** Use estimation to check your answer. \$86.50 is about \$90. So 20% off would be about −0.20 × \$90 = −\$18. So the discounted price is about \$70. The tax 7.5% is about 8%, so about \$70 × 0.08 = \$5.60. So the total is around \$75, close to the \$74.39 in the problem. |

Choose a Strategy

# YOUR TURN

## Choose the Right Word

absolute value    divide    multiply
negative    positive

**Fill in each blank with the correct word or phrase from the box.**

1. A negative number times a negative number is a ______________ number.
2. A positive number divided by a negative number is a ______________ number.
3. To ______________ or divide a positive number by a negative number, multiply or ______________ the absolute values and make the sign of the answer negative.
4. To multiply two negative numbers, multiply the ______________ of the numbers.

## Yes or No?

**Answer these questions and be ready to explain your answers.**

5. Can you multiply by negative numbers? ________
6. Can you divide by negative numbers? ________
7. Is a negative number times a negative number a negative number? ________
8. Is a negative number divided by a positive number a negative number? ________
9. Can changing to simpler numbers in a problem help you to solve it? ________

## Show That You Know

**Multiply or divide the integers.**

10. $5 \times (-6)$
11. $-7 \times 9$
12. $-8 \times (-8)$
13. $-4 \times 2 \times (-3)$
14. $-16 \div 2$
15. $-99 \div (-9)$

**Solve each word problem by multiplying or dividing integers.**

16. Sarah earned $795 in net pay on her most recent paycheck. She spent 12% of her paycheck on groceries. How much money does she have left over?
17. For the last half of the game, the attendance dropped off by 38% of what it was at halftime. If the attendance was 7,285 fans at the end of the game, what was it at halftime?

# READ on Your Own

## Reading Comprehension Strategy: Questioning

## Money: Earn It, Save It, Spend It, *pages 13–14*

### VOCABULARY

Watch for the words you are learning about.

**deductions:** amounts taken out of a paycheck for taxes

**minimum wage:** the lowest hourly wage that employers can legally pay a person over 20 years of age

### Fluency Tip

Read complex material at a natural pace but slowly enough to make sense of difficult concepts.

### Before You Read

Think about what you read about credit cards in "Buy Now; Pay Later." Do you think credit cards help you manage your money? Why or why not?

### As You Read

**Preview page 13 of "Who Took What?"** 

In the first column of the chart, write three to five questions that come to mind as you read the page.

**Carefully read pages 13–14 of "Who Took What?"** 

In the second column of the chart, write the answers you found in the reading. Some questions may not have an answer in the reading.

| What Will I Learn? | Answers I Found in the Reading |
|---|---|
| | |
| | |
| | |
| | |
| | |
| | |
| | |

### After You Read

Do you think it is fair to have some of your money taken out of your paycheck for taxes and other things? Explain your answer.

# SOLVE on Your Own

## Money: Earn It, Save It, Spend It, *page 15*

### Organize the Information

**Read the magazine article. Then complete the following table with a budget for yourself.**

| Monthly Fixed Expenses | | Monthly Flexible Expenses | |
|---|---|---|---|
| Rent | | Groceries | |
| Renter's Insurance | | Eating Out | |
| Car Payment | | Entertainment | |
| Car Insurance | | Clothes | |
| Heat | | Miscellaneous | |
| Electricity | | Savings | |
| Telephone | | | |
| Cable | | | |

| | |
|---|---|
| Total Monthly Budget | |
| Net Income Needed (Monthly Budget × 12) | |
| Salary Needed (Net Income + 20%) | |

Making a table for your budget may help you answer the magazine questions.

### You Do the Math

Use the budget information to answer these questions. Write your answers in the space provided.

**1.** Why are all of the numbers in the budget negative?

______________________________________________

______________________________________________

**2.** How can you find the annual amount spent in each category?

______________________________________________

### After You Solve

How do you think you could save money so that you will have more to spend on things that you want?

______________________________________________

______________________________________________

## The Four-Step Problem-Solving Plan

| Step 1: Read | Step 2: Plan | Step 3: Solve | Step 4: Check |
| --- | --- | --- | --- |
| Make sure you understand what the problem is asking. | Decide how you will solve the problem. | Solve the problem using your plan. | Check to make sure your answer is correct. |

**Read the article below. Then answer the questions.**

### The Gold Standard

Countries have not always used currency, or money, the way they do now. In the past, many countries, including the United States, used the gold standard. The gold standard was an agreement by countries to fix the prices of their currencies in relation to a given amount of gold. That nation's money was then converted, or changed, into gold at the agreed-upon price. For example, a country might have set a price at $100 an ounce. This would then mean that $1 would be worth $\frac{1}{100}$ of an ounce of gold.

The U.S. Gold Standard Act was passed in 1900 and established gold as the official way to exchange paper money. It ended in 1933 when President Franklin D. Roosevelt made it against the law for individuals to own gold (except for jewelry). The Bretton Woods System, made into law in 1946, created fixed exchange rates that allowed governments to sell their gold to the United States at the price of $35 per ounce. This system ended on August 15, 1971, when President Richard Nixon ended trading of gold at the fixed price. The gold standard has not been used in any major economy since that time.

1. How did the gold standard bring together different currencies?

______________________________

______________________________

2. Suppose the set price for gold was $250 an ounce. How many ounces of gold would $1,000 buy?

______________________________

______________________________

Application

# YOUR TURN

**Read the article below. Then answer the questions.**

## Floating Currencies

Floating currency is a currency that uses a flexible exchange rate to set its value. It is a system in which a country's currency value is allowed to shift back and forth according to the foreign exchange market.

Countries that use a floating currency include the United States, Canada, Japan, Australia, Great Britain, and other countries in Europe. Canada uses the floating currency in the true sense of the word since its central bank has not changed its rate since 1998. The United States has introduced few changes in its foreign reserves, unlike Japan and Great Britain who constantly change the rates of their currencies.

From 1946 to the early 1970s, the Bretton Woods system made fixed currencies the standard. In 1971, the United States government departed from the gold standard so that the U.S. dollar was no longer a fixed currency. Most of the world's currencies followed.

1. How does a floating exchange rate differ from a fixed exchange rate?

______________________

______________________

______________________

______________________

2. How does the British exchange rate differ from the Canadian rate?

______________________

______________________

______________________

______________________

3. If one U.S. dollar is valued at 0.52 British pounds, how much, in pounds, would you receive for $150?

______________________

### Fluency Tip

Reread sentences that you have trouble with. Rereading should help you read more smoothly.

# READ on Your Own

## Reading Comprehension Strategy: Questioning

## Money: Earn It, Save It, Spend It, *pages 16–18*

### VOCABULARY

Watch for the words you are learning about.

**convert:** to change

### Fluency Tip

Read complex material at a natural pace but slowly enough to make sense of difficult concepts.

### Before You Read

You read about deductions in "Who Took What?" What are some benefits of the money that is deducted from a paycheck?

### As You Read

**Read "Money Around the World," pages 16–18.** 

Think about "question word" questions that ask *Who?, What?, Where?, When?, Why?,* and *How?* as you read. Place sticky notes next to the answers. For each section, write one of the question-word questions and answer it in the chart below.

Fill in the chart below.

Fill in the chart below.

| What is a Euro? | Financial Markets |
|---|---|
| "Question word" question: ______ ______ ______ | "Question word" question: ______ ______ ______ |
| Answer: ______ ______ | Answer: ______ ______ |

### After You Read

What foreign currencies have you seen? How do they differ from U.S. currency?

______

______

# SOLVE on Your Own

## Money: Earn It, Save It, Spend It, *page 19*

### Organize the Information

**Use a table like the one below to organize the information you find in the Math Project on magazine page 19.**

| Foreign Currency | Rate of Exchange | U.S. Dollars |
|---|---|---|
| 73,000 Chinese yuan | | |
| 158,000 Mexican pesos | | |
| 258,093 Sri Lankan rupees | | |

### Math Project

You can round the numbers to estimate your answers before solving.


Use the information in the table above to answer these questions. Write your answers in the space provided.

1. To convert from a foreign currency to U.S. dollars, should you divide or multiply?

2. To convert from U.S. dollars to a foreign currency, should you divide or multiply?

3. All of the exchange rates in the table are equal to one U.S. dollar. How could you quickly create a new table that included conversion rates for five U.S. dollars?

### After You Solve

How might you illustrate a comparison of the values of the different currencies?

# Put It Together

## Introducing Formulas with Fractions

You have learned how to solve simple equations of the form $ax = b$, where $a$ and $b$ are integers. Look at this example where integer values have been used for both $a$ and $b$.

$$5x = 35$$

Solve the equation by dividing both sides of the equation by 5.

$$\frac{5x}{5} = \frac{35}{5}$$
$$x = 7$$

Suppose the variables $a$ and $b$ are replaced with fractions. You can still solve the example easily. The rules for solving equations have not changed.

$$\frac{3}{4}x = \frac{2}{3}$$

Solve the equation by dividing both sides of the equation by $\frac{3}{4}$.

$$\frac{3}{4}x \div \frac{3}{4} = \frac{2}{3} \div \frac{3}{4}$$

Recall that dividing by a fraction is the same as multiplying by its reciprocal.

$$\frac{3}{4}x\left(\frac{4}{3}\right) = \frac{2}{3}\left(\frac{4}{3}\right)$$
$$x = \frac{2}{3}\left(\frac{4}{3}\right)$$
$$x = \frac{8}{9}$$

Be sure to check your answer by substituting the answer in the original equation.

Does $\frac{3}{4}\left(\frac{8}{9}\right) = \frac{2}{3}$? Yes, you have correctly solved the example.

## Practicing Formulas with Fractions

**Solve the following examples and check your answers.**

1. $\frac{3}{8}x = \frac{5}{6}$ ______________
2. $\frac{2}{7}x = \frac{4}{9}$ ______________
3. $\frac{7}{10} = \frac{3}{5}x$ ______________
4. $\frac{2}{3} = \frac{10}{11}x$ ______________
5. $1\frac{2}{3}x = 2\frac{1}{2}$ ______________

# YOUR TURN

## Thinking About Formulas With Fractions

You have learned one method to solve multiplication equations that contain fractions. There is another method you can use to solve this example.

$$\frac{3}{4}x = \frac{2}{3}$$

First, multiply both sides of the equation by 12, the common denominator of both fractions in the example.

$$12(\frac{3}{4}x) = 12(\frac{2}{3})$$

$$9x = 8$$

Now, divide both sides of the equation by 9.

$$\frac{9}{9}x = \frac{8}{9}$$

$$x = \frac{8}{9}$$

This second method changes the equation into an equivalent equation with no fractions. A simple division step then completes the solution. Of course, the answer may be a fraction.

1. Explain why multiplying both sides of an equation by 8 and then dividing both sides by 5 is the same as dividing both sides by $\frac{5}{8}$.

   ________________________________________

   ________________________________________

2. In the example $\frac{5}{9}x = \frac{3}{7}$, what is the common denominator of the two fractions? ________
3. What equivalent equation would you get if you multiplied both sides of the equation by the common denominator? ________
4. What is the solution of the equation? ________
5. How can you check this example?

   ________________________________________

   ________________________________________

# Show That You Know

Read the information below. Use what you read about solving formulas with fractions to answer the questions.

Use the space provided to show your work.

Use the information in the table below to help you answer the questions.

Sierra helped her family plan for a summer vacation. They investigated the value of American dollars in other countries, knowing that the exchange rates change from time to time. Sierra created a table using the current exchange rates. She replaced the decimal values with close fractional values. Simple fractional equations made it easy for the family members to calculate the exchanges.

| What One American Dollar (*A*) Is Worth | | | |
|---|---|---|---|
| 1.18751 | Australian dollar | (*D*) | $1\frac{1}{5}$ |
| 0.50449 | British pound | (*P*) | $\frac{1}{2}$ |
| 0.746213 | euro | (*E*) | $\frac{3}{4}$ |
| 5.5538 | Danish krone | (*K*) | $5\frac{1}{2}$ |
| 123.67 | Japanese yen | (*Y*) | 124 |
| 10.7665 | Mexican peso | (*Pe*) | 11 |

Sierra wrote $\left[\frac{1}{2}(A) = P\right]$ to exchange British pounds for American dollars, or American dollars for British pounds.

To exchange 60 pounds for American dollars, substitute 60 for *P* and then solve for *A*.

$\frac{1}{2}(A) = 60.$

$A = 60(2)$

$A = 120$

So, $120 American is about the same as 60 British pounds.

1. What equation can Sierra write to exchange American dollars for Danish krones?

2. How many dollars would be exchanged for 99 krones?

## Show That You Know (continued)

3. What equation can Sierra write to exchange American dollars for euros?

4. How many euros would be exchanged for $120?

5. Which is worth more, 248 yen or 22 Mexican pesos?
(Hint: Change both to American dollars.)

6. Write a fraction equation that exchanges British pounds for Australian dollars.

7. Use your equation to exchange 600 pounds for Australian dollars.

## Review What You've Learned

8. What have you learned in this Connections lesson about solving formulas?

9. What have you learned in this Connections lesson that you did not already know?

10. What have you learned in this lesson about writing equations to simplify calculations?

# Review and Practice

## Skills Review

**Integers and rational numbers:**

Whole numbers may be positive or negative.

$-1$, 3, $-13$, $-2$, and 2 are examples of integers.

Rational numbers can be written as $\frac{a}{b}$;

$a$ and $b$ are integers, but $b$ cannot be zero.

$\frac{1}{2}$, 3.5, $\frac{2}{1}$, and 113.3 are rational numbers.

$\frac{3}{0}$ is *not* a rational number.

**Absolute value:**

A number's distance from zero is its absolute value.

$-2$ and 2 are the same distance from 0.

The absolute value of both $-2$ and 2 is 2.

The absolute value of $-1.13$ is 1.13.

$|-345| = 345 \quad |4.391| = 4.391$

**Addition with negative numbers:**

$-13 + 10 = -3$

$-12 + (-12) = -24$

$-6 + 6 = 0$

$-6$ and $+6$ are examples of opposites, or additive inverses.

**Subtraction with negative numbers:**

Subtracting an integer is the same as adding the opposite of that integer.

$-2 - 6 = (-2) + (-6) = -8$

$-3 - (-4) = -3 + 4 = 1$

$-16 - (-7) = -16 + 7 = -9$

**Multiplication with negative numbers:**

$-2 \times (-2) = 4$

$-2 \times 2 = -4$

$-3 \times 17 = -51$

$3 \times (-17) = -51$

**Division with negative numbers:**

$-50 \div 5 = -10$

$-50 \div (-5) = 10$

$\frac{-28}{7} = -4$

$\frac{28}{-7} = -4$

## Strategy Review

- Draw a number line to help compare negative and positive integers.
- Tables also organize information that you need to make calculations.
- Make a list of the values you know and the values you are trying to find when solving problems that involve adding, subtracting, and multiplying negative numbers.

## Skills and Strategies Practice

**Complete the exercises below.**

**1.** What is a rational number between 234 and 235?

______________________

**2.** Put these money values in order from least to greatest: \$5.67, –\$6.26, \$4.00, \$0.10, –\$0.70.

______________________

**3.** What is $|-15| \div 150$? ______________

**4.** Find the sum or difference.

$-134 - 10 =$ ______________

$|-134| - 10 =$ ______________

**5.** A river level rose from 12 feet below flood stage to 2 feet below flood stage. How much did the level of the river change? ______________

**6.** What is $|-1{,}005|$? ______________

**When studying for a test, work with a partner or group to write your own test problems. Then solve each other's problems. Write addition, subtraction, multiplication, and division problems that have positive and negative integers, and combinations of positive and negative integers. Help each other to determine whether the answers to your problems should be positive or negative, and why.**

# Mid-Unit Review

**Circle the letter of the correct answer.**

**1.** −212 ________ 0

A. ≥ C. >
B. = D. <

**2.** −15 + 134 = ________

A. −149 C. 119
B. −119 D. 149

**3.** 52.5 written as a ratio is ________.

A. $\frac{525}{1}$ C. $\frac{525}{10}$
B. $\frac{52}{0.5}$ D. $\frac{52.5}{100}$

**4.** What is the additive inverse of $7\frac{2}{3}$?

A. $7\frac{2}{3}$ C. $-7\frac{3}{2}$
B. $-7\frac{2}{3}$ D. $7\frac{3}{2}$

**5.** 25 − (−25) = ________

A. 0 C. 50
B. −50 D. −25

**6.** 35 + (−75) + 12 = ________

A. −28 C. 98
B. 28 D. −98

**7.** 5,134 ÷ (−17) = ________

A. 302 C. −203
B. 304 D. −302

**8.** |−45| ________ 47

A. ≥ C. <
B. = D. >

**9.** 1,243 + (−1,243) = ________

A. −2,468 C. −1,234
B. 0 D. 2,468

**10.** 156 × (−22) = ________

A. 3,432 C. 3,234
B. −3,432 D. −3,234

**11.** −10 + (−100) + (−15) = ________

A. −75 C. −125
B. 75 D. 125

**12.** −11 × (−11) = ________

A. 1 C. −22
B. −121 D. 121

**13.** |34| ________ 34

A. = C. >
B. ≠ D. <

**14.** $7\frac{2}{5}$ written as a ratio is ________.

A. $\frac{37}{5}$ C. $\frac{14}{5}$
B. $\frac{9}{5}$ D. $\frac{5}{37}$

**15.** 5.2 ÷ (−2.6) = ________

A. −2 C. −2.6
B. 2 D. $\frac{2}{6}$

**16.** −18 ________ 15

A. = C. >
B. ≥ D. <

# Mid-Unit Review

**17.** 3, −3, 2, 12, and 59 in order from least to greatest is ________.

A. −3, 3, 2, 12, 59
B. 59, 12, −3, 3, 2
C. −3, 2, 3, 12, 59
D. 2, 3, −3, 12, 59

**18.** −25 + 75 = ________

A. −100
B. 50
C. 25
D. 100

**19.** (−112)(10) + 1 = ________

A. 1,121
B. −1,121
C. 1,119
D. −1,119

**20.** 37 × (−5) = ________

A. 185
B. −175
C. 165
D. −185

**21.** (−1) − 1 − 1 − 100 = ________

A. 103
B. 97
C. −103
D. −97

**22.** −333 ÷ 22 is the same as ________.

A. $\frac{333}{22}$
B. $\frac{-333}{22}$
C. $\frac{3}{2}$
D. $\frac{-3}{2}$

**23.** $-\frac{1}{3}$, −3, 234, −17, and 9 in order from least to greatest is ________.

A. −17, −3, $-\frac{1}{3}$, 9, 234
B. $-\frac{1}{3}$, −3, −17, 9, 234
C. $-\frac{1}{3}$, −17, −3, 9, 234
D. 234, 9, $-\frac{1}{3}$, −3, −17

**24.** −625 ÷ 25 = ________

A. −25
B. 25
C. 5
D. −15

**25.** −999(−1) = ________

A. 999
B. −999
C. $\frac{-999}{1}$
D. 99

**26.** −50 + (−52) = ________

A. −100
B. −102
C. −2
D. 102

**27.** −0.5, −1.3, 0, −7, and 1.3 in order from least to greatest is ________.

A. −7, −0.5, −1.3, 0, 1.3
B. 1.3, 0, −0.5, −1.3, −7
C. −7, −1.3, −0.5, 0, 1.3
D. 0, −0.5, −1.3, 1.3, −7

**28.** 5 + (−120) + 2 = ________

A. −117
B. −113
C. 117
D. 113

**29.** |3.25| ________ −3.25

A. ≤
B. =
C. <
D. >

# Writing Linear Equations With Rational Numbers

## Learn the SKILL

Mrs. Small has kept a careful record of her deposits and withdrawals from her checking account. She started with $256. Her records show a deposit gave her a new balance of $293.

Two days later her records indicate a withdrawal and then a balance of $213. Mrs. Small plans to have her three children share the remaining balance equally. What **equation** can be written to find out how much they each receive?

### VOCABULARY

Watch for the words you are learning about.

**equation:** a mathematical sentence with an equal sign

**inverse operations:** operations that undo one another

**linear equation:** a two-variable expression, usually *x* and *y*, that when graphed forms a straight line

**variable:** a letter that stands for a number; the value of an algebraic expression varies, or changes, depending on the value of the letter given to the variable

| SKILL | EXAMPLE | WRITE AN EXAMPLE |
|---|---|---|
| Writing **linear equations** with rational numbers follows the same pattern as writing equations with whole numbers.<br>A deposit increases the amount of money in Mrs. Small's account. | The relationship of the deposit, the old balance, and the new balance in her checking account can be expressed with an addition equation. Represent her deposit using the **variable** *d*.<br>$256 + d = 293$ | What operation do you use to show an increase?<br>________________<br>Write an equation to show an increase.<br>________________ |
| A withdrawal decreases the amount of money in her account. | The relationship of the withdrawal, the old balance, and the new balance in her checking account can be expressed with a subtraction equation. Represent her withdrawal using the variable *w*.<br>$293 - w = 213$ | What operation do you use to show a decrease?<br>________________<br>Write an equation to show a decrease.<br>________________ |
| Sharing the amount equally can be written as either a division or multiplication equation because division and multiplication are **inverse operations.** | Represent an equal share with the variable *e*.<br>$(\frac{1}{3})213 = e$<br>$3e = 213$ | What operations can you use to show equal shares?<br>________________ |

Learn the Skill

# YOUR TURN

## Choose the Right Word

equation inverse operations
linear equation variable

**Fill in each blank with the correct word or phrase from the box.**

1. A mathematical sentence with an equal sign is a(n) ________________.
2. A letter that is used in place of an unknown value is a(n) ________________.
3. The solution to a(n) ________________ can be graphed as a straight line.
4. Multiplication and division are examples of ________________.

## Yes or No?

**Answer these questions and be ready to explain your answers.**

5. A woman withdraws $33 from her checking account on Tuesday and deposits $33 dollars on Wednesday. Can these be considered inverse operations? ________
6. Are all equations linear equations? ________
7. If a woman cuts a loaf of bread into eight pieces and then gives a piece to her son, can this be represented by an equation? ________
8. Is division used to find how many items are in each group if all of the items are shared equally? ________

## Show That You Know

**Write an expression with the same numbers using the inverse operation.**

9. $\frac{g}{229}$
10. $\frac{f}{v}$
11. $m - 568$
12. $678 + n - y$

**Tell whether these situations are represented by addition or subtraction equations.**

13. Jacob takes $x$ cans of soup out of the cupboard every day.
14. Dawn deposits $45 into her account every week.
15. City workers put $20 into a charity account once a month.

# SOLVE on Your Own

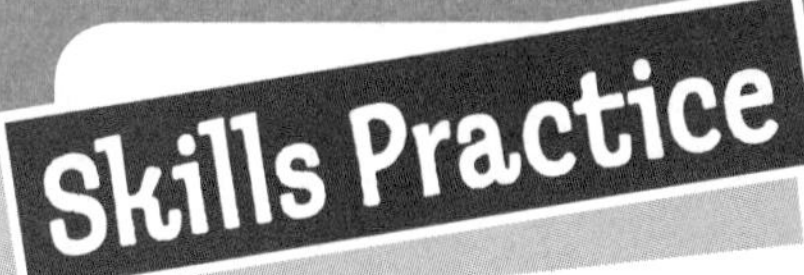

Say words in a problem to yourself to make sure you understand what is being described.


**Write equations that represent each situation.**

1. Levi deposits $12 into his bank account. His new balance is $55.
   ________________

2. Joshua divides his baseball card collection into four categories. There are 13 cards in each category. ________________

3. Una keeps three times as many pennies as nickels in her piggybank, plus one more penny.
   ________________

4. Melinda makes half as many muffins as Bijou, plus three more muffins. Melinda makes a total of 27 muffins. ________________

5. Houston normally eats half as many grapes as Ryan. Ryan eats *r* grapes. ________________

6. Delphine drives 5 hours going 50 miles per hour. How far does she travel?
   ______________________________

7. Water leaks out of a bathtub at 0.5 gallon each hour. How much water has leaked out after *t* hours? __________________________

8. Katrina adds *x* books to her shelf every day. After 7 days she has *g* books. ________________

9. Sung takes three rocks out of his collection. He has 24 rocks left. ________________

10. Kitty walks *x* blocks every hour. After 2 hours she has walked 45 blocks. ________________

Choose a Strategy

# Writing Linear Equations with Rational Numbers

## Strategies

### Make a Table or a Chart, Find a Pattern

**Step 1: Read** Did you know that it costs more to produce a penny than a penny is actually worth? A penny is made mostly of zinc, and in 2005 the cost of zinc per pound increased. In 2005, the cost of producing one penny went from 0.97 cent to 1.4 cents. Some people predict that when the cost of producing a penny jumps to 2 cents, the penny will be discontinued. If the price changes 0.1 cent every year, in what year should we discontinue the penny? Write a linear equation to show your answer.

| STRATEGY | SOLUTION |
|---|---|

**Make a Table or a Chart**

Sometimes using values in a table will help you work backward to find an equation.

**Step 2: Plan** Start in the year 2005. You know the value. So if the price change is 0.1 cent from 2005 to 2006, what would be the value? What about in 2007, or in 2012?

**Step 3: Solve** Make a table like this:

| Year | Cost at the Start of the Year | Cost at the End of the Year | Change in Cost of a Penny |
|---|---|---|---|
| 2006 | 1.4 | 1.5 | +0.1 |
| 2007 | 1.5 | 1.6 | +0.1 |

Fill in several more steps, until you reach the cost of 2 cents. Remember the equation form of $ax + b = y$, where $a$ is the constant change, $b$ is the starting cost, $y$ is the end cost, and $x$ is the variable. What is the variable in this case? When you figure that out, you can find the equation: $0.1x + 1.4 = 2$. The penny will be discontinued in 2012.

**Step 4: Check** Use your formula to check against the table.

**Find a Pattern**

In any linear equation you will find a pattern. There is a constant increase, so you'll be able to find any part.

**Step 2: Plan** Create an equation by solving it. If you know the price of the penny in 2005, then how can you find it in 2006?

**Step 3: Solve** Use the equation form of $ax + b = y$. Try to see by finding the price of a penny at different years if you can figure out what changes and what stays constant.

$0.1x + 1.4 = y$ $\quad\quad$ $0.1 \times 6 + 1.4 = 2$

The penny should be discontinued in the year 2012.

**Step 4: Check** Once you have an equation, check your answers.

# YOUR TURN



## Choose the Right Word

equation inverse operations
linear equation variable

**Fill in each blank with the correct word or phrase from the box.**

1. Operations that undo one another are ________________.
2. A(n) ________________ shows two expressions that have the same value.
3. A(n) ________________ is a letter or symbol that stands for a number.
4. A particular type of equation is a ________________.

## Yes or No?

**Answer these questions and be ready to explain your answers.**

5. If the variable $x$ is used in one equation and variable $y$ is used in another equation, can they ever equal the same number? ________
6. Is division an inverse operation of addition? ________
7. If the variable $x^2$ is used in an equation, can it still be a linear equation? ________

## Show That You Know

**Write a linear equation given the description.**

8. Marge has $m$ more marbles than eight.
9. Peter has $b$ bagels and is buying two more.
10. Andy had 12 dollars and lost $d$ dollars.
11. Fifteen people are at a party and $p$ more arrive.
12. Don gave away $c$ of his 20 cards.

**Write the inverse operation using the same values.**

13. $10 + r$
14. $rt$
15. $r - 18$
16. $\frac{12}{r}$
17. $\frac{155}{r}$

# READ on Your Own

## Reading Comprehension Strategy: Questioning

## Money: Earn It, Save It, Spend It, *pages 20–21*

### VOCABULARY

Watch for the words you are learning about.

**counterfeit:** fake; made to look like something else to deceive others

### Fluency Tip

Read with expression. Use expression in your reading of expository text as well as narrative text. Emphasize unusual facts and details.

### Before You Read

Think about what you read about the euro in "Money Around the World." Do you think replacing all the different currencies with the euro made it easier or harder to manufacture money? Why?

### As You Read

**Preview pages 20–21 of "How Is Money Made?"** 

What do you hope to learn from reading this text?

______________________________________________________________________

**Read "How Is Money Made?", pages 20–21.** 

What are some of the most important details you learned about how money is made?

______________________________________________________________________

Would you recommend this article to another person? Why?

______________________________________________________________________

### After You Read

What did you learn in the article about efforts to stop the making of counterfeit money? What should you do if you think you have money you think may be counterfeit?

______________________________________________________________________

______________________________________________________________________

______________________________________________________________________

______________________________________________________________________

# SOLVE on Your Own

## Money: Earn It, Save It, Spend It, *page 22*

*page 22*

### Organize the Information

**Read the magazine article. Then fill out the following table with more information about money.**

| Fun Fact | Equation | What It Means |
|---|---|---|
| If you had 10 billion \$1 notes and gave one away every second of every day, it would take you a little more than 317 years to go broke. | $60 \times 60 \times 24 \times 365 \times 317 =$ 9,996,912,000 | |
| | | |
| | | |
| | | |
| | | |

### You Do the Math

Try writing many different equations. Record your favorites.

Use the information in the table above to write your answers to these questions.

1. What can you say about the length of our currency today and its original length before 1929?

______________________________

2. What can you say about the width of our currency today and its original width before 1929?

______________________________

### After You Solve

Why do you think the U.S. prints so many bills each year?

______________________________

______________________________

# Solving Linear Equations With Rational Numbers

## Learn the SKILL

Jeremy earns money by working part-time at the pet store every Friday evening and Saturday. Each week he works for a total of 8 hours and earns \$52. Sometimes he receives a bonus and his total weekly earnings are \$65.

| SKILL | EXAMPLE | COMPLETE THE EXAMPLE |
|---|---|---|
| Addition equations can be solved by subtracting the same number from both sides of the equation or by adding the opposite of the number to both sides of the equation. | How much is Jeremy's weekly bonus?<br>$52 + b = 65$<br>$52 + b - 52 = 65 - 52$ or<br>$52 + b + (-52) = 65 + (-52)$<br>$b = 13$ | How can you solve an addition equation?<br>__________<br>__________<br>__________<br>__________ |
| Multiplication equations can be solved by dividing both sides of the equation by the same number or by multiplying both sides of the equation by the reciprocal of the number. | How much does Jeremy earn per hour?<br>$8h = 52$<br>$8h \div 8 = 52 \div 8$ or<br>$8h(\frac{1}{8}) = 52(\frac{1}{8})$<br>$h = \$6.50$ | How can you solve a multiplication equation?<br>__________<br>__________<br>__________<br>__________ |
| Use the same equation-solving rules for solving equations with negative numbers.<br>Be sure to also obey the rules for computation with negative numbers. | $-12x = -84$<br>$\frac{-12x}{-12} = \frac{-84}{-12}$<br>$x = +7$ | What must you remember when solving equations with negative numbers?<br>__________<br>__________<br>__________<br>__________ |

# YOUR TURN



## Choose the Right Word

equation   linear equation   variables

**Fill in each blank with the correct word or phrase from the box.**

1. In a(n) ________________, the expressions on both sides of the equal sign must have the same value.
2. A(n) ________________ is a special type of equation that can be graphed as a straight line.
3. One or more ________________ may be found in an equation.

## Yes or No?

**Answer these questions and be ready to explain your answers.**

4. Is the solution to a variable in an equation always a positive number? ________
5. Must only one operation be used to solve an equation? ________
6. Are multiplication and division inverse operations? ________
7. Are the same rules followed for solving equations that have negative numbers as for solving equations that have positive numbers? ________

## Show That You Know

**Solve for *y*.**

8. $y + 3.9 = 12.4$   $y =$
9. $y - 16 = -22$   $y =$
10. $y$ is 10% of 340   $y =$
11. $y + 2 - 3 = 19$   $y =$

**Solve for *x*.**

12. $(\frac{3}{7})x = 3$   $x =$
13. $38x = -950$   $x =$

# SOLVE on Your Own

## Skills Practice

Be sure to correctly identify the operation in each equation. Then you will choose the correct inverse operation to solve the problem.

**Solve for the variable in each equation.**

1. $689 + d = 294$ ________

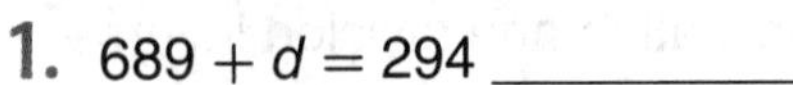

2. $25x = 4{,}000$ ________

3. $\frac{z}{2.4} = \$48$ ________

4. $g - 0.11 = 22.03$ ________

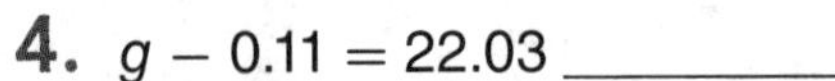

5. $-324.4g = -40.55$ ________

**Use an equation to solve each problem. Write your equation below your answer.**

6. Juniper makes $5.25 an hour babysitting. How much will she make if she babysits for 8 hours? ________

7. Jenna worked for 5 hours. She made $65. How much does she earn per hour?

8. Shakira rode her bike for 2 hours. She went for 11 miles. How fast did she go (in miles per hour)? ________

9. Daphne gathered shells for 2.5 hours. If she gathered them at a rate of 20 per hour, how many shells did she gather altogether?

10. Sharat put 12 books on his shelf. He took away two, then added $x$ more. In the end, there were 26 books on his shelf. How many books is $x$ equal to? ________

# Solving Linear Equations with Rational Numbers

## Strategies

### Try a Simpler Form of the Problem, Find a Pattern

Step 1: Read Every week at work you earn *d* dollars. After you get your paycheck, you use \$300 to pay bills and the rest goes into your savings account. How can you find out how much money (*m*) you have in your savings account after *w* weeks?

| STRATEGY | SOLUTION |
|---|---|
| **Try a Simpler Form of the Problem**<br>Break down the problem. Understand what each part means before you attempt to solve. | Step 2: Plan Write out the equation. What looks odd about it? You should see there are actually three variables. What does this mean? Simply put, there is no exact answer to this problem.<br>Step 3: Solve Write the equation.<br>$m = w \times (d - 300)$<br>If $w = 10$ weeks and $d = \$500$, solve for $m$. $m = \$2{,}000$<br>If $m = \$800$ and $w = 5$ weeks, solve for $d$. $d = \$460$<br>Step 4: Check Work backward after you solve for one variable. Then insert one of the known values and try to solve for the final value to see if it all matches. |
| **Find a Pattern**<br>Each piece of a pattern is simply part of the whole. So look at the pattern in pieces and see how the pieces react. | Step 2: Plan Create an equation and apply values. Use a table to chart them.<br>Step 3: Solve Hold one variable constant. Make *d* dollars 500. What do you notice about the pattern as you change from week to week? Then make the week variable constant. For example, it could be 10. How much money would you need to make just to break even? How about to save \$300? What is the pattern?<br>Step 4: Check When holding variables constant, use the variable answer to work backward to get the constant. |

Choose a Strategy

# YOUR TURN

## Choose the Right Word

equation    linear equation    variables

**Fill in each blank with the correct word or phrase from the box.**

1. A letter or symbol that stands in the place of an unknown number is called a(n) ________________.
2. An equation is a(n) ________________ when the graph of its solution is a straight line.
3. $2x = y$ is an example of a(n) ________________ because of the equal sign.

## Yes or No?

**Answer these questions and be ready to explain your answers.**

4. A percent compares a number to 100. Can there be more than 100% of something? ________
5. Can you have an infinite number of variables in an equation? ________
6. Can multiplication be used in a linear equation? ________
7. Are percents allowed in linear equations? ________

## Show That You Know

**Solve for the variable in each equation.**

8. $y + 7 = 12$
9. $x - 12 = 32$
10. $7z - 12 = 58$
11. $0.1p = 6.7$
12. $1.5n + 18 - 1.1n = 22$
13. $(\frac{5}{7})q + (\frac{1}{7})q - (\frac{4}{7})q = 18$
14. $75 + 7e - 6e - 3e = 33$
15. $5j + 6j - 42j + 18j + 9j = -16$
16. $(\frac{7}{12})h + 77 = 91$
17. $(\frac{2}{5})r - 7 + 1.2r = 97$

# READ on Your Own

## Reading Comprehension Strategy: Questioning

## Money: Earn It, Save It, Spend It, *pages 23–24*

### Before You Read

Remember what you read in "How Is Money Made?" How does money get from the manufacturer to the general public?

### As You Read

**Preview "What Can My Bank Do for Me?", pages 23–24.** 

Write a goal-setting and details question in the chart below.

**Read "What Can My Bank Do for Me?", pages 23–24.** 

Write your answers in the chart below.

| Before You Read | After You Read |
|---|---|
| Goal-setting question: | Answer: |
| Details question: | Answer: |

### After You Read

Do you have any money in a bank account? What kind of account is it, and how is the interest paid?

## VOCABULARY

Watch for the words you are learning about.

**annual:** yearly; happening once a year

**collateral:** property used to back a loan; if the loan is not paid, the property is taken

**compound interest:** interest paid on previous interest earned

**equity:** the amount of the principle that is paid off

**mortgage:** a loan for buying a house

**penalty:** a fee charged for withdrawing money too soon

**principle:** the amount borrowed or deposited

**secured loans:** loans that are backed with collateral

## Fluency Tip

Look for words that might be difficult to pronounce. Check a dictionary or ask someone to help you pronounce those words.

# SOLVE on Your Own

## Money: Earn It, Save It, Spend It, *page 25*

### Organize the Information

**Read the magazine article. Then fill out the following table with information on the amount in your account in a certain period of time.**

The CD I chose has an APR of _____ for a __________ term and is compounded __________.

| Period | Account Value at Start of Period | Annual Interest Rate (APR) | Amount of Interest Earned in Period | Interest Earned in Period | Account Value at End of Period |
|---|---|---|---|---|---|
| January 2008 | $580 | | | | |
| | | | | | |
| | | | | | |
| | | | | | |

### You Do the Math

Use the information in the table above to answer these questions. Write your answers in the space provided.

Making a table will help you answer the magazine questions.


1. How can you find the total interest earned?

______________________________________________

2. If the APR is 5.3% and the account is compounded quarterly, what percentage rate will you earn for each period?

______________________________________________

3. How did you use the percentage rate for the period to determine the interest earned during that period?

______________________________________________

______________________________________________

### After You Solve

If you had a large sum of money to invest, how would you invest it?

______________________________________________

## The Four-Step Problem-Solving Plan

| Step 1: Read | Step 2: Plan | Step 3: Solve | Step 4: Check |
|---|---|---|---|
| Make sure you understand what the problem is asking. | Decide how you will solve the problem. | Solve the problem using your plan. | Check to make sure your answer is correct. |

**Read the article below. Then answer the questions.**

### Inflation

Inflation is an increase in the level of prices for goods and services. It is measured as an annual percentage. The value of a dollar shifts back and forth in response to inflation. The value of a dollar is measured in terms of purchasing power—that is, how many things it can buy. When inflation increases, the value of the dollar goes down. For example, suppose the inflation rate is 3% for the year. So a $1 pack of gum will cost $1.03 a year later. After inflation, your dollar cannot buy the same amount of goods it previously could.

There are two situations that cause inflation to increase:

**Demand-Pull Inflation**—When there is more demand than supply, prices will increase. This usually occurs in countries that are trying to build a strong system of goods and services. These are countries that have growing economies.

**Cost-Push Inflation**—When the costs to produce an object increase, the price on that object increases so that the business that produces the object can make enough money to produce more. Such costs can include costs of goods, wages, and taxes.

1. How does a rise in inflation affect our lives?

   ______________________________

   ______________________________

2. Suppose the yearly inflation rate was 2%. How much would a car that originally cost $20,000 cost in a year?

   ______________________________

   ______________________________

Application

# YOUR TURN

**Read the article below. Then answer the questions.**

## Inflation and Interest

In the United States, the Federal Reserve determines the interest rates. The people who run the Federal Reserve meet eight times a year to set short-term interest rate targets. During these meetings, the Consumer Price Index (CPI) is taken into account as they make their decision. The CPI is a measure of the average change in price of goods and services over time. It is also called the cost-of-living index.

The goal of the Federal Reserve in changing the interest rate is to have the greatest number of people working, to hold prices steady, and to encourage good production levels. When interest rates are lowered, spending increases, and this in turn helps the economy grow.

When the economy of a country grows a lot, it can be detrimental, or harmful. On the other hand, an economy with no inflation signals a weak economy. It is the Federal Reserve's job to strike a balance between the two extremes.

1. If you purchased a used car for $2,500 and borrowed the full cost of the car at an interest rate of 8%, how much would you have to pay in interest? (Assume the interest does not compound. It is a one-time payment.)

   ______________________________

2. How important is the Federal Reserve to our economy?

   ______________________________

   ______________________________

   ______________________________

3. Why is it good for an economy to experience some inflation?

   ______________________________

   ______________________________

### Fluency Tip

Read and reread to practice maintaining an even pace throughout the text.

# READ on Your Own

## Reading Comprehension Strategy: Questioning

## Money: Earn It, Save It, Spend It, *pages 26–28*

### Before You Read

You read about borrowing and saving in "What Can My Bank Do for Me?" How is interest related to both of these topics?

### As You Read

**Read "Money's Ups and Downs," pages 26–28.** 

Think about the different types of questions you learned to ask. Then write three questions, the type of questions they are, and the answers.

| Question | Type of Question | Answer |
|---|---|---|
| | | |
| | | |
| | | |

### VOCABULARY

Watch for the words you are learning about.

**deflation:** an overall decrease in the prices that people pay for goods and services over time

**economists:** people who study how money is earned and spent

**inflation:** an overall increase in the prices that people pay for goods and services

### Fluency Tip

Pause briefly for dashes that indicate explanations.

### After You Read

How has inflation affected your life? Explain your answer.

# SOLVE on Your Own

## Money: Earn It, Save It, Spend It, *page 29*

### Organize the Information

**Use a list like the one below to organize the information you find in the Math Project on page 29 in the magazine.**

| Price of the commodity ________________ |
|---|
| Reference year ________________ |
| Price of the commodity today ________________ |
| CPI ________________ |

A list will help you keep track of the benchmark figures you are using.

### Math Project

Use the information in the list above to answer these questions. Write your answers in the space provided.

1. Which year did you choose as your reference year? Why?

____________________________________________

____________________________________________

2. How do you solve proportions?

____________________________________________

3. If the price is less than the price in the reference year, what type of CPI should you expect?

____________________________________________

### After You Solve

How else might you express the same information in the list?

____________________________________________

# Choosing the Best Procedures to Solve Linear Equations

## VOCABULARY

Watch for the words you are learning about.

**equivalent equations:** equations with the same solutions

## Learn the SKILL

Once a linear equation has been written to solve a problem, the next step is to choose the procedure to solve the problem. In each step the properties of equality are used to express the equation in a new way. Solutions that are obtained for the new equation also solve the original equation.

| SKILL | EXAMPLE | COMPLETE THE EXAMPLE |
|---|---|---|
| Equations can be expressed in many ways. Equations that have the same solutions are **equivalent equations.** | Equivalent equations:<br>$x + 8 = 12$<br>$x - 9 = -5$<br>$-7x = -28$<br>$-\frac{x}{2} = -2$<br>These equations all have a solution of 4. | How can you change an equation into an equivalent equation?<br>____________________<br>____________________<br>____________________ |
| Equivalent equations can be obtained by using the properties of equality, which state that adding, subtracting, multiplying, or dividing both sides of an equation by the same number result in equivalent equations. | Start with the equation $-9 + x = 3$.<br>Multiply both sides of the equation by 6.<br>The equivalent equation is<br>$6(-9 + x) = 18$ or<br>$-54 + 6x = 18$ | Starting with the equation $4x = -20$, what four equivalent equations can be obtained by adding, subtracting, multiplying, or dividing both sides of the equation by $-3$?<br>____________________<br>____________________<br>____________________<br>____________________ |
| Solve equations by choosing a procedure that will simplify the equation and find the value of the variable. | Multiplying both sides of an equation by $-\frac{2}{3}$ would give an equivalent equation but could make the equation more complicated. Choose a strategy that simplifies the equation. | What efficient step simplifies $\frac{4}{5}x = -\frac{3}{4}$?<br>____________________<br>____________________ |

Learn the Skill

# YOUR TURN

## Choose the Right Word

simplify   equivalent equation   variable

**Fill in each blank with the correct word or phrase from the box.**

1. To ________________ an equation is to make it less complicated.
2. Solving an equation means to find the value of the ________________.
3. Two equations with the same solution are ________________.

## Yes or No?

**Answer these questions and be ready to explain your answers.**

4. Do equivalent equations have to have the same operations? ________
5. If you multiply the expression on one side of an equation by 6, must you also multiply the expression on the other side by 6? ________
6. Do equivalent equations have the same variable? ________
7. Is there only one way to express an equation?________

## Show That You Know

**Write two equivalent equations.**

8. $3x - 3 = 27$

9. $2x = 44$

**Solve the equations.**

10. $2x - 1 = 97$

11. $2(3 + x) = 12$

12. $(\frac{3}{57})\,x = 27$

# SOLVE on Your Own

## Skills Practice

Write out every step to solving a problem. If you make a mistake, you can go back to check all of your work.

**Solve each equation. Then write an equivalent equation.**

1. $4s + 13 = 29$ ________________

2. $s - 2.4 = 2.4$ ________________

3. $(\frac{2}{3})m = 4$ ________________

4. $n - 2 = -6$ ________________

5. $123n = 123$ ________________

**Use the properties of equality to write an equivalent equation.**

6. $3s + 3 = 60$ ________________

7. $d - 2 = 12$ ________________

8. $t \times \frac{1}{35} = \frac{2}{7}$ ________________

9. $s - 15 = 156$ ________________

10. $2s + 5.5 = 124$ ________________

11. $36m = 72$ ________________

Choose a Strategy

# Choosing the Best Procedures to Solve Linear Equations

## Strategies

### Make a Table or a Chart, Try a Simpler Form of the Problem

**Step 1: Read** A couple receives a loan for $1,000 with 4% monthly interest. The bank requires that they make a $120 payment each month. The couple would like to repay the money within 6 months. Should they pay more than the bank requires each month?

| STRATEGY | SOLUTION |
|---|---|

**Make a Table or a Chart**

Use a table to organize information about the couple's loan. Figure out how much the couple will still owe after their first monthly payment. Use this amount to determine how much they will owe after their second, third, fourth, fifth, and then sixth monthly payment. Take into account that interest is added every month.

**Step 2: Plan** Plug the payment amount into the table and use it to figure out how much the couple will owe after 6 months if they pay only $120 a month.

**Step 3: Solve**

| Monthly Payment | Expression for Amount Owed | Amount Owed | Payment | Expression for Amount Still Owed | Amount Still Owed |
|---|---|---|---|---|---|
| 1 | $1,000 + (0.04)1,000 | $1,040 | $120 | $1040 – $120 | $920 |
| 2 | $920 + (0.04)920 | $956.8 | $120 | $956.8 – $120 | $836.8 |
| 3 | $836.8 + (0.04)836.8 | $870.27 | $120 | $870.27 – $120 | $750.27 |
| 4 | $750.27 + (0.04)750.27 | $780.28 | $120 | $780.28 – $120 | $660.28 |
| 5 | $660.28 + (0.04)660.28 | $686.69 | $120 | $686.69 – $120 | $566.69 |
| 6 | $566.69 + (0.04)566.69 | $589.36 | $120 | $589.36 – $120 | $469.36 |

**Step 4: Check** At the end of 6 months the couple still owes $469.36. They need to make more than a $120 payment each month.

**Try a Simpler Form of the Problem**

For a moment, imagine that there is no interest on the loan. Determine how much they would have to pay each month if there were no interest, and compare that to $120.

**Step 2: Plan** Determine what monthly payments would be to repay the entire loan in 6 months if there were no interest on the loan.

**Step 3: Solve**

$1,000 ÷ 6 = $166.67. They would have to pay this amount each month to repay a loan with no interest in 6 months.

With interest, the couple would have to pay more than this amount to repay their loan in 6 months.

**Step 4: Check** Compare $1,000 ÷ 6 with the minimum payment required by the bank. Would the couple be able to repay the loan in 6 months if they paid only $120 each month? No.

# YOUR TURN

Choose a Strategy

## Choose the Right Word

interest rate percent solve

**Fill in each blank with the correct word or phrase from the box.**

1. The percent of the balance of a loan charged by a bank every month or year is the ________________.
2. A ________________ is a part of 100.
3. To find the value of a variable that makes an equation true is to ________________ the equation.

## Yes or No?

**Answer these questions and be ready to explain your answers.**

4. Is 112% of $x$ the same as $1.12x$? ________
5. Is it possible to pay more in interest than the amount of a loan itself? ________
6. Is $5.35x = 2$ the same as $x = \frac{5.35}{2}$? ________
7. If you take a long time to pay off a loan, will you pay less in interest than if you take a short time? ________

## Show That You Know

**Solve for x or y.**

8. $1.04x = 20.8$
9. $\$560 - y = \$320$
10. $(\frac{2}{3})y = \frac{22}{33}$
11. $90 = 0.01x$
12. $3x - 1 = 5$
13. $12y - 480 = 0$

# READ on Your Own

## Reading Comprehension Strategy: Questioning

### Money: Earn It, Save It, Spend It, *pages 30–31*

**VOCABULARY**

Watch for the words you are learning about.

**deficit:** the yearly amount that the nation spends beyond what it takes in

**securities:** bonds or treasury notes the government sells to raise money for its programs

**Fluency Tip**

Read the text more than once. You will read more smoothly and you will be more likely to remember what you read.

#### Before You Read

Recall what you read about inflation in "Money's Ups and Downs." How does inflation affect the economy? Why?

#### As You Read

**Read "Debt and Bankruptcy," pages 30–31.** 

As you read, ask yourself, "What important details can I find in the text?" Record your results in the graphic organizer below.

| Detail | Why It Is Important |
|---|---|
| | |
| | |
| | |
| | |

#### After You Read

What do you think should be done about the national debt?

# SOLVE on Your Own

## Money: Earn It, Save It, Spend It, *page 32*

### Organize the Information

**Read the magazine article. Then fill out the following table with values using the graph. Extend the *x*-axis and *y*-axis and the line of the graph. Use the line to estimate the national debt in 2007, 2008, and 2009.**

| Year ($x$) | National Debt ($y$) |
|---|---|
| 1999 | |
| 2003 | |
| 2006 | |
| 2007 | |
| 2008 | |
| 2009 | |

Listing values in a table may help you answer the questions in the article.


### You Do the Math

Use the information in the table above to answer these questions. Write your answers in the space provided.

1. What factors did you consider when you made your first guess of the year?

_______________

_______________

2. After you extended the axes of the graph and the line, how did you use the graph to help adjust your guess?

_______________

_______________

### After You Solve

How else could you display the information in the chart above?

_______________

Application

## The Four-Step Problem-Solving Plan

| Step 1: Read | Step 2: Plan | Step 3: Solve | Step 4: Check |
|---|---|---|---|
| Make sure you understand what the problem is asking. | Decide how you will solve the problem. | Solve the problem using your plan. | Check to make sure your answer is correct. |

**Read the article below. Then answer the questions.**

### Presidential Coins

In 2007 the United States began making $1 coins showing images of presidents from George Washington through Gerald Ford. The face of each coin shows the picture of a president's head, the president's name with the dates he served, and the order in which he served. On the back of each coin is a picture of the Statue of Liberty. "E Pluribus Unum," "In God We Trust," the mint mark, and the year of the coin is sent out are carved around the edge of the coin. The size, weight, and metal composition of the coin are similar to that of the $1 Sacagawea coin.

These coins are being made in the order in which the presidents served, beginning with coins for presidents Washington, Adams, Jefferson, and Madison in 2007. The United States Mint will make and send out four presidential coins each year through 2016.

1. How will the $1 president's coin be similar to previously released coins?

______________________________

______________________________

______________________________

2. If a dollar coin costs 12 cents to make and a dollar bill costs 4 cents to make, what is the difference in production costs if you have $20 in coins as opposed to $20 in $1 bills?

______________________________

# YOUR TURN

Application

**Read the article below. Then answer the questions.**

## The Golden Coin

The Sacagawea golden dollar coin was first released in January 2000. This new dollar coin replaced the Susan B. Anthony dollar coin, which had been in circulation since 1979. Because demand had increased for a dollar coin in commerce, the government's supply of Susan B. Anthony dollars was nearly exhausted, creating a need for a new dollar coin. The coin's design had to address complaints that the Susan B. Anthony coin and the quarter were much too similar.

This new coin was different from any other coin in use—it was gold. The eye-catching color made it different from the other coins and its edge had a different feel to it than that of the Susan B. Anthony coin or the quarter. The striking image of Sacagawea on the face and the bald eagle on the back made it one of the most pleasing coins made by the U.S. Mint.

1. A money sack contains 2,000 gold dollar coins. A second sack contains the same value of money in quarters. How many quarters are in the second sack?

______________________________

2. How was the Sacagawea coin different from the Susan B. Anthony coin?

______________________________

______________________________

3. Why was changing the feel of the edge of the Sacagawea coin important?

______________________________

______________________________

______________________________

### Fluency Tip

Vary loudness and softness when reading phrases to add to the excitement of what you are reading.

# READ on Your Own

## Reading Comprehension Strategy: Questioning

## Money: Earn It, Save It, Spend It, *pages 33–35*

### VOCABULARY

Watch for the words you are learning about.

**seigniorage:** the difference between the cost to produce a coin and the value of the coin

### Fluency Tip

To help you manage long sentences, mark a slash at the end of each phrase. Then read and reread the paragraph.

### Before You Read

In "Debt and Bankruptcy," you read about the national debt. What do you think would happen if the government borrowed less money?

### As You Read

As you read "The 50 State Quarters Program," look for between-the-lines questions and beyond-the-text questions. The concept map below provides "question starters" for between-the-lines questions on the left side of the circle. "Question starters" for beyond-the-text questions are on the right side.

**Read page 33.** 

Fill in two of the concept map questions.

**Read pages 34–35.** 

Fill in two of the concept map questions.

**The 50 State Quarters Program**

- Why was it important for each state to
- Why did the Secretary of the Treasury have final say
- What other coins
- What if a state wanted to

### After You Read

Choose one question from the concept map and answer it.

______________________________

______________________________

# SOLVE on Your Own

## Money: Earn It, Save It, Spend It, *page 36*

### Organize the Information

**Use a table like the one below to organize the information you find in the Math Project on page 36 in the magazine.**

| Coin | Quantity |
|---|---|
| Quarter | |
| Dime | |
| Nickel | |
| Penny | |

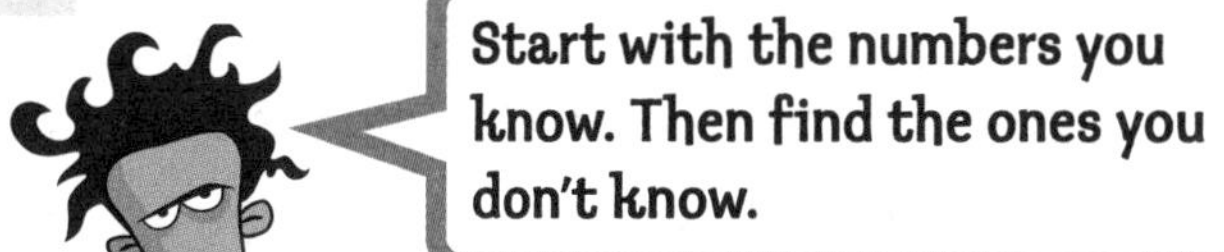

Start with the numbers you know. Then find the ones you don't know.


### Math Project

Use the information in the table above to answer these questions. Write your answers in the space provided.

1. What variables should you use to write the equations? What does each variable stand for?

2. Why is it helpful to use numbers such as 3, 5, and 10 instead of 3 billion, 5 billion, and 10 billion?

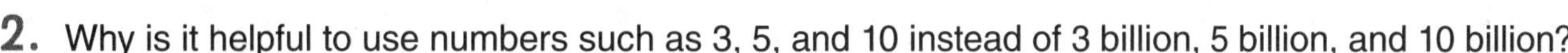

3. Using your equation and the table above, how much will the Treasury earn this year?

### After You Solve

If you could design a coin to honor someone, what would it look like?

# Put It Together

## Introducing Prime Numbers and Prime Factorization

You have learned that some numbers have many factors. If the number of factors is greater than two, then the number is called a composite number.

$24 = 1 \times 24 = 2 \times 12 = 3 \times 8 = 4 \times 6$

The number 24 has eight different factors: 1, 2, 3, 4, 6, 8, 12, and 24.

Numbers that have exactly two different factors are prime numbers.

$5 = 5 \times 1 \qquad 13 = 13 \times 1 \qquad 29 = 29 \times 1$

The number 0 is neither prime nor composite. Zero has every number as a factor. The factors cannot be counted. The number 1 is also neither prime nor composite. The number 1 has only one factor, 1.

Composite numbers can be expressed as the product of prime numbers. Break the number into smaller factors until all the factors are prime. There is often more than one way to do this.

$$\begin{aligned} 48 &= 6 \times 8 \\ &= 2 \times 3 \times 2 \times 4 \\ &= 2 \times 3 \times 2 \times 2 \times 2 \\ &= 2^4 \times 3 \end{aligned}$$

$$\begin{aligned} 48 &= 4 \times 12 \\ &= 2 \times 2 \times 2 \times 6 \\ &= 2 \times 2 \times 2 \times 2 \times 3 \\ &= 2^4 \times 3 \end{aligned}$$

$$\begin{aligned} 48 &= 3 \times 16 \\ &= 3 \times 4 \times 4 \\ &= 3 \times 2 \times 2 \times 2 \times 2 \\ &= 2^4 \times 3 \end{aligned}$$

Notice the answers are all the same and easy to compare when the factors are written in order from least to greatest. Exponents should be used when a factor occurs more than once.

## Practicing Using Prime Numbers and Prime Factorization

**Write the prime factorization.**

1. 60 ________________
2. 128 ________________
3. 211 ________________
4. 3,150 ________________

# Thinking About Prime Numbers and Prime Factorization

Eratosthenes, a Greek mathematician famous for his work on prime numbers, suggested a way of finding prime numbers less than a given number. First, list the numbers in order from 1 to the given number. You know 1 is not a prime. Cross it out. Second, circle the smallest prime number in your list, 2. Cross out every second number in your list, the even numbers. These numbers are all divisible by 2. Next, circle 3, the smallest number left in your list. Cross out every third number, the multiples of 3. Some of these numbers are already crossed out because they are also multiples of 2. Continue by always circling the smallest number and then crossing out multiples of that number.

The first 10 prime numbers are 2, 3, 5, 7, 11, 13, 17, 19, 23, and 29.

1. How many prime numbers are even?

2. How can you recognize multiples of 5?

3. Write the numbers 1 to 100 and use the method of Eratosthenes to find prime numbers. There are 25 prime numbers between 1 and 100.

4. If you are testing to find the prime factors of 5,767, what is the greatest possible prime factor you need to test? Factors must occur in pairs. Start testing with 2, then 3, and then 5. Continue using the prime numbers in order.

5. Find the prime factorization of 5,767. (Hint: Use what you learned about the greatest prime factor of 5,767.)

## Show That You Know

**Read the information below. Use what you read about prime numbers and prime factorization to answer the questions. Use the space provided to show your work.**

Kyra's uncle is a math professor. He gives her money each year for her birthday. The amount of the gift is always the next prime number.

| Birthday | Amount in Dollars | Total |
|---|---|---|
| 1 | 2 | 2 |
| 2 | 3 | 5 |
| 3 | 5 | 10 |
| 4 | 7 | 17 |
| 5 | 11 | 28 |
| 6 | 13 | 41 |
| 7 | 17 | 58 |
| 8 | 19 | 77 |
| 9 | | |
| 10 | | |
| 11 | | |
| 12 | | |
| 13 | | |
| 14 | | |
| 15 | | |
| 16 | | |

Use your list of prime numbers between 1 and 100.

1. Complete the chart through Kyra's sixteenth birthday.

2. How much money did Kyra get on her sixteenth birthday?

3. What is the total amount Kyra has received from her uncle in 16 years?

4. What are the two prime factors of the total amount?

## Show That You Know *(continued)*

5. Some years the total amounts are also prime numbers. List the years and the total amounts.

6. What pattern do you see in the totals for the even number of years and odd number of years?

7. In what years is Kyra's gift total evenly divisible by 20?

8. In which year did the total amount have an odd number of factors?

## Review What You've Learned

9. What have you learned in this Connections lesson about prime numbers?

10. What have you learned in this Connections lesson that you did not already know?

11. How will this lesson help you find common factors and least common denominators?

# Review and Practice

## Skills Review

**Inverse operations:**

Addition and subtraction are **inverse operations:**
$a + 36 = b \quad b - 36 = a$

Multiplication and division are **inverse operations:**
$23g = f \qquad \frac{f}{23} = g$

**Equations:**

Mathematical sentences that contain an equal sign are **equations.**

The graph of a solution to a **linear equation** is a straight line.

**Solving linear equations:**

Use inverse operations to solve equations. Be sure to apply the same operation to both sides of the equation.

$d - 13.5 = 134$

$d - 13.5 + 13.5 = 134 + 13.5$

$d = 147.5$

**Linear equations with negative numbers:**

Linear equations that have negative numbers are solved in the same way as equations that have only positive numbers.

$\frac{c}{(-12.6)} = 138.6$

$-12.6 \times (\frac{c}{-12.6}) = -12.6 \times 138.6$

$c = -1{,}746.36$

**Equivalent equations:**

Equations are equivalent equations if they have the same solution. Use properties of equality to find equivalent equations.

$x - 3.2 = 6.4$

$2(x - 3.2) = 2(6.4)$

$2x - 6.4 = 12.8$

**Simplifying equations:**

$(\frac{4}{6})z = -\frac{4}{3}$

Multiply both sides by $\frac{6}{4}$ to simplify.

$(\frac{4}{6})z \times (\frac{6}{4}) = (-\frac{4}{3})(\frac{6}{4})$

$z = -\frac{6}{3}$

$z = -2$

## Strategy Review

- To solve problems in which there is a constant change over time, if you do not have an equation, you can use a table to work backward or you can find a pattern.
- Use a table to organize information when solving linear equations.
- When solving linear equations, often you can solve simpler problems by first carefully examining each part of the problem. Make sure you understand each part and the meanings of variables before continuing.

## Skills and Strategies Practice

**Complete the exercises below.**

**1.** Which of the following shows an inverse operation?

$s + 6 = n, n - 6 = s$

$\frac{r}{t} = 2, \frac{t}{r} = \frac{1}{2}$

______________________

**2.** Imagine the cost of a pound of nails increases 5 cents every year. If a pound of nails costs 55 cents in 2007, what will it cost in 2010?

______________________

**3.** Solve for $x$.

$x - 1.24 = 6.34$

______________________

**4.** Jennifer ate 3 times as many carrot sticks as May. May ate 3 sticks. How many did Jennifer eat?

______________________

**5.** Write an equivalent equation.

$s + 3 = 9$

______________________

**Whenever you solve an open equation and find the value of a variable, always check your answer. Substitute the value you found into the equation. Then evaluate the equation to be sure it is true.**

## Unit Review

**Circle the letter of the correct answer.**

**1.** $7 + h = 1{,}204.6$ $h =$ ________

A. 172.09 C. 1,197.6
B. 1,190.7 D. 1,211.6

**2.** What is an equivalent equation of $2s + 36 = 40$?

A. $s + 36 = 20$ C. $2s - 36 = 40$
B. $s + 18 = 20$ D. $2s = 16$

**3.** Solve for $z$.

$17.3 + z = 51.9$

A. 69.2 B. 3 C. 34.6 D. 33.7

**4.** Julianna eats twice as many grapes as raisins, plus three more. Which expression represents the number of grapes she eats?

A. $3r - 3$ B. $2r + 2$ C. $3r + 3$ D. $2r + 3$

**5.** What would you do to solve this equation?
$\frac{g}{2} = 770$

A. subtract 2 from each side
B. multiply both sides by $\frac{1}{2}$
C. multiply both sides by 2
D. divide both sides by 2

**6.** Edward drove for 6.25 hours. He went 440 miles. How fast did he drive?

A. 60 miles per hour C. 35.2 miles per hour
B. 73.3 miles per hour D. 70.4 miles per hour

**7.** Solve for $x$.

$2x = 125$

A. 60 B. 62.5 C. 41.7 D. 6.25

**8.** Which of these are equivalent expressions of $d = 4$?

A. $4 + d = 8; \frac{16}{d} = 4$
B. $4 + d = 12; \frac{16}{d} = 4$
C. $8 + d = 12; \frac{16}{d} = 8$
D. $d + 2 = 6; \frac{d}{2} = 12$

**9.** Which pair shows inverse operations?

A. $2 + 6 = t; 6 - t = 2$
B. $\frac{3}{4} = \frac{x}{y}; 3 - x = 4 - y$
C. $3d = 1; \frac{1}{3} = d$
D. $4 - r = 24; \frac{24}{4} = r$

**10.** Carol's shop has three times more jeans than sweaters. She has 45 jeans and sweaters together. Which equation shows this?

A. $3s + s = 45$ C. $45 - s = 3$
B. $3s = 45$ D. $s + 45 = 30$

**11.** $t - 1{,}000 = 12.47$ $t =$ ________

A. 1,012.47 C. 1,247
B. 987.53 D. –1,012.47

**12.** George has five fewer posters than Jorge. Jorge has 33. Which expression represents the number of George's posters?

A. $33 + 5$ C. $\frac{33}{5}$
B. $33 - 5$ D. $33 \times 5$

**13.** Su runs 4 miles per hour. How far does she run in 2.2 hours?

A. 8.8 miles C. 0.55 miles
B. 8 miles D. 10 miles

**14.** What is the inverse operation of $2{,}346 - c + 10$?

A. $2{,}346 + 10 - c$
B. $\frac{2{,}346}{10} + c$
C. $2{,}346 \times 10 - c$
D. $2{,}346 - 10 + c$

**15.** $-13d = -39$ $\qquad d =$ ________

A. $-3$ C. $-13$
B. 13 D. 3

**16.** Sho throws half as many pitches as Danny, plus 15. Sho makes a total of 65 pitches. Which equation represents this?

A. $\frac{d}{2} - 15 = 65$
B. $2d + 15 = 65$
C. $\frac{d}{2} + 15 = 65$
D. $\frac{65}{2} + 15 = d$

**17.** Gino gave two baseball cards to his sister. If he has 45 left over, how many did he have originally?

A. 43 B. 47 C. 45 D. 49

**18.** Della drives five miles in $x$ minutes. Which expression shows her speed (miles per minute)?

A. $\frac{5}{x}$ C. $5 + x$
B. $5x$ D. $x - 5$

**19.** Solve for $g$.

$12.4g = 62$

A. $-5$ C. 74.4
B. 5 D. 49.6

**20.** Solve for $t$.

$\frac{t}{11} = 2$

A. 122 C. 22
B. 11 D. 111

**21.** What is an equivalent equation of $d - 22 = 4$?

A. $4d - 88 = 12$
B. $3d - 66 = 4$
C. $2d - 44 = 2$
D. $2d - 44 = 8$

**22.** What is an equivalent equation of $16s + 160 = 32$?

A. $s + 10 = 2$ C. $8s + 20 = 32$
B. $s + 8 = 2$ D. $4s + 40 = 80$

**23.** What is an equivalent equation of $3s - 27 = 15$?

A. $s - 9 = 15$ C. $s - 6 = 16$
B. $s - 9 = 5$ D. $2s - 18 = 27$

**24.** Martin starts with \$56 dollars in his savings account. He then deposits $x$ dollars into his bank account. His new balance is \$569. What equation represents this situation?

A. $\$56 + \$569 = x$
B. $\$56 - \$569 = x$
C. $\$569 + x = \$56$
D. $\$56 + x = \$569$

**25.** What is an equivalent equation of $t - 33 = 41$?

A. $3t - 66 = 82$
B. $3t - 99 = 82$
C. $2t - 66 = 41$
D. $2t - 66 = 82$

# Unit 3 Reflection

Money: Earn It, Save It, Spend It

## MATH SKILLS

The easiest part about solving linear equations is

Integers are useful because

## MATH STRATEGIES & CONNECTIONS

For me, the math strategies that work the best are

The number 13 is a prime number because

## READING STRATEGIES & COMPREHENSION

The easiest part about questioning is

One way that questioning helps me with reading is

The vocabulary words I had trouble with are

## INDEPENDENT READING

My favorite part of Money: Earn It, Save It, Spend It is

I read most fluently when

# UNIT 4
# Systems of Linear Equations

## MATH SKILLS & STRATEGIES

After you learn the basic **SKILLS**, the real test is knowing when to use each **STRATEGY.**

## READING STRATEGY

Learn the power of **Previewing and Predicting.**

## AMP LINK MAGAZINE

**You Do the Math and Math Projects:** After you read each magazine article, apply what you know in real-world problems.

**Fluency:** Make your reading smooth and accurate, one tip at a time.

## CONNECTIONS

You own the math when you make your own connections.

## VOCABULARY

MATH WORDS:
Know them!
Use them!
Learn all about them!

# Reading Comprehension Strategy: Previewing/Predicting

## How to Preview and Predict

| **Preview** the article by reading the **title** and **subtitles.** | Look at the **photos.** Read the **captions.** | Think about **what you already know** about the topic or related topics. | Now **predict** what you think the article is about. What will you learn about as you read? | As you read, use what you learn to **check your prediction.** You may change it at any time. |
|---|---|---|---|---|

To **preview,** look through the pages you are going to read. Read the **title, subtitles,** and **captions.** Study the **photos.** Look at the last paragraph of the article to see how it ends. If there are review questions, they can tell you what you should look for while reading. When you preview, also look for **bold** words.

### Chasing Tornados

The sky darkens suddenly. It takes on a greenish color as the wind picks up. Rain has been falling for a while, but now it falls harder. Then hail begins to fall, clicking and clattering on sidewalks, cars, and house windows. In the corner of the television screen, a little weather radar pops up. Storms are approaching! "Stay inside," says the weather forecaster. "Be prepared to seek shelter!"

1. What does the title tell you about the subject of the passage?

______________________________

______________________________

______________________________

Before you read, look at photos and read their captions. Use what you see and read to **predict** something about the article. Try to add to your prediction by using details from the photos.

Most people are glad to follow these instructions. For storm chasers, however, bad weather is an invitation to go outside. As their name suggests, they chase strong storms, looking for tornados. Tornados are powerful, twisting storms that form in the clouds and drop to the ground. They can produce wind speeds up to 250 miles per hour. You have probably seen pictures of the damage such a storm can do.

Tornados can cause great amounts of damage.

2. What do this image and the image on the next page show? Make a detailed prediction about what the passage will tell you about storm chasers.

______________________________

______________________________

______________________________

______________________________

______________________________

______________________________

You have previewed the text and made predictions based on titles, subtitles, and photos. Before you read, think about **what you already know** about the topic. You can use your knowledge and experience to predict what the article will tell you.

### Why Do Storm Chasers Chase Storms?

Why do storm chasers want to get close to these storms rather than get away from them? Scientists who study the weather chase storms to study them. They measure a tornado's shape, wind speeds, and path. Their research is used to better understand tornados and so better protect people from these storms. Other storm chasers photograph tornados. They sell their pictures to news groups.

**3.** What do you already know about tornados and other powerful storms?

As you read on, check the predictions you have made. Make new predictions as you read. Check them as you learn more.

### How Do Storm Chasers Chase Storms?

Storm chasing is hard work. The best storm chasers do their homework to predict when and where tornados may happen. When tornados are rare, storm chasers read books, research, and reports. During "tornado season," they study the weather, looking for signs.

When the storms hit, storm chasers start driving. They can drive up to 500 miles to follow stormy weather systems. Their cars are packed with useful technology to tell them where to go, how to get there, and what to look for. Food, water, and first aid supplies are needed, and of course they have their cameras! Every storm chaser hopes to get close enough to a tornado to film it. Still, they stay far enough away to be safe.

**4.** Look at the predictions you have made so far. Were you right? How can you add to or change your prediction so that it is correct?

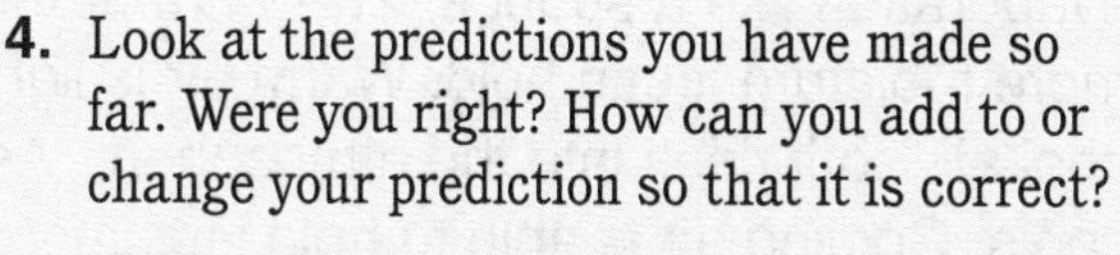

When you **predict,** you make smart guesses about what an article will tell you. You add your knowledge and experience to what you read to **make and check predictions.** Making predictions helps you understand and remember more of what you read.

### Do Not Try This at Home!

Back at home, your family is ready for bad weather. You have water, flashlights, and batteries ready. You hear sirens or wind so loud it reminds you of a train. Quick! Move away from windows so that you do not get hit by debris. Take shelter in a basement, closet, or bathroom. Let the storm chasers study storms while you stay safe inside!

**5.** Make a smart guess about how to protect yourself from a tornado's strong winds.

**6.** Which step of previewing and predicting do you find most useful?

**7.** Think of another strategy for predicting. Describe it below.

# Use the Strategies

**Use the reading comprehension strategies you have learned to answer questions about the article below.**

## Not-So-Gentle Rainfall

The word *rainfall* may bring to mind a gentle patter on the roof or a softly caressing spring shower. Yet rain, like other forces on earth, can be destructive.

### What Makes Rain Fall?

Heat from the sun draws water out of the oceans in a process called evaporation. Earth's air absorbs this evaporation like a sponge. The warmer the air is, the more moisture it can hold. Warm air is lighter than cool air, so it rises into the atmosphere. As air rises, it cools. Cooling air is able to hold less moisture, so the water vapor condenses into tiny water droplets. These droplets join together to make raindrops.

Sometimes, vast amounts of water vapor get swept high into the atmosphere very quickly. In hurricanes, clouds form as high as 8 miles, and in thunderstorms, clouds may tower to 10 miles. Such conditions cause raindrops to form so fast that they fall in torrents.

### Rain Monsters

Some places, such as India, experience seasonal rains called monsoons. Though they can provide much needed rain, they can also cause a lot of damage. On one July day in 2005, a monsoon rainstorm dumped 37.1 inches of rain on Mumbai, India. Mumbai, one of the world's largest cities, was overwhelmed by flooding, which led to more than 200 deaths.

In many parts of the world, extreme rainfall is associated with tropical storms or hurricanes. On one day in October 2005, Hurricane Wilma dumped 64.3 inches of rain on Isla Mujeres, an island off Mexico.

Hurricanes and tropical storms have triggered monster rainstorms in the United States, too. In July 1979, Tropical Storm Claudette dumped 42 inches of rain on the town of Alvin, Texas. It set an all-time one-day record for rainfall in the United States.

1. Based on the title, what might this article be about?

______________________

______________________

______________________

2. Look at the subheads. What do you think is the main topic of the article?

______________________

______________________

______________________

3. Preview the paragraphs. How does the content match or not match your prediction?

______________________

______________________

______________________

______________________

4. How does the first paragraph prepare you, the reader, for the topic of the article?

______________________

______________________

______________________

______________________

______________________

## Reading Strategies: Summarizing, Questioning, Previewing/Predicting

**Use the reading comprehension strategies you have learned in this and previous units to answer the questions below.**

1. How did previewing the article help you understand the content?

2. What did you first predict this article would be about? As you read the article, did you have to change your prediction about the topic? Explain.

3. Identify a statistic in the article and explain why it probably would not figure into your previewing and predicting.

4. What factors lead to extreme rainfall, according to the article?

## Problem-Solving Strategies: Draw a Picture or Use a Model, Find a Pattern, Make a List

**Use the problem-solving strategies you have learned to answer the questions below.**

1. Rainfall is part of a cycle, or circular pattern, of distribution of moisture on Earth. Based on what you have read, describe this pattern in your own words.

2. On another sheet of paper, draw a scale model of clouds in a hurricane and clouds in a thunderstorm. Label heights both with standard American measurements and metric measurements.

3. On a separate sheet of paper, make a bar graph showing record one-day rainfall totals for Mumbai, India; Alvin, Texas; and Isla Mujeres, Mexico.

# Linear Functions, Linear Equations, and Systems of Linear Equations

## VOCABULARY

Watch for the words you are learning about.

**function:** a relation that assigns exactly one value in the range (set of all values of *y*) to each value of the domain (set of all values of *x*)

**linear function:** a function that has a constant rate of change and can be modeled by a straight line

**system of linear equations:** two or more linear equations using the same variables

## Learn the SKILL

Jen is given two expressions. One is $f(x) = 3x + 4$. The other is $y = 2x - 5$. Which of the two expressions is a linear function? Which is a linear equation? Use the linear equation to create a system of linear equations.

| SKILL | EXAMPLE | COMPLETE THE EXAMPLE |
|---|---|---|
| A **function** is a relationship that can be described by $f(x)$ = an expression involving a variable, $x$. The set of values of $x$ is called the domain. The set of values of $f(x)$ is called the range. If any value of $x$ can result in more than one $f(x)$, then the relation is not a function.<br>In a **linear function,** the two values $x$ and $f(x)$ change at the same rate. This creates a straight line when graphed. For graphing purposes, $f(x)$ is called $y$. | Decide if $f(x) = 3x + 4$ or $y = 2x - 5$ is a function.<br>The definition shows that $f(x)$ is a characteristic of a function, so $f(x) = 3x + 4$ is a function.<br>If $f(2) = 3$ and $f(2) = 4$, $f(x)$ is not a function. | Decide if $y = 2x - 3$ or $f(x) = 5 - 3x$ is a function.<br>____________________ |
| A linear equation has two variables, $x$ and $y$. They can be put in the sentence $ax + by = c$, where $a$, $b$, and $c$ are numbers, and where $a$ and $b$ are not both zero. When graphed, a linear equation creates a straight line. | Decide if $f(x) = \frac{1}{2}x + 6$ or $y = 4x + 7$ is a linear equation.<br>The definition tells us that a linear equation has two variables, $x$ and $y$. So, $y = 4x + 7$ is a linear equation. | Decide if $f(x) = 7 - 2x$ or $y = 4 - 5x$ is a linear equation.<br>____________________ |
| A **system of linear equations** is a collection of two or more linear equations.<br>For example:<br>$2x - y = 5$<br>$4x + y = -3$ | Create a system of linear equations. We know that $y = 2x - 5$ is a linear equation. Find one more linear equation. Assign a value for the constants $a$, $b$, and $c$ and place them in the form $ax + by = c$. | Create a system of linear equations.<br>____________________<br>____________________<br>____________________ |

# YOUR TURN



## Choose the Right Word

system of linear equations
linear function  function

**Fill in each blank with the correct word or phrase from the box.**

1. A ________________________ is a collection of linear equations.
2. A ________________ is a relationship that assigns exactly one value from the range to the domain.
3. A ________________ has the characteristic $f(x)$ and is a straight line when it is graphed.

## Yes or No?

**Answer these questions and be ready to explain your answers.**

4. Do linear equations have two variables?

   ________

5. Is a linear function a circle when graphed?

   ________

6. Does a function have to be linear?

   ________

7. Can a system of linear equations have more than two equations? ________

## Show That You Know

**Determine if each expression is a linear function or a linear equation.**

8. $f(x) = 2x + 3$
9. $4x + 2y = 5$
10. $y = 4 - 3x$
11. $f(x) = 3 - 5x$
12. $y = 3x$
13. $f(x) = -3 - 8x$
14. $9x = 2y$

# SOLVE on Your Own

## Skills Practice

Now that you know how to tell the difference between linear functions and linear equations, show it by solving these!


**Determine if each is a linear function or a linear equation.**
**If it is a linear equation, create a system of linear equations.**

1. $f(x) = 2x + 4$ ______________________

2. $4x - 3 = f(x)$ ______________________

3. $-x - 4 = y$ ______________________

4. $x + y = 6$ ______________________

5. $f(x) = 6x + 12$ ______________________

6. $5x - 6y = 15$ ______________________

7. $f(x) = x + 8$ ______________________

8. $6x + 3y + 10 = 10x$ ______________________

9. $3x - 3 + 4x = f(x)$ ______________________

10. $\frac{1}{2}x + \frac{3}{4}y = 3$ ______________________

11. $x + 2x + 3x = y$ ______________________

12. $f(x) = 2 + 2x + 3x + 19$ ______________________

# Linear Functions, Linear Equations, and Systems of Linear Equations

## Strategy

### Make a List

**Step 1: Read** A conveyor belt in a factory travels at a constant speed of 0.2 meters per second. If the foreman lets the conveyor belt run for 40 seconds before stopping it, how far will items on the line have traveled?

| STRATEGY | SOLUTION |
|---|---|
| **Make a List**<br>You can make a list to help you decide what method to use to solve a problem. If you make a list of the identifying attributes of each method, you can easily see which one will be best to use. | **Step 2: Plan** List each method and write the identifying attributes of each.<br>Linear Function: $y = f(x)$; used to portray constant rate of change<br>Linear Equation: $y = mx + b$; used to graph a line<br>Systems of Linear Equations: uses linear equations to solve the system; used to graph two lines<br>Now, look at your list to decide which would be best to solve the problem in Step 1. Use the linear function formula $y = f(x)$ to solve the problem.<br>**Step 3: Solve** Analyze the facts in the problem. The speed of the conveyor belt is a constant, 0.2 meters per second ($\frac{\text{m}}{\text{sec}}$). The time that the foreman lets it run is a variable because he could change it. The desired result is distance moved, which can be regarded as a function of multiplying the speed by time. If the foreman does change the time, the distance will change at the same rate as the time is changed. Given all these facts, the best choice is a linear function.<br>Let $x$ = time, or 40 sec.<br>Multiply $x$ by the constant, $\frac{0.2\text{ m}}{\text{sec}}$.<br>Let $f(x)$ be the distance—the outcome or result of the function.<br>$f(x) = 0.2\,\frac{\text{m}}{\text{sec}}\,(40\text{ sec})$<br>$f(x) = 8$ m, the distance covered<br>**Step 4: Check** Substitute the distance, 8 m, for $f(x)$ in the original function and solve.<br>$8 = 0.2\,(40)$<br>$8 = 8$ |

Choose a Strategy

# YOUR TURN

## Choose the Right Word

linear function    linear equation
system of linear equations    variable

**Fill in each blank with the correct word or phrase from the box.**

1. The variable *y* is a function of the variable *x* in a ________________.
2. Two equations solved for a common point on a graph make a ________________.
3. A letter that represents a value in an equation is a ________________.
4. The equation $y = mx + b$ is called a ________________.

## Yes or No?

**Answer these questions and be ready to explain your answers.**

5. Can a variable represent an unknown value? ________
6. Can an equation have more than one unknown variable? ________
7. Does a system of linear equations use one equation to solve the system? ________
8. Are linear functions and linear equations the same? ________

## Show That You Know

**Tell whether to solve the word problem with a linear function, a linear equation, or a system of linear equations.**

9. At a fair, rides cost $1.50 each. If you buy a discount card for $12, each ride costs $1.00. How many rides would you have to take to make the discount card worthwhile?

10. A train averages a speed of 20 mph between stops, but the stops are not equally spaced. If it takes 1 minute to get from Stop A to Stop B, what is the distance between those two stops?

11. Kim is measuring the height and length of a ramp. For every foot of length she measures, the height increases by one-half of a foot. Kim wants to graph her measurements. What can she use?

12. Marley's song plays at 60 beats per minute. The song is 4 minutes long. How many minutes would the song play at 45 beats per minute?

# READ on Your Own

## Reading Comprehension Strategy: Previewing/Predicting

## Extremes of Nature, *pages 3–4*

### VOCABULARY

Watch for the words you are learning about.

**moisture:** tiny, fine droplets of water

**tsunami:** a series of sea waves that start from a massive disturbance under the ocean

**water vapor:** water droplets floating in the air, often forming steam or fog

### Fluency Tip

If you come to a word you do not know, skip it and read the rest of the sentence. Then reread the sentence and use context to figure out what the word means.

### Before You Read

Think about what you know about weather. What kinds of weather do you think might be considered extreme?

### As You Read

**Preview by reading the first paragraph of "Extreme Natural Events," pages 3–4.** STOP

Think about the natural weather events you have experienced. Make a list of all the natural weather events you can think of. Then circle the events you think would be considered extreme.

If necessary, revise your prediction as you read.
Then answer the question in the right column of the table.

| Extreme Natural Events | |
|---|---|
| **Prediction:** ______ ______ ______ | Did your prediction match what you read about or did you have to revise your prediction as you read? Explain. ______ ______ |

### After You Read

Have you ever experienced extreme natural weather events? If so, explain your experience. If not, what do you think it would be like?

______

______

# SOLVE on Your Own

## Extremes of Nature, *page 5*

### Organize the Information

**Read You Do the Math on magazine page 5. Then complete the table below with information from the magazine.**

| Time | Seconds Between Lightning and Thunder | Distance from the Storm |
|---|---|---|
| 2:45 | | |
| 2:50 | | |
| 3:00 | | |

Drawing a picture may help you answer some of these questions.

### You Do the Math

Use the information in the table above to answer these questions. Write your answers in the space provided.

1. How can you write a system of equations to help you solve the problem?

______________________________________________

______________________________________________

2. How fast is the storm traveling in kilometers per hour? Describe the process you went through to find your answer.

______________________________________________

______________________________________________

______________________________________________

______________________________________________

### After You Solve

Think about other natural events. How can you use a table and an equation to record the features of other natural events?

______________________________________________

______________________________________________

# The Equation of a Line

## Learn the SKILL

The local hospital needs to build a ramp at the front entrance. The height of the ramp is 2 feet and the distance to the entrance is 20 feet. What would be the slope of the ramp?

### VOCABULARY

Watch for the words you are learning about.

**slope-intercept form:** $y = mx + b$, where $m$ is the slope and $b$ is the $y$-intercept of the line

**$y$-intercept:** the $y$-coordinate of the point where the line crosses the $y$-axis

| SKILL | EXAMPLE | COMPLETE THE EXAMPLE |
|---|---|---|
| The slope of a line measures how steep the line is. To find the slope on a graph, you can count the rise ($y$) over the run ($x$). Slopes can be positive or negative. When the slope is negative, the graphed line *falls* from left to right.<br>The hospital ramp is 2 feet high and runs 20 feet. The slope is $\frac{2}{20}$, or $\frac{1}{10}$. | The slope of line $AB$ is $\frac{4}{4} = 1$.<br>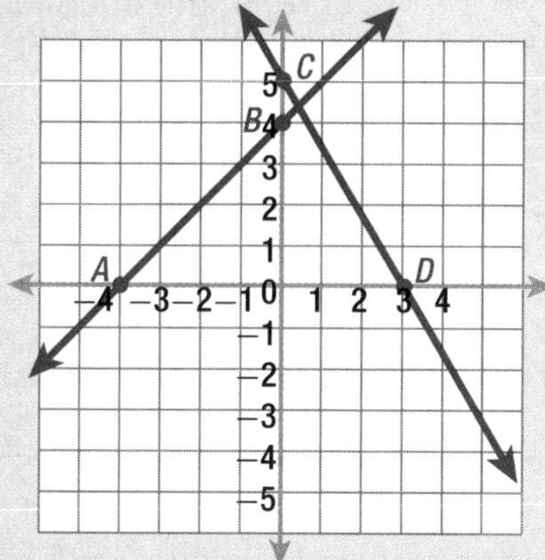<br>The slope of line $CD$ is $-\frac{5}{3}$. The slope of line $CD$ is negative, because the change in $y$-value is negative (downward). | Tell whether the slope of a line passing through the given points is positive or negative.<br>(1, 2) and (3, 3)<br>____________ |
| Another way to find slope $m$ of given points is to solve for change in $y$ over change in $x$. | Find the slope of (6, 9), (2, 3).<br>$m = \frac{(y_2 - y_1)}{(x_2 - x_1)}$<br>$m = \frac{(9 - 3)}{(6 - 2)} = \frac{6}{4} = \frac{3}{2}$<br>So, the slope is $\frac{3}{2}$. | Find the slope of (−10, 3), (−4, −2).<br>____________ |
| The ***y*-intercept** is where $x = 0$. | In line $CD$ above, the $y$-intercept is at point $C$ (0, 5), when $x = 0$, $y = 5$. | What is the $y$-intercept of line $AB$ in the graph? ______ |
| Linear equations can be written in the **slope-intercept form.**<br>$y = mx + b$<br>↑ slope ↑ $y$-intercept | To graph $y = \frac{3}{2}x + 1$, start from the $y$-intercept 1. Use the slope $\frac{3}{2}$ to move 3 units up and 2 units right. | Identify the slope and the $y$-intercept of the equation.<br>$y = \frac{1}{2}x + 9$.<br>$y$-intercept = ________<br>slope = ________ |

Learn the Skill

# YOUR TURN

## Choose the Right Word

slope-intercept form   *y*-intercept   slope

**Fill in each blank with the correct word or phrase from the box.**

1. A ________________ describes the tilt of a line.
2. The ________________ is the *y*-coordinate of the point where the graph crosses the *y*-axis and the value of *x* is zero.
3. The equation $y = mx + b$ is also called the ________________.

## Yes or No?

**Answer these questions and be ready to explain your answers.**

4. Is the slope of (0, 0) and (3, 4) positive? ________
5. Is the slope of (0, 0) and (–4, 5) positive? ________
6. In the equation $y = \frac{1}{2}x - 4$, is the slope negative? ________
7. In the equation $y = -\frac{3}{4}x + 5$, is 5 the *y*-intercept? ________

## Show That You Know

**Find the slope of the line containing the given points.**

8. (7, 9), (2, 4)
9. (8, 3), (–12, 13)
10. (4, 4), (1, –6)
11. (3, 6), (0, 0)

**Write in slope-intercept form.**

12. The slope is 4, and the *y*-intercept is 12.
13. The slope is $\frac{1}{2}$, and the *y*-intercept is 0.
14. The slope is $-\frac{2}{3}$, and the *y*-intercept is –8.
15. The slope is –7, and the *y*-intercept is $\frac{1}{4}$.

# SOLVE on Your Own

## Skills Practice

You can count up and to the right from the y-intercept to find a point on the line. Then repeat to find more points.


**Graph the *y*-intercept and the given slope.**

**1.** *y*-intercept = −1; slope = 2

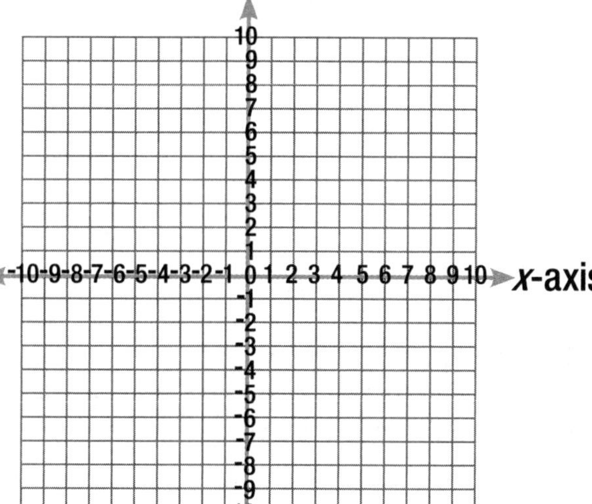

**2.** *y*-intercept = 2; slope = −3

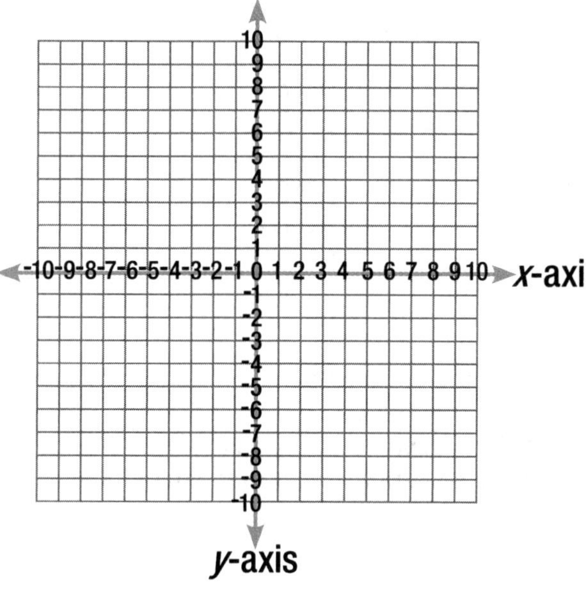

**Graph the equation.**

**3.** $y = \frac{1}{2}x + 4$

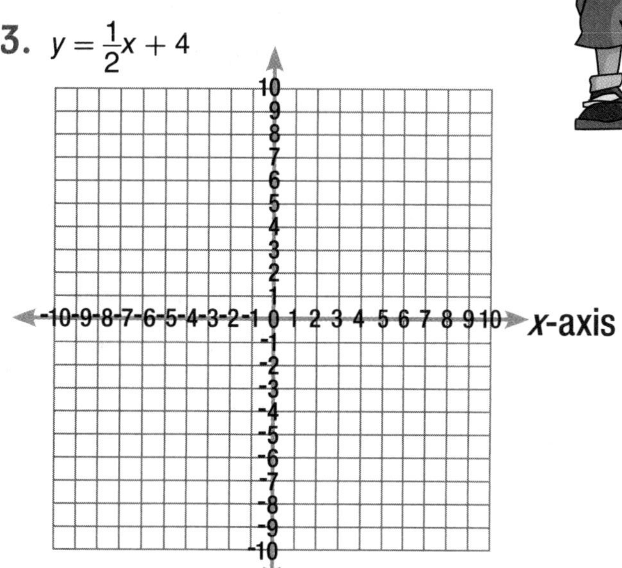

**4.** $y = -3x - 2$

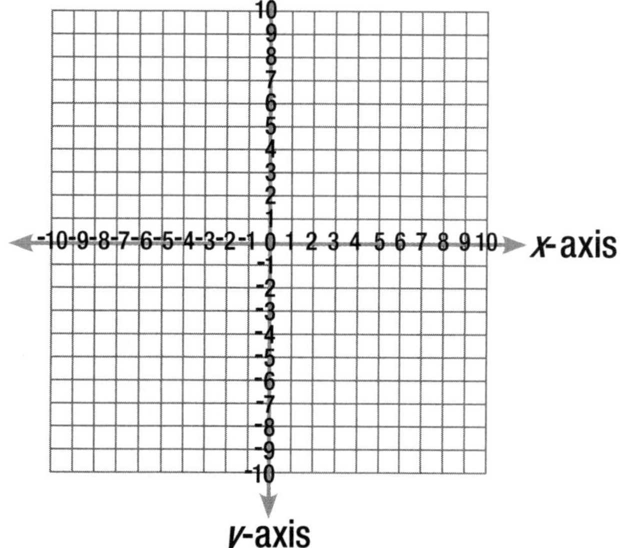

# The Equation of a Line

## Strategy

### Make a Table or a Chart

**Step 1: Read** Mr. Jordan is building a staircase and is using the equation $y = \frac{3}{2}x + 2$. How can he show the staircase on a graph in order to visually inspect the slope?

| STRATEGY | SOLUTION |
|---|---|

**Make a Table or a Chart**

When you need to organize your information to solve a problem, a table or chart will help you.

**Step 2: Plan** Make an input/output table of ordered pairs to graph the equation of the line $y = \frac{3}{2}x + 2$. Start with the $x$- and $y$-coordinates for the one point you know: the $y$-intercept (where $x = 0$). Then substitute $y$-values of $-1$ and $-4$ in the equation to obtain $x$-output values to complete the chart.

| $x$ | $y$ |
|---|---|
| 0 | 2 |
| −2 | −1 |
| −4 | −4 |

**Step 3: Solve** Plot each ordered pair on a graph. Then use a straightedge to connect the points. Identify the slope from the equation and then visually inspect the slope in the graph. Do you think the slope would be satisfactory for a staircase?

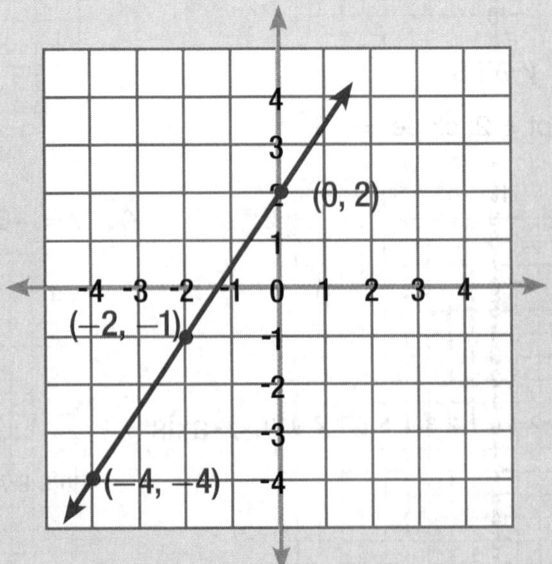


**Step 4: Check** If you cannot plot a straight line from plots you have made, then you know there must be a mistake either in the data table or in one of the plots.

# YOUR TURN



## Choose the Right Word

$y = mx + b$ slope input/output table

**Fill in each blank with the correct word or phrase from the box.**

1. The ______________ of a line is found by plotting points on a graph and connecting them with a straight line.
2. A(n) ______________ helps you organize ordered pairs to make it easier to graph a line.
3. A straight line can be represented by the linear equation ______________.

## Yes or No?

**Answer these questions and be ready to explain your answers.**

4. Can a line graphed from a linear equation be anything other than a straight line? ________
5. Can the slope of a line ever be a negative slope? ________
6. Can an input/output table have more than two columns of data? ________
7. Can $x$ and $y$ values in an input/output table be negative values? ________

## Show That You Know

**Graph each linear equation by organizing ordered pairs in an input/output table.**

8. $y = 4x + 4$

9. $2x + 3y = 12$

**Plot each set of ordered pairs and graph the line.**

10. (2, 4) (4, –5)
11. (3, –3) (7, 2)
12. (9, 6) (–8, 1)

13. Identify ordered pairs for points A and B and for the $y$-intercept on the line of the graph below.

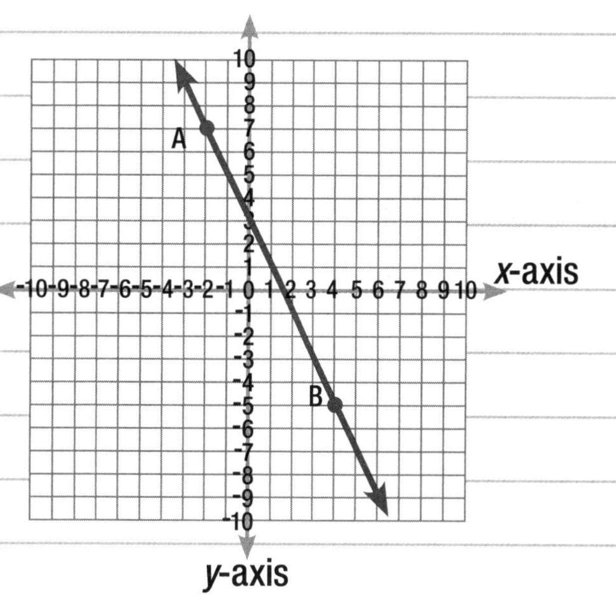

# READ on Your Own

## Reading Comprehension Strategy: Previewing/Predicting

## Extremes of Nature, *pages 6–7*

### Before You Read

Recall what you read about in "Extreme Natural Events." Would you call a hailstorm an extreme natural event? Why or why not?

### As You Read

**Preview by reading the first paragraph of "Twister!", pages 6–7.** 

In the chart below, write a prediction of what you think the reading will be about. Be sure to elaborate on your prediction with some details.

**Read pages 6–7.** 

If necessary, revise your prediction as you read. Then answer the question in the right column of the table.

| Twister! | |
|---|---|
| **Prediction:** | Did your prediction match what you read about or did you have to revise your prediction as you read? Explain. |

### After You Read

Have you ever experienced a tornado or known someone who has? What was it like? If not, what do you think the experience would be like? Explain.

**VOCABULARY**

Watch for the words you are learning about.

**funnel:** a column shape that narrows to a small opening at the bottom

**meteorologists:** people who study the atmosphere and weather for a region

**Fluency Tip**

Reread difficult text at a slower pace. Try reading aloud to aid comprehension.

# SOLVE on Your Own

## Extremes of Nature, *page 8*

### Organize the Information

**Read You Do the math on magazine page 8. Then use the grid below to graph the line for the tornado's path.**

Drawing a simple map may help you understand how the tornado is traveling.


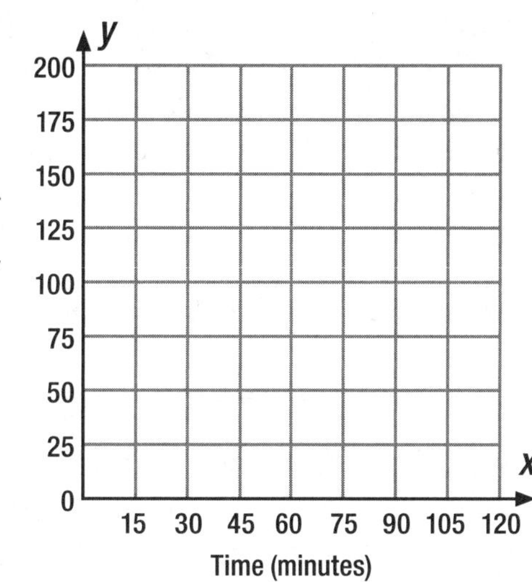


### You Do the Math

Use the information in the coordinate grid above to answer these questions. Write your answers in the space provided.

1. What is the slope of your line? How did you find it?

2. Write an equation for your line in slope-intercept form.

3. Use the graph of the line to find the speed at which the tornado is traveling in miles per hour.

### After You Solve

Describe how you think someone who studies tornadoes might use linear equations in their research.

Application

## The Four-Step Problem-Solving Plan

| Step 1: Read | Step 2: Plan | Step 3: Solve | Step 4: Check |
|---|---|---|---|
| Make sure you understand what the problem is asking. | Decide how you will solve the problem. | Solve the problem using your plan. | Check to make sure your answer is correct. |

**Read the article below. Then answer the questions.**

### Rating Hurricanes

If you heard that a Category 3 hurricane was upgraded to a Category 4 hurricane, you would probably conclude that the hurricane is now more dangerous. If you know how hurricanes are classified, you can also figure out how much damage the hurricane is likely to cause.

The system used to classify hurricanes is called the Saffir–Simpson Hurricane Scale. Saffir was an engineer and Simpson was director of the National Hurricane Center. They combined their knowledge to create a useful scale based on wind speeds and storm surge height. Here are the categories:

**Category 1:** winds 74–95 mph, storm surge 4–5 ft, minimal damage

**Category 2:** winds 96–110 mph, storm surge 6–8 ft, moderate damage

**Category 3:** winds 111–130 mph, storm surge 9–12 ft, extensive damage

**Category 4:** winds 131–155 mph, storm surge 13–18 ft, extreme damage

**Category 5:** winds over 155 mph, storm surge over 18 ft, catastrophic damage

1. A hurricane has winds of 99 mph and is predicted to have a storm surge of 7.5 ft. What category is this hurricane and what type of damage would it be expected to cause?

______________________

______________________

______________________

2. Suppose a hurricane has maximum wind speeds of 98 mph. By how much would the wind speeds have to increase for the hurricane to be classified as Category 4?

______________________

______________________

______________________

______________________

# YOUR TURN

Application

**Read the article below. Then answer the questions.**

## Hurricane Wilma

Recall Hurricane Wilma from the reading. Let's look at how Wilma changed categories as it moved and changed. Using the Saffir-Simpson scale makes it easier to keep track of Wilma's strength.

Wilma became a Category 1 hurricane when its wind speeds exceeded 74 mph on October 18. At 11 PM, wind speeds hit 110 mph, making Wilma a Category 2 hurricane. At 1 AM on October 19, only 2 hours later, wind speeds hit 150 mph, making Wilma a Category 4 hurricane. A few hours later it hit Category 5.

Wilma gradually weakened, dropping to Category 4 before hitting Mexico and Category 2 before heading into the Gulf of Mexico. Wilma was back up to Category 3 strength by the time it hit Florida. Then it dropped to Category 2 over land, but went back up to Category 3 as it headed into the Atlantic. It gradually dropped back down before fading out.

1. What happened each time Hurricane Wilma crossed over land?

_______________

_______________

2. How is the Saffir–Simpson scale useful?

_______________

_______________

3. By how much per hour did Hurricane Wilma's wind speeds increase between 11 PM on October 18 and 1 AM on October 19?

_______________

_______________

4. Hurricane Wilma took 4 hours to cross Florida. As it did, its wind speeds dropped from 125 mph to 100 mph. By approximately how much per hour did Hurricane Wilma's wind speeds decrease as it crossed Florida?

_______________

_______________

### Fluency Tip

As you read and reread, pay attention to punctuation marks that are clues to correct phrasing.

# READ on Your Own

## Reading Comprehension Strategy: Previewing/Predicting

## Extremes of Nature, *pages 9–11*

### VOCABULARY

Watch for the words you are learning about.

**forecasters:** people who are trained to analyze weather reports and predict weather conditions for the near future

**storm surge:** a dome of water that a hurricane pushes ahead of it

### Fluency Tip

Identify words that you do not know. Find out how to pronounce them before reading.

### Before You Read

Think about the last time you heard about a hurricane on the news. What did the news story say about the hurricane?

### As You Read

**Preview by reading the first paragraph of "Hurricanes" on page 9.** 

In the space below, write a prediction of how you think the damage caused by a hurricane might compare to the damage caused by a tornado. Be sure to explain the reasons for your prediction.

______________________________________________

______________________________________________

**Read pages 9–11.** 

In the space below, describe one type of damage from hurricanes that tornadoes do not usually cause.

______________________________________________

______________________________________________

### After You Read

Do you think it is important to pay attention to news stories about hurricanes? Why or why not?

______________________________________________

______________________________________________

# SOLVE on Your Own

## Extremes of Nature, *page 12*

### Organize the Information

**Use a table like the one below to organize the information you find in the Math Project on magazine page 12.**

| Hurricane | City of Landfall | Slope of Line | Equation of Line |
|---|---|---|---|
| A | | | |
| B | | | |
| C | | | |

### Math Project

Use the information in the table above to answer these questions. Write your answers in the space provided.

Use the formula $y = mx + b$ to find the slope-intercept form of the line.


1. How did you find the slope of each line?

2. Should the slope of your lines be negative or positive? Why?

3. Where will each of the hurricanes hit?

### After You Solve

How could you express the same information in the table using a different strategy?

# Using the x- and y-Intercepts to Graph a Linear Equation

## VOCABULARY

Watch for the words you are learning about.

***x*-intercept:** the *x*-coordinate of the point where the line crosses the *x*-axis

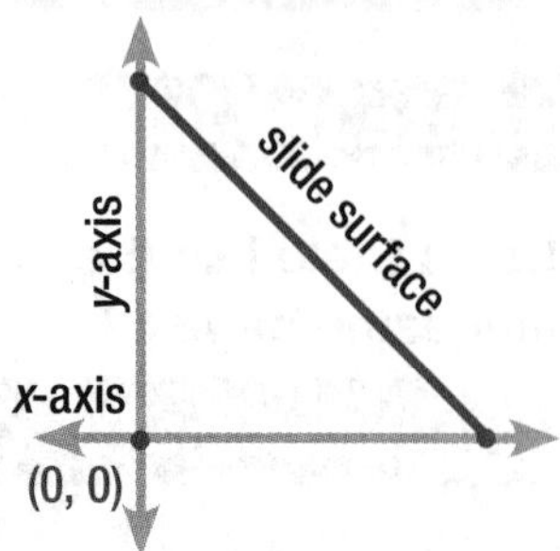


## Learn the SKILL

In a factory that makes playground equipment, the dimensions and slope of a slide are represented in a blueprint by the following equation: $3x + 4y = 12$. The numbers are understood to be dimensions in feet. How can a factory worker determine the slope of the slide from this equation?

| SKILL | EXAMPLE | COMPLETE THE EXAMPLE |
|---|---|---|
| The $y$-intercept is the point on the graphed line where $x = 0$.<br>To find the $y$-intercept, substitute 0 for $x$. Then solve for $y$. | Find the $y$-intercept of $3x + 4y = 12$.<br>$3x + 4y = 12$<br>$3(0) + 4y = 12$<br>$4y = 12$<br>$y = \frac{12}{4} = 3$<br>So, the $y$-intercept is 3. | Find the $y$-intercept:<br>$5x + 4y = 16$<br>$y =$ ________ |
| The ***x*-intercept** is the point on the graphed line where $y = 0$.<br>To find the $x$-intercept, substitute 0 for $y$. Then solve for $x$. | Find the $x$-intercept of $3x + 4y = 12$.<br>$3x + 4y = 12$<br>$3x + 4(0) = 12$<br>$3x = 12$<br>$x = \frac{12}{3} = 4$<br>So, the $x$-intercept is 4. | Find the $x$-intercept:<br>$7x + 4y = 21$<br>$x =$ ________ |
| Use the intercepts of the line to graph $3x + 4y = 12$.<br>The $y$-intercept $= 3 \rightarrow (0,3)$.<br>The $x$-intercept $= 4 \rightarrow (4,0)$. | Graph<br>$3x + 4y = 12$.<br>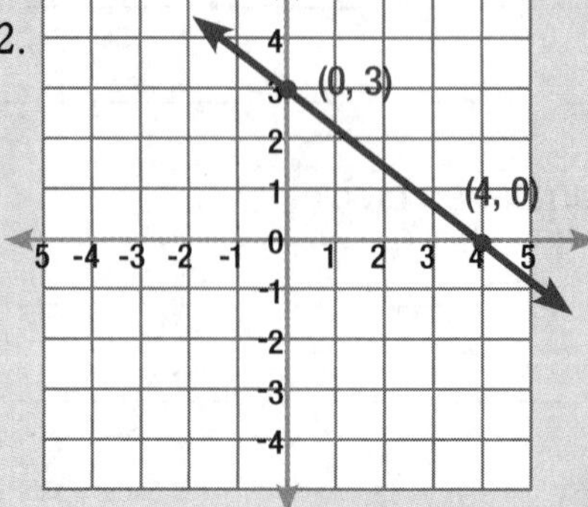 | Graph $2x + 5y = 10$ |
| To get the slope, you can either count the rise over the run in the graph or you can compute for the change in $y$ over the change in $x$. | Find the slope.<br>$\frac{3-0}{0-4} = -\frac{3}{4}$<br>Slope $= -\frac{3}{4}$ | Find the slope.<br>(5,0), (0,2) ________ |

# YOUR TURN



## Choose the Right Word

*x*-intercept  *y*-intercept  straight  slope

**Fill in each blank with the correct word or phrase from the box.**

1. The ratio of the vertical change (rise) over the horizontal change (run) is called the _______________.

2. The _______________ is the *x*-coordinate of the point where the graph crosses the *x*-axis.

3. The graph of a linear equation is a _______________ line.

4. In the equation $y = mx + b$, $b$ is known as the _______________.

## Yes or No?

**Answer these questions and be ready to explain your answers.**

5. Is $-\frac{1}{2}$ the slope of the line containing (2, 2) and (4, 3)? ________

6. Is $\frac{4}{3}$ the slope of the line containing (5, 3) and (0, 2)? ________

7. Is 6 the *x*-intercept of the equation $2x + 3y = 12$? ________

8. Is 4 the *y*-intercept of the equation $2x + 3y = 12$? ________

## Show That You Know

**Graph two lines with the same *y*-intercept and the given slopes: *y*-intercept = 2; slope *A* = 1; slope *B* = –1.**

9.

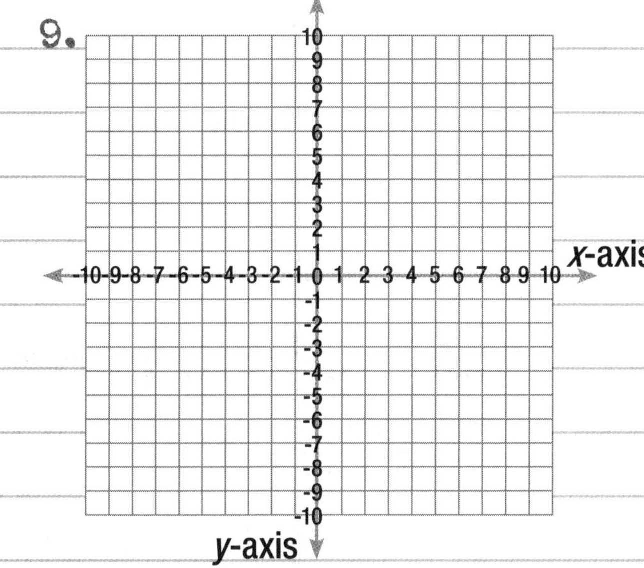


**Graph two lines with the same *y*-intercept and the given slopes: *y*-intercept = 0; slope *A* = $\frac{1}{2}$; slope *B* = 2.**

10.

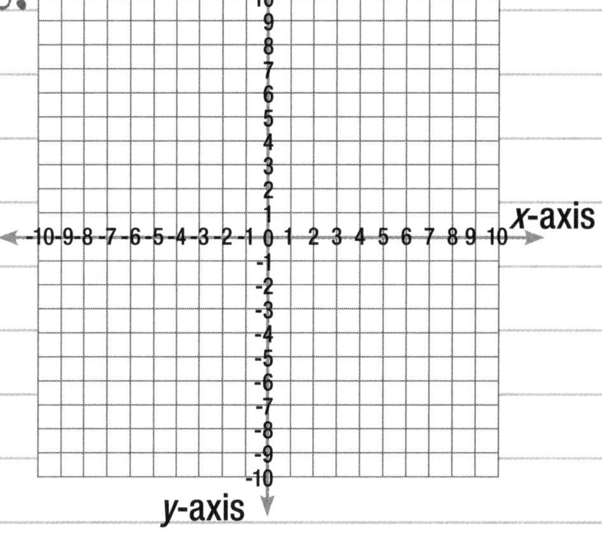

# SOLVE on Your Own

## Skills Practice

You can graph a line by drawing a line through the x-intercept and the y-intercept.


**Find the x-intercept and the y-intercept. Use the intercepts to graph the equation.**

**1.** $x + y = 8$

$x$-intercept = ________ $y$-intercept = ________

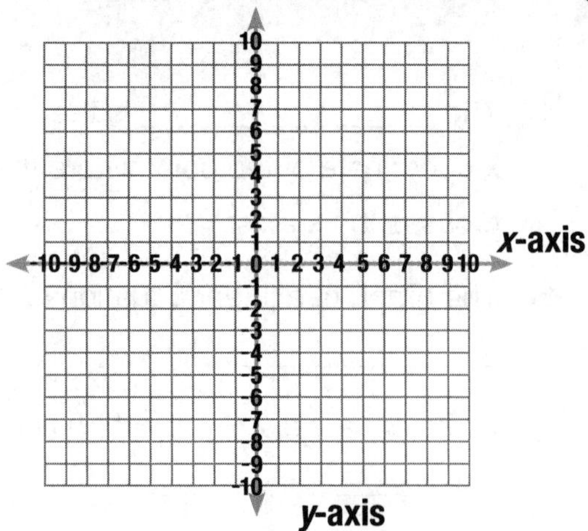


**2.** $3x + y = 9$

$x$-intercept = ________ $y$-intercept = ________

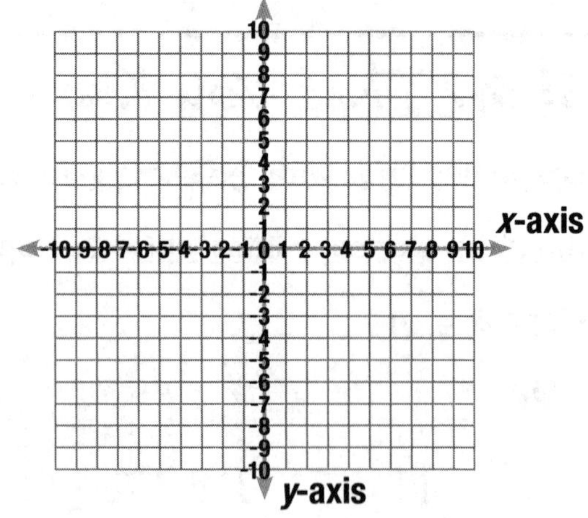


**3.** $5x + 5y = 25$

$x$-intercept = ________ $y$-intercept = ________

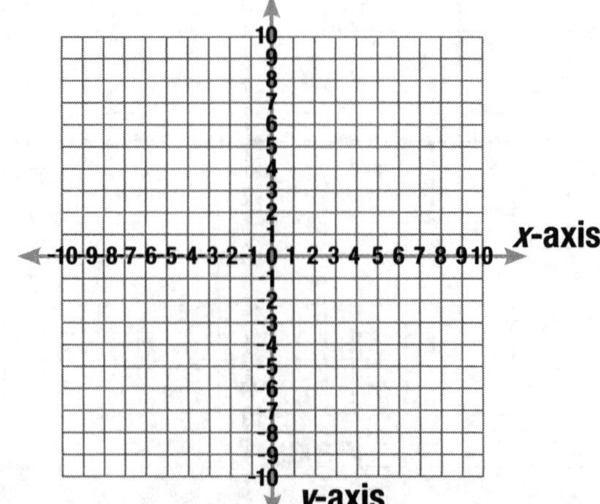

# Using the x- and y-Intercepts To Graph a Linear Equation

## Strategy

### Draw a Picture or Use a Model

**Step 1: Read** Rickie wants to build the roof of his garage to be steep enough for the winter snow to slide down. The roof has a height of 9 feet and a base of 24 feet. How can Rickie find the slope of the roof?

| STRATEGY | SOLUTION |
| --- | --- |

**Draw a Picture or Use a Model**

When constructing anything, it is always helpful to draw or make a scale model of what is being constructed.

**Step 2: Plan** Plot the points associated with the specifications of the roof.

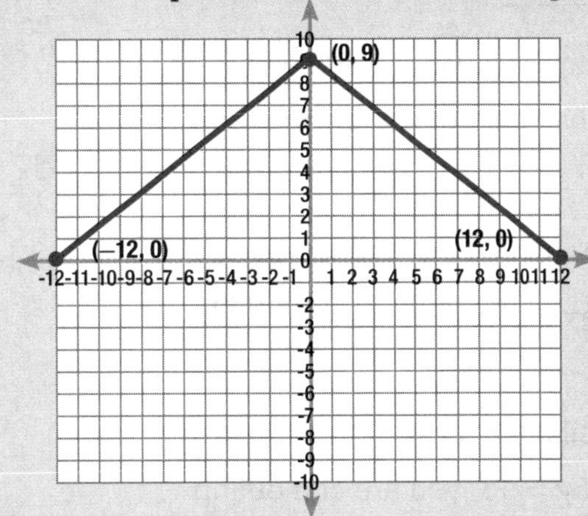


The roof has a height of 9 feet. So, the $y$-intercept is 9. The base is 24 feet. In the coordinate grid, the base, which is the $x$-axis, runs from $-12$ to $+12$. The $x$-intercepts are on $-12$ and $+12$.

Once plotted, it is easy to see the $x$-intercepts and the $y$-intercept.

The $y$-intercept is at (0,9). The $x$-intercepts are at (12,0) and (–12,0).

**Step 3: Solve** Choose ordered pairs to solve for the slope: (0, 9) and (12, 0).

$$m = \frac{y_1 - y_2}{x_1 - x_2} \longrightarrow m = \frac{9-0}{0-12} \longrightarrow m = \frac{9}{-12} \quad \text{or} \quad \frac{3}{-4}$$

So, the slope is $-\frac{3}{4}$ on the right. It is $\frac{3}{4}$ on the left.

**Step 4: Check** You can use the slope-intercept form to check your answer.

Replace each variable with the known value. Note that when $y = 0, x = 12$.

$y = mx + b$

$0 = (-\frac{3}{4})(12) + 9$

$0 = (-\frac{3}{4})(\frac{12}{1}) + 9$

$0 = -9 + 9; 0 = 0$

So, your answer is correct.

Choose a Strategy

# YOUR TURN

## Choose the Right Word

slope   x-intercept   y-intercept
slope-intercept form

**Fill in each blank with the correct word or phrase from the box.**

1. The equation $y = mx + b$ is known as the ________________.
2. The change in the value of $y$ divided by the change in the value of $x$ is the formula for ________________.
3. When you substitute 0 for $x$ in the equation $2x + 5y = 15$, you are computing the ________________.
4. When you substitute 0 for $y$ in the equation $2x + 5y = 15$, you are computing the ________________.

## Yes or No?

**Answer these questions and be ready to explain your answers.**

5. Is the equation $y = 3x + 5$ an example of a linear equation? ________
6. Is the equation $f(x) = 2x - 4$ an example of a function? ________
7. Is 5 the slope in the equation $y = 2x + 5$? ________
8. Is 7 the $y$-intercept in the equation $y = 7x + 13$? ________

## Show That You Know

9. Complete the table. Then write and graph the ordered pairs and linear equation.

| x | −1 | 0 | 1 | 2 |
|---|---|---|---|---|
| y | 2 | 0 | −2 | |

10. Complete the table. Then write and graph the ordered pairs and linear equation.

| x | 0 | 1 | 2 | 3 |
|---|---|---|---|---|
| y | 1 | 4 | 7 | |

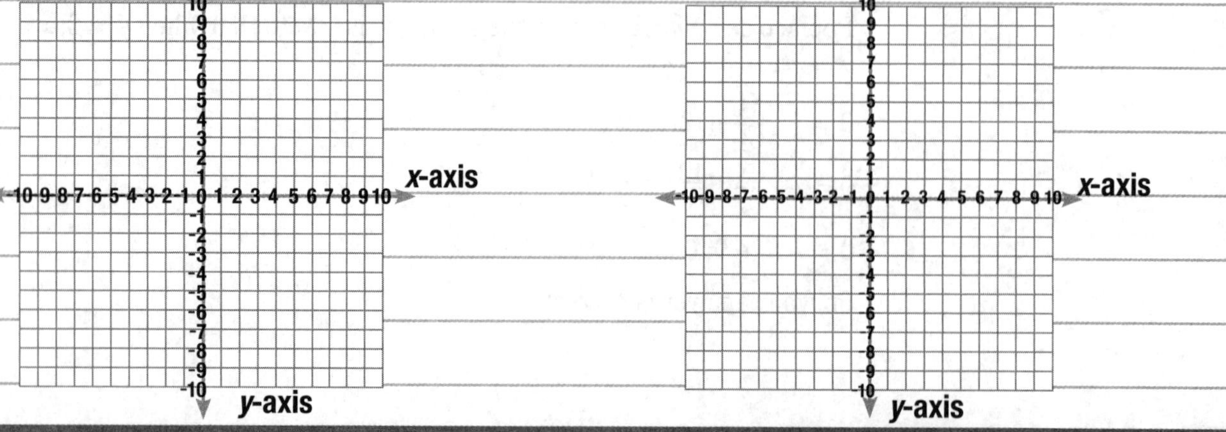

# READ on Your Own

## Reading Comprehension Strategy: Previewing/Predicting

## Extremes of Nature, *pages 13–14*

### VOCABULARY

Watch for the words you are learning about.

**radar:** a device that emits radio waves and is used especially for detecting and locating objects or surface features

**satellites:** manufactured objects or vehicles intended to orbit the earth, the moon, or other celestial bodies

### Fluency Tip

If you come to a word you do not know, skip it and read the rest of the sentence first. Then reread the sentence and use context to figure out what the word means.

### Before You Read

What is the weather forecast for today? How can a meteorologist make accurate predictions about the weather?

### As You Read

It is important to check your predictions as you read to help you know whether or not you understand the text. As you read, remember to ask, "Was my prediction about what I am reading correct?"

**Preview "What Will the Weather Be?",**

**pages 13–14.** 

Use what you know to predict what this reading will be about. Write your prediction in the chart below.

**Now read pages 13–14.** 

Complete the chart.

| Preview, Read, and Predict | Read and Check |
|---|---|
| I predict "What Will the Weather Be?" will be about<br>______<br>______<br>______ | Did your prediction match the text, or did you have to revise it? Explain.<br>______<br>______<br>______ |

### After You Read

In which states do you think weather forecasters or meteorologists are most in demand? Why?

______

______

# SOLVE on Your Own

## Extremes of Nature, *page 15*

### Organize the Information

**Read You Do the Math on magazine page 15. Then use a graph like the one shown on magazine page 15 to organize the information. Draw your own graph on a sheet of graph paper.**

### You Do the Math

Use the information in the from your graph to answer these questions. Write your answers in the space provided.

1. How could you calculate how fast the front is moving?

_______________________________________________

_______________________________________________

2. How can you write equations for the storm's movement at slower and faster speeds?

_______________________________________________

_______________________________________________

3. How can you use the graph to find out when the storm will hit Yourtown if its speed does not change? When will it hit?

_______________________________________________

_______________________________________________

### After You Solve

Could you use an equation to predict the movement of other types of weather? Explain.

_______________________________________________

_______________________________________________

## The Four-Step Problem-Solving Plan

| Step 1: Read | Step 2: Plan | Step 3: Solve | Step 4: Check |
|---|---|---|---|
| Make sure you understand what the problem is asking. | Decide how you will solve the problem. | Solve the problem using your plan. | Check to make sure your answer is correct. |

**Read the article below. Then answer the questions.**

### New Orleans and Storm Surges

New Orleans, Louisiana, was built mostly below sea level. The city lies between the Mississippi River and Lake Pontchartrain near the Gulf of Mexico. People who live there have long worried about storms possibly flooding the city. To help prevent this possibility, levees were built to protect the city. A levee is a raised mound of earth.

An unnamed hurricane in 1947 caused a storm surge of 3 meters, killed 51 people, and flooded areas near New Orleans. In response, levees were built south of Lake Pontchartrain. These levees were overtopped by a 3-meter storm surge brought by Hurricane Betsy in 1965. The levees were then raised to about 4 meters.

Hurricane Camille hit the New Orleans area in 1969, bringing a storm surge as high as 9 meters. Although this storm caused great damage along the coast, it did not hit New Orleans directly.

Hurricane Georges, which hit the area in 1998, also missed New Orleans. Georges, however, showed what might have happened and prompted measures to improve the levees.

1. If existing levees had a height of 4 meters, how much higher would they have to be built to protect New Orleans from a storm surge like that from Hurricane Camille?

______________________________

______________________________

______________________________

______________________________

2. Why do you think the New Orleans levees have not been built high enough to protect against a storm surge like that from Hurricane Camille?

______________________________

______________________________

______________________________

______________________________

Application

# YOUR TURN

**Read the article below. Then answer the questions.**

## Hurricane Katrina Storm Surge

On August 28, 2005, Hurricane Katrina was just off the coast of Louisiana. It was classified as a Category 5 hurricane, with winds of up to 160 mph. Based on the available information, a storm surge of at least 8 meters was predicted.

As Katrina made landfall on August 29, it had moved to Category 3 status. The storm surge, however, maintained most of its strength. The surge water rushed into Lake Pontchartrain. The lake rose from a normal height of 0.3 meters above sea level to a maximum height of 2.6 meters.

At first, the levees between Lake Pontchartrain and New Orleans held back the extra water. However, on August 30 they failed in dozens of places. Water flooded much of the city and surrounding areas.

The New Orleans levees were designed to hold back the waters of up to Category 3 hurricanes. They initially did so for Katrina, but eventually failed. The reasons for this failure, and what should be done to strengthen the levees, have been widely debated.

1. What would likely have happened if Hurricane Katrina had still been at Category 5 strength when it reached land?

______________________________

______________________________

______________________________

2. If the entire predicted storm surge had entered Lake Pontchartrain, to what height would the lake have risen?

______________________________

______________________________

3. Why did New Orleans flood after Hurricane Katrina struck?

______________________________

______________________________

______________________________

### Fluency Tip

Read the text more than once. You will read more smoothly and you will be more likely to remember what you read.

# READ on Your Own

## Reading Comprehension Strategy: Previewing/Predicting

## Extremes of Nature, *pages 16–18*

**VOCABULARY**

Watch for the words you are learning about.

**tide:** the regular rise and fall of ocean water levels due to the moon's and sun's gravity

**Fluency Tip**

Emphasize certain words and phrases that you think are important.

### Before You Read

What causes a storm surge?

### As You Read

**Preview "How High Will the Water Go?", pages 16–18.** STOP

Write down what you know about tides and storm surges after previewing these pages.

________________________________________________________________________

________________________________________________________________________

________________________________________________________________________

________________________________________________________________________

Make two predictions about what the article will tell you.

________________________________________________________________________

________________________________________________________________________

________________________________________________________________________

________________________________________________________________________

### After You Read

Are you safe from hurricanes if you do not live near the ocean? Why or why not?

________________________________________________________________________

________________________________________________________________________

________________________________________________________________________

________________________________________________________________________

# SOLVE on Your Own

## Extremes of Nature, *page 19*

### Organize the Information

**Use a list like the one below to organize the information you find in the Math Project on magazine page 19.**

Low tide height = ______________

Low tide time = ______________

High tide height = ______________

High tide time = ______________

Hurricane distance = ______________

Hurricane speed = ______________

Predicted storm surge = ______________

Levee height = ______________

**Use this list to help graph the changes in tides.**

### Math Project

Use the information in the table above to answer these questions. Write your answers in the space provided.

1. How can you calculate when the hurricane will reach land? What time will the hurricane reach land?

______________________________

2. What do you need to know about the tides to find out how high the water level will be when the storm surge hits?

______________________________

3. How high will the storm surge be? Is the levee high enough to save Shoretown?

______________________________

### After You Solve

How could you show the movement of the hurricane visually?

______________________________

# Put It Together

## Introducing Connections Between Nonlinear Equations and Their Graphs

You have learned about linear equations and their graphs. The equation of a line can be easily recognized in the form $y = mx + b$. There are many other types of equations that generate interesting and unique graphs. There are even equations that generate u–shapes, circles, and ellipses (ovals). These equations are nonlinear.

Look at the equation: $y = x^2$. You should first notice there is an exponent in this equation. Exponents are not found in linear equations. To graph this equation, complete a table of values with positive and negative integer values for $x$ and the corresponding values for $y$.

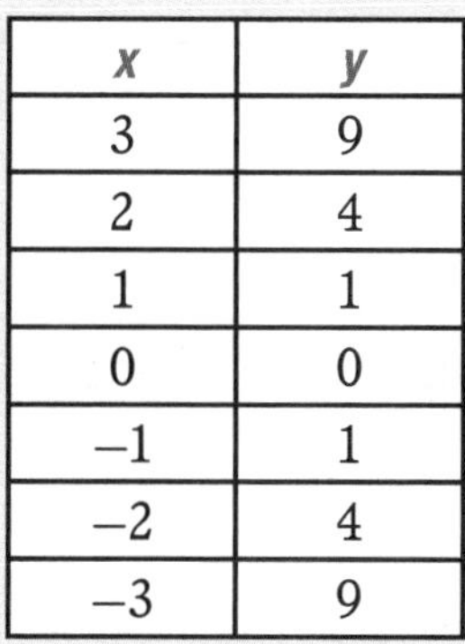

| $x$ | $y$ |
|---|---|
| 3 | 9 |
| 2 | 4 |
| 1 | 1 |
| 0 | 0 |
| –1 | 1 |
| –2 | 4 |
| –3 | 9 |

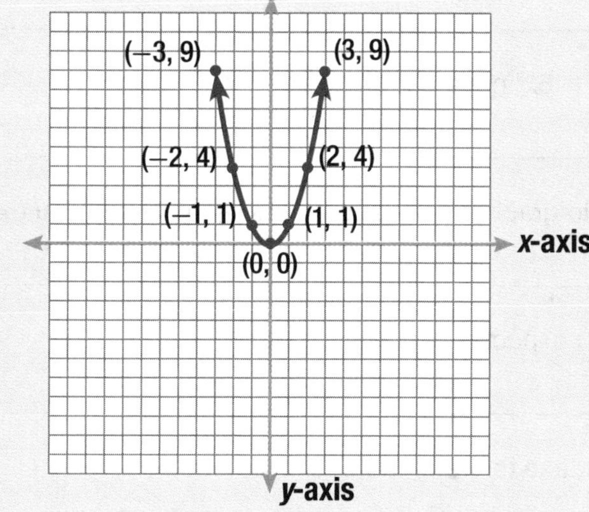


Notice that the equation generates a curve that is almost u–shaped. The curve is called a parabola.

## Practicing Recognizing Nonlinear Equations

**Classify each of the following equations as linear or nonlinear.**

1. $y = 3x$ ________________
2. $y = x^3$ ________________
3. $7x - 8 = y$ ________________
4. $y = x^2 + 9x + 20$ ________________
5. $y = 9$ ________________

Connections

# YOUR TURN

## Thinking About Nonlinear Equations and Their Graphs

The equation of a line in the form $y = mx + b$ allows you to quickly graph a straight line using the slope ($m$) and $y$-intercept $(0, b)$. The equation of a parabola in the form $y = ax^2 + bx + c$ also allows you to quickly graph the parabola. Equations of this form are called quadratic equations. The parabola equation must have an $x^2$ term but does not necessarily have an $x$ term or a constant term.

1. How can you recognize a linear equation?

2. How can you recognize a quadratic equation?

3. Why is the equation $y = 6x^3$ not a quadratic equation?

4. Suppose you wanted to graph the equation $y = x^2 + 4$. Would you expect a straight line?

5. What shape would you expect?

6. What steps would you take to graph the equation?

7. Use the equation $y = x^2 + 4$. What are the missing $y$-values for the $x$-values? (−3, ), (−2, ), (−1, ), (0, ), (1, ), (2, ), (3, ).

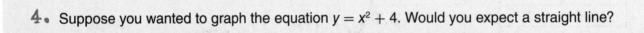

8. How does the graph of the equation in #7 differ from the graph of $y = x^2$?

9. How are the two parabolas the same?

10. Compare the two equations $y = x^2$ and $y = x^2 + 4$. How would you expect the graph of $y = x^2 + 5$ to look?

## Show That You Know

**Read the information below. Use what you know about graphing nonlinear equations to complete the items and answer the questions.**

Raj read a newspaper report of a mild earthquake that could be felt by people in a neighboring town 25 miles from the epicenter, the point on Earth's surface that is directly above the point where the earthquake originated. Raj knows there are equations to represent different types of curves and wonders if there is an equation to represent the distance 25 miles from the epicenter. Can he guess the equation?

Let every space on the graph equal 5 miles.

1. Put a dot at (0, 0) on the graph below to represent the epicenter.

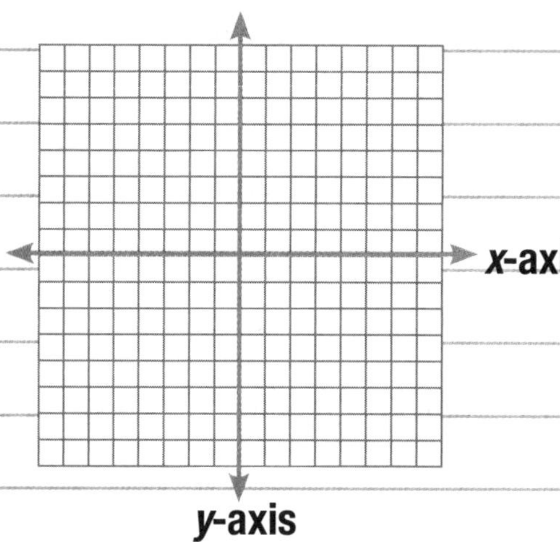


2. Mark the points that represent 25 miles north, 25 miles east, 25 miles south, and 25 miles west of the epicenter.

3. What are the coordinates of these points on the graph?

## Show That You Know (continued)

4. What do you know about 3–4–5 right triangles that could help you find other points that are 25 miles (5 units on the graph) from the epicenter?

5. What eight points on the graph can be found using 3–4–5 right triangles?

6. What geometric figure are your graphed points starting to form?

7. The equation for a circle is $x^2 + y^2 = r^2$, where $r$ is the radius of a circle. Do the points on your graph fit the equation $x^2 + y^2 = 5^2$?

## Review What You've Learned

8. What have you learned in this Connections lesson about the graphs of nonlinear equations?

9. What have you learned in this Connections lesson that you did not already know?

10. What have you learned in this lesson that will help you graph new equations?

# Review and Practice

## Skills Review

**Functions and linear functions:**

A **function** shows the relationship between an input, $x$, and an output, $f(x)$.

A **linear function** is a special type of function that when graphed makes a straight line.

**Linear equations:**

There are two variables in a linear equation, $x$ and $y$. These variables are raised only to the first power ($x^1$ and $y^1$).

A graph of a linear equation is a straight line.

Two or more linear equations are a system of linear equations.

**Slope and $y$-intercept of a line:**

$$\text{Slope} = \frac{(\text{change in } y)}{(\text{change in } x)}$$

Slope may be positive or negative.

The **$y$-intercept** is where the line crosses the $y$-axis of a graph (or where $x = 0$).

**Slope-intercept form of linear equations:**

$y = mx + b$ is the **slope-intercept form** of a linear equation.

$m$ is the slope

$b$ is the $y$-intercept

**Using linear equations to find slope:**

$5x + y = 325$

Change to slope-intercept form:

$5x + y - 5x = -5x + 325$

$y = -5x + 325$, slope $= -5$

**Using linear equations to find intercepts:**

The $x$-intercept is where $y = 0$.

Substitute 0 for $x$ or $y$ to find intercepts.

$5x + y = 325$; $5(0) + y = 325$, $y = 325$

$y$-intercept $= 325$

$5x + y = 325$; $5x + 0 = 325$

$x = \frac{325}{5} = 65$, $x = 65$, $x$-intercept $= 65$

## Strategy Review

- When solving problems involving linear equations, it may help to make a list of all the information you have.
- Make a table of $x$ and $y$ values to help you find the slope of a line. Plot the ordered pairs of a graph and find the slope of the line that runs through these points.
- Scale drawings are helpful when finding slopes of real objects such as roofs.

## Skills and Strategies Practice

**Complete the exercises below.**

**1.** Is $y = x^2 + 3$ a linear equation? Why or why not?

______________________

______________________

**2.** What is the $y$-intercept of the line represented by $32x + y = 16$? What is the $x$-intercept?

______________________

**3.** What is the slope of the line represented by $32x + y = 16$?

______________________

**4.** $y = 3x + 2$
Fill in the table with values of $x$ and $y$.

| x | y |
|---|---|
| 0 | |
| 1 | |
| 2 | |

**5.** What is the slope of a line that runs through points (1, 4) and (3, 17)?

______________________

**6.** $y = 11x + 10$. What is the slope of this line?

______________________

When you study for a math test, review any formulas and example problems. Then practice the step-by-step procedures for solving problems. For instance, there are several ways that you can find the slope of a line. Review examples of each. Then practice finding the slope by using two points in the line and using the slope-intercept form of a linear equation.

# Mid-Unit Review

**Circle the letter of the correct answer.**

**1.** A system of linear equations is a collection of ________ linear equation(s).

A. 1
B. $\geq 3$
C. $\geq 2$
D. exactly 2

**2.** What is the slope of a line that runs through points (0, 2) and (3, 11)?

A. 3
B. $\frac{13}{3}$
C. $\frac{3}{13}$
D. $-3$

**3.** What is the slope of the line represented by $y = -2x + 36$?

A. $-2$
B. 2
C. 36
D. $-\frac{1}{2}$

**4.** What is the slope of the line represented by $4x + y = 32$?

A. 5
B. 4
C. $-8$
D. $-4$

**5.** What is the slope of a line that runs through points (1, 6) and (2, 10)?

A. 4
B. 2
C. $\frac{1}{2}$
D. $-4$

**6.** What is the $x$-intercept of the line represented by $11x + y = 33$?

A. 11
B. 33
C. 3
D. $-3$

**7.** Which is an equation for a line that has slope $\frac{1}{2}$ and $y$-intercept 33?

A. $y = \frac{1}{2}x + 33$
B. $y = -\frac{1}{2}x - 33$
C. $y = \frac{1}{2}x - 33$
D. $y = x + 33$

**8.** What is the $y$-intercept of the line represented by $15x + y = 121$?

A. 15
B. $-15$
C. 121
D. $-121$

**9.** What is the $y$-intercept of the line represented by $y = 16x + 21$?

A. 16
B. 1
C. 21
D. $-21$

**10.** Which of these is a linear equation?

A. $y = \frac{1}{3}x + 23$
B. $y = x^2 + 5$
C. $y = x^2$
D. $x^2 + y = 5$

**11.** What is the $x$-intercept of the line represented by $-2x + y = 8$?

A. 4
B. $-4$
C. $-2$
D. 8

**12.** What are the variables in a linear equation?

A. $x$ and $y$
B. $x$ only
C. $m$
D. $b$

**13.** What is the slope of the line represented by $-\frac{2}{3}x + y = 17$?

A. 17
B. $-17$
C. $-\frac{2}{3}$
D. $\frac{2}{3}$

**14.** What is the slope of a line that runs through points (–11, 6) and (5, 18)?

A. $\frac{4}{3}$
B. $-2$
C. $\frac{3}{4}$
D. $\frac{12}{15}$

# Mid-Unit Review

**15.** What is the slope of the line represented by $y = 12x - 6$?

A. 12 C. 6
B. $-6$ D. $-12$

**16.** What is the slope of the line represented by $-3x + y = 16$?

A. 3 C. $\frac{16}{3}$
B. $-3$ D. $-\frac{16}{3}$

**17.** What is the slope of a line that runs through points $(0, -6)$ and $(3, 9)$?

A. $-5$ C. 5
B. 1 D. $-1$

**18.** What is the slope of a line that runs through points $(0, 17)$ and $(4, 9)$?

A. 4 C. $-4$
B. 2 D. $-2$

**19.** What is the $y$-intercept of the line represented by $-\frac{3}{2}x + y = -5$?

A. 5 C. $-\frac{3}{2}$
B. $-5$ D. $\frac{10}{3}$

**20.** Which is an equation for a line that has slope $-6$ and $y$-intercept 2?

A. $y = -6x + 2$
B. $y = 6x - 2$
C. $y = 6x + 2$
D. $y = -6x - 2$

**21.** What is the $y$-intercept of this line: $x + y = 16$?

A. $-16$ C. 16
B. 0 D. 8

**22.** Which of these is a linear equation?

A. $y = 2x + 7$ C. $y = x^2 + x - 6$
B. $x^2 = 17$ D. $x + y^2 = 5$

**23.** What is the $y$-intercept of the line represented by $y = \frac{5}{3}x - 18$?

A. $-18$ C. $\frac{5}{3}$
B. 18 D. $-\frac{5}{3}$

**24.** Which is an equation for a line that has slope of 4 and $y$-intercept $-7$?

A. $y = -7x + 4$ C. $y = 4x - 7$
B. $y = 4x + 7$ D. $y = -7x - 4$

**25.** What information can be found from a slope-intercept form of a linear equation?

A. $y$-intercept only
B. slope and $y$-intercept
C. slope only
D. $x$-intercept only

**26.** What is the slope of a line that runs through points $(-1, 16)$ and $(3, 7)$?

A. $-\frac{4}{7}$ C. $\frac{9}{4}$
B. $\frac{4}{9}$ D. $-\frac{9}{4}$

**27.** What is the $x$-intercept of this line: $x - y = 3$?

A. 3 C. 1
B. $-1$ D. $-3$

**28.** Which is an equation for a line that has slope 132 and $y$-intercept 57?

A. $y = -132x + 57$
B. $y = -132x - 57$
C. $y = 132x + 57$
D. $y = 132x - 57$

# Solving Systems of Linear Equations with Two Variables

**VOCABULARY**

Watch for the words you are learning about.

**consistent system:** a system of linear equations that has at least one solution

**inconsistent system:** a system of linear equations that does not have a solution

## Learn the SKILL

Jane is given this pair of linear equations: $5x - 3y = -6$ and $x + y = 2$. She will solve to find the values of $x$ and $y$.

| SKILL | EXAMPLE | COMPLETE THE EXAMPLE |
|---|---|---|
| To solve by substitution, first, convert each equation into slope-intercept form, $y = mx + b$. Next take the $y$-value from the first equation—that is, the expression on the right side of the equation—and substitute it for $y$ in the other equation. Then solve for $x$. Finally, substitute the value of $x$ into either equation and solve for $y$. | $y = \frac{5}{3}x + 2$<br>Substitute $\frac{5}{3}x + 2$ for $y$ in the second equation: $\frac{5}{3}x + 2 = -x + 2$.<br>Solve. Multiply both sides by 3.<br>$5x + 6 = -3x + 6$ Add $3x$ to each side.<br>$8x + 6 = 6$ Subtract 6 from each side.<br>$8x = 0$ Divide both sides by 8. $x = 0$<br>Substitute 0 for $x$ in the first equation:<br>$y = \frac{5}{3}(0) + 2$ Solve: $y = 2$<br>So, the solution is $x = 0$, $y = 2$, or (0, 2). | Use the $y$-value from the first equation to solve for $x$ in the second equation.<br>$y = -\frac{1}{2}x + 8$<br>$y = x - 4$<br>________________ |
| To solve by elimination, use the unconverted form of the equation. Add the equations so as to eliminate either the $x$ or the $y$, then solve for the remaining symbol. | $5x - 3y = -6$<br>$3x + 3y = 6$ $x = 0$<br>$8x + 0y = 0$<br>Substitute 0 for $x$ in either equation and solve for $y$:<br>$x + y = 2 \longrightarrow 0 + y = 2; y = 2$<br>So, the solution is (0, 2). | Use elimination to solve for $x$ and $y$ in the following equations:<br>$2x + 5y = 21$<br>$x - 5y = 6$<br>________________ |
| A system of equations that has at least one solution is called a **consistent system.**<br>A system of equations that has no solution is an **inconsistent system.** | Is this system of linear equations consistent or inconsistent?<br>$y = -\frac{3}{4}x + 2$ $y = -\frac{3}{4}x + \frac{1}{2}$<br>Substitute the $y$-value from the first equation, $-\frac{3}{4}x + 2$, for $y$ in the second equation and solve:<br>$-\frac{3}{4}x + 2 = -\frac{3}{4}x + \frac{1}{2} \longrightarrow 2 = \frac{1}{2}$ Not true.<br>There is no solution. The system is inconsistent. | Determine whether this system of equations is consistent or inconsistent.<br>$y - 2x = 5$<br>$y = 2x + 7$<br>________________ |

Learn the Skill

# YOUR TURN

## Choose the Right Word

system of linear equations
inconsistent system consistent system

**Fill in each blank with the correct word or phrase from the box.**

1. A system of equations is called a(n) ________________ when there is a solution to the system.
2. A system of equations is called a(n) ________________ when there is no solution to the system.
3. A ____________________ has two or more linear equations that have the same variable.

## Yes or No?

**Answer these questions and be ready to explain your answers.**

4. Is a system of equations inconsistent if there is a solution? ________
5. Are substitution and elimination two methods for solving a system of linear equations? ________
6. Is it necessary to convert equations to slope-intercept form to solve a system of linear equations by elimination? ________
7. Would the graph of an inconsistent system of linear equations show parallel lines? ________

## Show That You Know

**Show the substitution you would make to solve each system of linear equations.**

8. $y = -x - 1$

   $y = 3x + 7$

9. $y = 7x + 2$

   $2x = y + 8$

**Show how you could modify the first equation in each system of equations in order to eliminate a variable.**

10. $x + y = 7$ $\quad 5x + 3y = 11$

11. $x - 3y = 2$ $\quad 4x + 10y = 10$

# SOLVE on Your Own

## Skills Practice

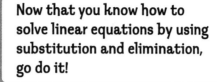

Now that you know how to solve linear equations by using substitution and elimination, go do it!

**Find the solution for these equations**

1. $y = 8$

   $2y = 4x + 8$ ________

2. $x = y$

   $3x + 2y = 15$ ________

3. $x + 4 = 16$

   $2y - 3x = 10$ ________

4. $x + 2 = -3$

   $x + 5y = 14$ ________

**Find the solutions of these equations using elimination.**

5. $y = -3x + 3$

   $y = -2x + 4$ ________

6. $x + 3y = 5$

   $-x - 2y = -3$ ________

7. $8x + 2y = 6$

   $2x - 6y = 8$ ________

8. $2x + \frac{1}{2}y = 2$

   $6x - y = 1$ ________

**State whether each system of linear equations is consistent or inconsistent.**

9. $3x - 2y = 8$

   $-6x + 4y = 10$ ___________

10. $x = 7 - \frac{1}{2}y$

    $8x - y = -4$ ___________

11. $y = 18x + 8$

    $y - 18x = 12$ ___________

# Solving Systems of Linear Equations with Two Variables

## Strategy

### Draw a Picture or Use a Model

**Step 1: Read** Jane was given this pair of linear equations: $5x - 3y = -6$ $x + y = 2$
She had to determine if they had a common solution. How can she do this?

**STRATEGY**

**Draw a Picture or Use a Model**

Systems of linear equations can be graphed on the coordinate plane. If the graphed lines intersect, there is a common solution. If the lines are parallel and do not intersect, then there is no common solution.

**SOLUTION**

**Step 2: Plan** Put both the equations in the slope-intercept form for graphing.

$5x - 3y = -6 \longrightarrow y = \frac{5}{3}x + 2$

$x + y = 2 \longrightarrow y = -x + 2$

Take note of the slope and the $y$-intercept of each equation. To find the $x$-intercept of each equation, substitute 0 for $y$. When you have all this data, you can graph the equations.

| $y = \frac{5}{3}x + 2$ | $y = -x + 2$ |
|---|---|
| slope $= \frac{5}{3}$ | slope $= -1$ |
| $y$-intercept = (0, 2) | $y$-intercept = (0, 2) |
| $x$-intercept = $(-\frac{6}{5}, 0)$ | $x$-intercept = (2, 0) |

**Step 3: Solve** Graph the two equations. Do they have a common solution? If so, what is it?

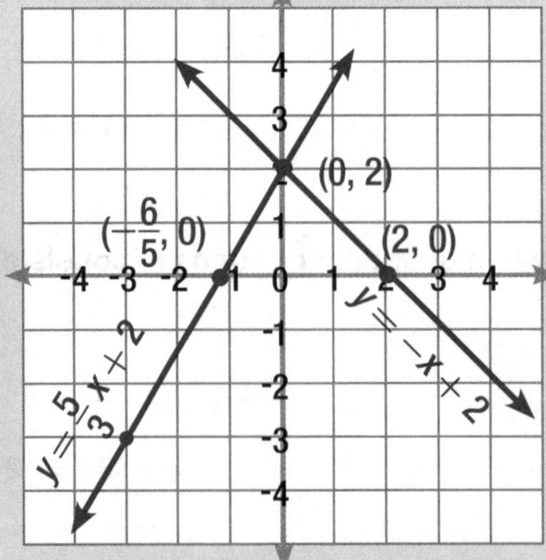


The lines intersect at (0, 2) so that is the common solution of this system of equations.

**Step 4: Check** Check your answer by using substitution (replacing a variable with a number) or elimination (removing a variable) to find actual solutions.

$5x - 3y = -6 \longrightarrow 5x - 3y = -6$

$x + y = 2 \longrightarrow$ Multilply by 3. $\longrightarrow + 3x + 3y = 6$

$8x + 0 = 0$

$x = 0$, so $y = 2$. So the solution is (0, 2).

# YOUR TURN

Choose a Strategy

## Choose the Right Word

parallel linear intersecting

**Fill in each blank with the correct word or phrase from the box.**

1. A(n) ________________ equation is an equation that can be graphed as a straight line.
2. A graph with ________________ lines indicates a solution to a system of linear equations.
3. A graph with________________ lines indicates that there is no solution to the system of linear equations.

## Yes or No?

**Answer these questions and be ready to explain your answers.**

4. When writing an ordered pair, does *x* always come first? ________
5. Can you graph a line if you have only two ordered pairs? ________
6. Do perpendicular lines have the same slope? ________
7. Is the slope of a line always positive? ________
8. If two lines cross each other, will there be one common solution for both? ________

## Show That You Know

**Graph each system of linear equations. Estimate the coordinates for the intersection if there is one. Then use substitution or elimination to check your estimate of the solution. If there is no intersection, you should conclude that the system is inconsistent.**

9. $4y - 12x = -8$

   $15 = 3x - 3y$

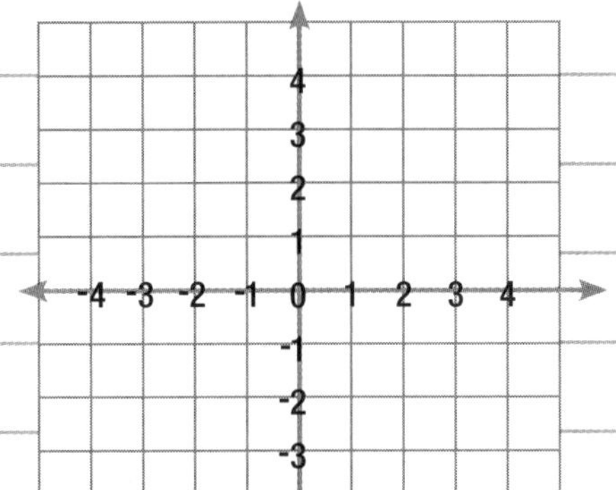

10. $4x + 2y = 8$

    $3y + 6x = -3$

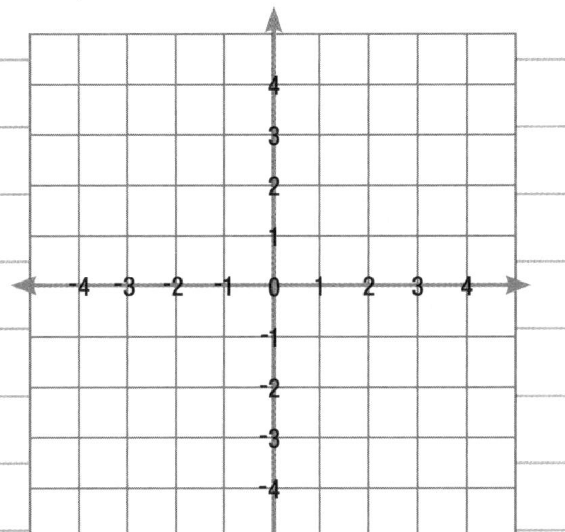

# READ on Your Own

## Reading Comprehension Strategy: Previewing/Predicting

### VOCABULARY

Watch for the words you are learning about.

**policy:** a plan or contract between an insurance company and an individual or organization buying insurance

**premium:** the amount paid for a contract of insurance

**topography:** the physical or natural features of a place

### Fluency Tip

If you come to a word you do not know, skip it and read the rest of the sentence first. Then reread the sentence and use context to figure out what the word is.

## Extremes of Nature, *pages 20–21*

### Before You Read

What kinds of insurance do you know about? Why do people need insurance?

### As You Read

Use what you know to predict what this reading will be about. Write your prediction in the chart below. As you read, remember to ask, "Was my prediction correct about what I am reading?"

**Preview "Disaster Insurance," pages 20–21.** 

Complete the left column of the chart.

**Read pages 20–21.** 

Complete the right column of the chart.

| Preview and Predict | Read and Check |
|---|---|
| | Did your prediction match the text, or did you have to revise it? Explain. |
| ________________ | ________________ |
| ________________ | ________________ |
| ________________ | ________________ |
| ________________ | ________________ |

### After You Read

If disaster happens, who pays for the repair and the damages?

________________________________________

________________________________________

# SOLVE on Your Own

## Extremes of Nature, *page 22*

### Organize the Information

**Complete the table comparing two insurance plans. Remember, each column should include the total amount the person has paid so far.**

| Cost | | | | | | | | | | |
|---|---|---|---|---|---|---|---|---|---|---|
| | Year 1 | Year 2 | Year 3 | Year 4 | Year 5 | Year 6 | Year 7 | Year 8 | Year 9 | Year 10 |
| **Plan A** | | | | | | | | | | |
| **Plan B** | | | | | | | | | | |

### You Do the Math

Write your answers in the space provided.

1. How did you find the costs of the policies after 10 years?

_______________________________________________

2. Let's say the owner of Plan B had another car accident. How much would the driver pay after 10 years?

_______________________________________________

### After You Solve

What types of insurance should people have? Why do some people have higher insurance rates than others?

_______________________________________________

_______________________________________________

# Verbal, Algebraic, and Graphical Representations of Functions

## Learn the SKILL

Ryan's teacher verbally gave him the following function:
"*f* of *x* equals four times a number plus three."
Write the algebraic representation of this function.

| SKILL | EXAMPLE | WRITE AN EXAMPLE |
|---|---|---|
| Start by breaking the verbal function into parts in order to better understand each part. Begin with "*f* of *x* equals" and replace it with its algebraic equivalent. | Replace: "*f* of *x* equals"<br>When you see or hear "*f* of *x*" this tells you that the expression is a function. To write "*f* of *x*" simply write an "*f*" with an *x* in parentheses beside it: $f(x)$. For "equals" write an equals symbol, $=$.<br>Put them together to get: $f(x) =$. | Replace: "equals *f* of *x*"<br>____________________ |
| Next, work on the first part of the expression on the right side of the equals symbol, "four times a number." | Replace: "four times a number"<br>When you see "a number," this refers to a variable. Since the function is "of *x*," the variable will be *x*. "Four times" tells you that the variable is being multiplied four times: $4x$. | Replace: "negative six times a number"<br>____________________ |
| The last part of the equation is "plus three." Replace this with its algebraic equivalent, then put the expression back together to get the function. | Replace: "plus three"<br>Since the "three" is standing alone, no variable is associated with it. "Three" is the constant. "Plus" tells us that "three" is positive. So, we have: $+ 3$. When you put the expression back together, you get $f(x) = 4x + 3$. | Replace: "minus twelve"<br>____________________ |

# YOUR TURN

## Choose the Right Word

constant function verbal
algebraic representation

**Fill in each blank with the correct word or phrase from the box.**

1. A(n) ________________ is an expression that uses the verbal saying "*f* of *x*."
2. An expression is called a(n) ______________________ when it is written with a variable.
3. A function is a(n) ________________ function when it is said out loud.
4. A(n) ________________ is a number in a function or equation that stays the same.

## Yes or No?

**Answer these questions and be ready to explain your answers.**

5. Can a constant have more than one value? ________
6. Can a variable be written with any letter? ________
7. Does a function have to have a variable and a constant? ________
8. Can any function that is written be said verbally? ________

## Show That You Know

**Replace each verbal function with its algebraic equivalent.**

9. "*f* of *x* equals two minus a number"
10. "*f* of *x* equals three times a number plus five"
11. "*f* of *x* equals negative two times a number minus three"
12. "*f* of *x* equals eight times a number plus seven"
13. "*f* of *x* equals ten minus a number multiplied by three"

# SOLVE on Your Own

## Skills Practice

Now that you know how to write the algebraic reorientation of a verbal function, listen for those functions!


**Write the algebraic representation of the verbal function or write a verbal function using the algebraic representation.**

1. "*f* of *x* equals ten times a number minus three" ______________

2. $f(x) = 6x + 4$ ______________

3. $8x - 3 = f(x)$ ______________

4. "three times a number added to 5 equals *f* of *x*" ______________

5. $f(x) = 7 + 2x$ ______________

6. "*f* of *x* plus 5 equals two times a number" ______________

7. "four plus a number divided by 2 equals *f* of *x*" ______________

8. $f(x) = -2x - 3$ ______________

9. "a number times six equals *f* of *x*" ______________

10. "eight multiplied by a number and added to five gives you *f* of *x*" ______________

11. $\frac{1}{2}x - 5 = f(x)$ ______________

# Verbal, Algebraic, and Graphical Representations of Functions

## Strategy

### Make a Table or a Chart

**Step 1: Read** Karen recorded the high temperatures each day for 5 days. The temperatures she recorded were 73, 72, 74, 78, and 79 degrees Fahrenheit. She would like to see if there is a trend in the temperatures. How can she graph this information?

**STRATEGY**

**Make a Table or a Chart**

A table can help organize information, which can then help you to recognize patterns.

**SOLUTION**

**Step 2: Plan** First create a table that has two columns. The first column is for the days, and the second column is for the temperatures recorded on that day.

| Day | Temp |
|---|---|
| 1 | 73 |
| 2 | 72 |
| 3 | 74 |
| 4 | 78 |
| 5 | 79 |

**Step 3: Solve** Make a graph with days as the $x$-axis, and temperature as the $y$-axis. Use the information to make ordered pairs $(x, y)$ and graph each ordered pair. You can see the trend is increasing temperatures.

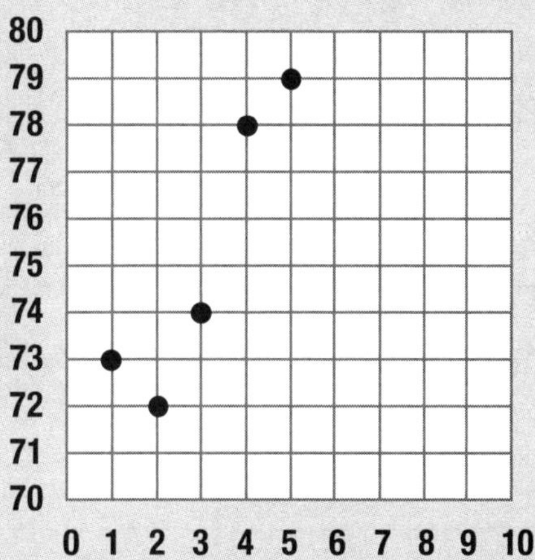


**Step 4: Check** Refer to your table. Double check the plotted points to make sure that the correct temperatures are paired with the correct days.

Choose a Strategy

# YOUR TURN

## Choose the Right Word

function ordered pair *x*-axis

**Fill in each blank with the correct word or phrase from the box.**

1. The numbers that represent a point on a coordinate plane are called a(n) ________________.
2. The ________________ is the horizontal line of a coordinate plane.
3. A(n) ________________ uses the words "*f* of *x*."

## Yes or No?

**Answer these questions and be ready to explain your answers.**

4. When writing an ordered pair, does *x* always come first? ________
5. Is the *y*-axis the horizontal axis? ________
6. Does every function have a domain? ________
7. Does the *x* represent the domain? ________
8. Does *y* represent the range? ________

## Show That You Know

**Graph these equations on graph paper.**

9. $y = x + 1$
10. $y = -x + 1$
11. $y = x$

**Graph these ordered pairs and connect them.**

12. (1, 0) and (2, 1)
13. (–3, 1) and (–3, 2)
14. (0, 0) and (5, 4)

**Graph the equations and write the ordered pair of their estimated solution.**

15. $y = 3x + 5$

    $y = -2x + 4$

# READ on Your Own

## Reading Comprehension Strategy: Previewing/Predicting

## Extremes of Nature, *pages 23–24*

### VOCABULARY

Watch for the words you are learning about.

**calving:** becoming detached or separating from an ice mass

**moraine:** rocks and debris left behind by melting glaciers

### Fluency Tip

Try to read smoothly and expressively, just as a storyteller or news reporter would.

### Before You Read

What do you think it might have been like to live in the ice age when glaciers covered much of North America?

### As You Read

**Preview by reading the first paragraph of "Slow Motion Geology—Glaciers," page 23.** 

In the chart below, write a prediction of what you think the reading will be about. Be sure to elaborate on your prediction with some details.

**Read pages 23–24.** 

Complete the chart.

| Predict and Check | |
|---|---|
| Prediction:<br>__________<br>__________<br>__________<br>__________ | Did your prediction match what you read about or did you have to revise your prediction as you read? Explain.<br>__________<br>__________<br>__________ |

### After You Read

Many people believe that global temperatures are rising. How might this affect formation of glaciers?

____________________

____________________

# SOLVE on Your Own

## Extremes of Nature, *page 25*

### Organize the Information

**Read magazine page 25. Then fill out the following flowchart.**

| Known: | | Estimate: | | Formulate: | | Calculate: |
|---|---|---|---|---|---|---|
| Glacier speed is between ____________ and ____________<br>Glacier width = ________<br>Glacier height = ________ | → | Speed of a glacier in meters per month<br>____________ | → | Write an equation for the length of glacier that goes into the ocean in one year. | → | Use $V = lwh$ to find the volume of glacier that goes into the ocean in one year. |

### You Do the Math

Use the information in the flowchart above to answer these questions. Write your answers in the space provided.

**1.** What did you use as an estimate for the speed of the glacier?

____________________________

You can use $l = st$ to find the length, $l$, of an iceberg that goes into the sea when the glacier travels at a speed $s$ (in meters per month) during a time $t$ (in months).

**2.** What equation can you use for the amount of ice that goes into the sea in one year?

____________________________

____________________________

**3.** About how much ice from the glacier will go into the sea in one year?

____________________________

### After You Solve

Is there another way you could calculate the amount of ice that goes into the sea in one year? Explain.

____________________________

____________________________

## The Four-Step Problem-Solving Plan

| Step 1: Read | Step 2: Plan | Step 3: Solve | Step 4: Check |
|---|---|---|---|
| Make sure you understand what the problem is asking. | Decide how you will solve the problem. | Solve the problem using your plan. | Check to make sure your answer is correct. |

**Read the article below. Then answer the questions.**

### Sumatra Tsunami

The worst tsunami on record is the Sumatra tsunami. It occurred in the Indian Ocean off the coast of Indonesia on December 26, 2004. The powerful earthquake that caused it measured 9.3 on the Richter scale. It was the second-most powerful earthquake ever recorded.

Shaking from the earthquake produced powerful tsunami waves that spread out in all directions. Waves up to 100 feet high crashed onto the Indonesian coastline. An estimated 130,000 people drowned or died from related injuries in the rushing water.

Within two hours, the waves reached the coastlines of Thailand, Sri Lanka, and India. Another 58,000 people died as the waves crashed ashore.

As the death toll rose, the huge loss of lives shocked the world. People demanded better tsunami alerts. Their governments agreed and took measures to improve their warning systems.

1. What was one result of the death toll from the Sumatra tsunami?

______________________________

______________________________

______________________________

2. The Richter scale is logarithmic. This means that every whole number added to a measurement represents an increase of 10 times in the strength of an earthquake. How much stronger is a 9.3 earthquake compared to a 7.3 earthquake?

______________________________

______________________________

______________________________

______________________________

Application

# YOUR TURN

**Read the article below. Then answer the questions.**

## 2006 Java Tsunami

Only two years after the devastating Sumatra tsunami, people in Indonesia had no idea that another tsunami was traveling toward them until it was too late. Over 600 people were killed and many buildings destroyed.

Despite efforts to improve warning systems, tsunamis are difficult to forecast. Warning systems do not always alert authorities in time. The power of the tsunami and the exact location of the coastline it targets are difficult to predict.

Many things add to the problem of accuracy. Even though the earthquake registered 7.8 on the Richter scale, people on land near the centroid (the place where the burst of energy was released) felt no land tremors. The focus or actual site of the earthquake was too deep below Earth's surface.

Scientists also think that a 7.8 earthquake would not normally cause the wall of water racing onto the beach to be 65 feet high. They think that the earthquake may have caused a submarine landslide or a collapse of one of Earth's submarine canyons. Either event could have increased the surface disturbance.

1. A friend says that the 2006 earthquake was about four-fifths as strong as the 2004 earthquake. Do you agree? Explain your answer.

______________________________

______________________________

______________________________

______________________________

2. Why did people near the centroid of the earthquake not feel it?

______________________________

______________________________

3. How big were the waves from the 2006 tsunami compared to the 2004 tsunami? Express your answer as a simple proportion.

______________________________

______________________________

______________________________

**Fluency Tip**

Let your voice fall at the end of a sentence.

# READ on Your Own

## Reading Comprehension Strategy: Previewing/Predicting

## Extremes of Nature, *pages 26–28*

### VOCABULARY

Watch for the words you are learning about.

**displaces:** moves aside

**disturbance:** a sudden change

**eruptions:** the release of materials from a volcano or other structure

**evacuations:** the removal of people from an area

**seismographs:** devices that detect an earthquake and measure and record its intensity and the energy released

### Fluency Tip

Pay attention to punctuation and pause between phrases and sentences.

### Before You Read

Recall what you have heard about earthquakes. What is an earthquake?

### As You Read

**Preview pages 26–28, "Predicting Tsunamis."** 

What information do you predict will be in the article? Write your prediction below.

What I predict:

______________________________

______________________________

**Read pages 26–28, "Predicting Tsunamis."** 

Fill in the remaining information.

Information in the article I predicted:

______________________________

______________________________

Information in the article that I did not predict:

______________________________

______________________________

### After You Read

How does previewing help you better understand the article? Explain your answer.

______________________________

______________________________

______________________________

# SOLVE on Your Own

## Extremes of Nature, *page 29*

### Organize the Information

**Use the table below to organize the information you find in the Math Project on magazine page 29.**

| Buoy | Distance to Buoy | Time Wave Was Recorded | Time Wave Traveled to Buoy | Speed = Distance ÷ Time |
|---|---|---|---|---|
| Hawaii | | 1:15 PM | 2 h 0 min | 460 mph |
| Buoy A | 2,300 miles | 3:12 PM | 3 h 57 min | |
| Buoy B | 2,750 miles | | | |
| Buoy C | | | | |
| Buoy D | | | | |
| Buoy E | | | | |

### Math Project

Use the information in the table above to answer these questions. Write your answers in the space provided.

**1.** Which buoy reading or readings do not fit with the rest of the data? Explain.

**2.** What was the speed of the tsunami? About when would it hit South America?

### After You Solve

How could you express the same information in the table by drawing a picture?

# Using Linear Equations, Linear Functions, and Systems of Linear Equations to Solve Problems

## Learn the SKILL

Ray is five years older than Lela. The sum of their two ages is 25. How can you find each of their ages?

| SKILL | EXAMPLE | WRITE AN EXAMPLE |
|---|---|---|
| This is a perfect opportunity to use a system of linear equations to solve a problem. One variable, $x$, can represent Lela's age; another variable, $y$, can represent Ray's age. Since two distinct relationships are expressed, we need two equations—not just one. | Let $x$ = Lela's age.<br>Let $y$ = Ray's age.<br>We will write two equations representing the two distinct relationships.<br>(1) Ray is five years older than Lela, so: $x + 5 = y$<br>(2) The sum of the ages is 25, so: $x + y = 25$.<br>We now have our system of linear equations. | Write equations to represent these relationships: Mr. Kannon weighs 20 pounds more than Mr. Lopez. The sum of their two weights is 320 pounds.<br>__________<br>__________<br>__________<br>__________<br>__________ |
| Rearrange the equations to be in slope-intercept form.<br>$x + 5 = y \rightarrow y = x + 5$<br>$x + y = 25 \rightarrow y = -x + 25$<br>Use elimination to solve. | Add the two equations.<br>$y = x + 5$<br>$y = -x + 25$<br>$2y = 30$<br>$y = 15$ (Ray's age) | Use elimination to solve for Mr. Lopez's weight.<br>__________<br>__________<br>__________<br>__________<br>__________<br>__________ |
| Substitute the value of $y$ in one of the equations to find Lela's age ($x$). | $y = 15$ (Ray's age)<br>$x + y = 25$<br>$x + 15 = 25$<br>$x = 10$ (Lela's age) | Substitute the value of $y$ in one equation to find Mr. Kannon's weight.<br>__________<br>__________<br>__________ |

Learn the Skill

# YOUR TURN

## Choose the Right Word

linear    linear function    slope-intercept form
system of linear equations

**Fill in each blank with the correct word or phrase from the box.**

1. A ______________________ is a set of two or more equations.
2. A ______________ equation is an equation that can be graphed as a straight line.
3. A ______________ can be graphed as a straight line and has a constant rate of change.
4. The ______________ has the format of $y = mx + b$.

## Yes or No?

**Answer these questions and be ready to explain your answers.**

5. Can you use a system of equations to solve a problem that expresses two separate mathematical relationships? ________
6. Should you put an equation in slope-intercept form before solving by substitution? ________
7. Does solving by elimination involve changing the value of a variable? ________

## Show That You Know

**Rearrange each equation into slope-intercept form. Simplify the equation if necessary.**

8. $x + y = 6$
9. $y + 5 = 7x$
10. $2x - y = 8$
11. $9x + 3y = 3$
12. $2x + 2y = 2$
13. $4y - 8x = 12$
14. $22x - 11y = -44$

# SOLVE on Your Own

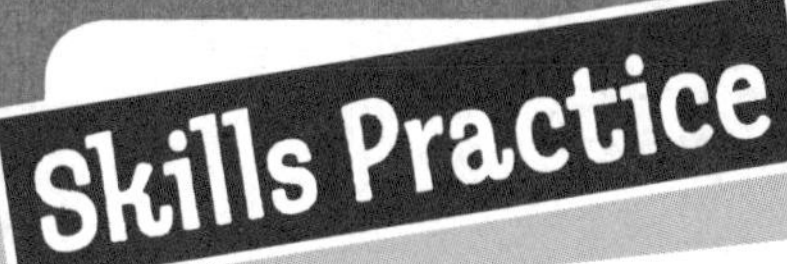

Now that you know how to solve systems of equations using algebra, show it!


**Solve each problem by setting up a system of linear equations.**

1. Tony's Uncle Ned is one year less than three times as old as Tony is. The difference between Uncle Ned's age and Tony's age is 27. How old are they both?

2. Mrs. Hong and Mrs. Dexter both like to travel. This year, Mrs. Hong has traveled 800 miles farther than Mrs. Dexter. In total, the two ladies have traveled 3,680 miles. How many miles has each of them covered?

# Using Linear Equations, Linear Functions, and Systems of Linear Equations to Solve Problems

## Strategy

### Make a Table or a Chart

**Step 1: Read** Karen is paid \$8.00 an hour to work as a lifeguard. She works 7 hours per day. She wants to know how many hours she needs to work to earn \$500. How can she find this answer?

**STRATEGY**

**Make a Table or a Chart**

An input/output table can help organize the information, and a chart can be used to graph the information.

Start by writing an equation to represent the facts.

In this problem, \$8 is the constant.

$x$ can represent the number of hours worked.

$y$ can represent the total amount earned.

So, the total, $y$, would equal the constant, \$8, multiplied by the number of hours, $x$.

$y = \$8x$

**SOLUTION**

**Step 2: Plan** Make a two–column table that has inputs ($x$) and outputs ($y$). Write in a value for $x$. Then calculate the $y$-value

| x | y |
|---|---|
| 0 | 0 |
| 5 | 40 |
| 10 | 80 |
| 15 | 120 |

**Step 3: Solve**

Now use these ordered pairs to graph the information. To get more ordered pairs, write greater values for $x$.

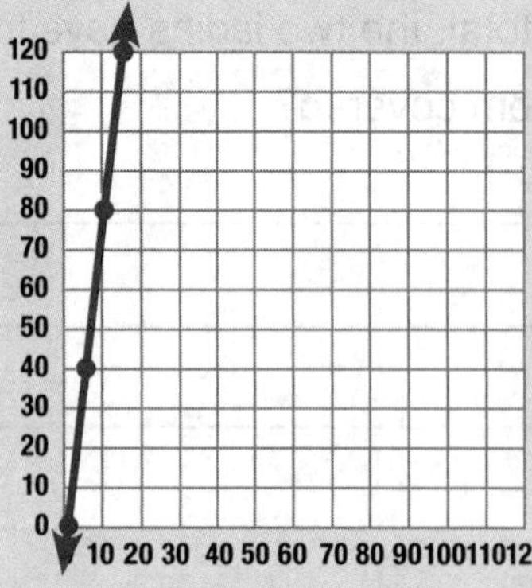


If you expand your input/output table and extend your graph, you will find that Karen will have to work about 63 hours to earn \$500. If she works 7 hours a day, she'll have to work about 9 days.

Karen could have put the value \$500 into the equation and solved for $x$ to find the number of hours she needed to work:

$y = 8x$

$x = \frac{y}{8}$ $\qquad y = 500$

$x = 62.5$ hours

**Step 4: Check** Check by multiplying.

# YOUR TURN



## Choose the Right Word

constant input/output table
dependent variable

**Fill in each blank with the correct word or phrase from the box.**

1. The variable that depends on the input value is the ________________.
2. A number in an equation that does not change is the ________________.
3. Using a(n) ________________ helps show ordered pairs.

## Yes or No?

**Answer these questions and be ready to explain your answers.**

4. When writing an ordered pair, does $x$ always come first? ________
5. Can equations be graphed? ________
6. Does a constant always have to be positive? ________
7. Does $y$ increase as $x$ increases on a positive slope? ________
8. Is $x$ usually the independent variable? ________

## Show That You Know

**Graph these equations on graph paper.**

9. $y = 2x + 3$

10. $5x + y = 6$

11. $y = x + 4$

12. $8x + 4y = 4$

**Find the value of $y$, given the value of $x$.**

13. $x = 6$

    $2y = 4x + 10$

14. $x = 6$

    $2y + 3x = 10$

15. $x = 1$

    $3x + 2y = 15$

**Graph the equations and write the ordered pair of their estimated solution.**

16. $y = 3x + 5$

    $y = 2x + 4$

# READ on Your Own

## Reading Comprehension Strategy: Previewing/Predicting

## Extremes of Nature, *pages 30–31*

### Before You Read

Think about what you know about earthquakes. What do you think it would be like to experience an earthquake?

### As You Read

**Preview by reading the first paragraph of "Tracking Earthquakes," page 30.** 

Predict what you think the reading will be about. Be sure to elaborate on your prediction with some details.

**Read pages 30–31.** 

If necessary, revise your prediction as you read.
Then answer the question in the right column of the table.

| Tracking Earthquakes | |
|---|---|
| **Prediction:** ____________________ ____________________ ____________________ ____________________ | Did your prediction match what you read about or did you have to revise your prediction as you read? Explain. ____________________ ____________________ ____________________ |

### VOCABULARY

Watch for the words you are learning about.

**epicenter:** the ground directly above the focus of an earthquake

**focus:** a place where the plates or slabs of Earth's crust break

**P–waves:** the primary, underground waves of an earthquake, also known as body waves

**S–waves:** the secondary and stronger underground waves that come after P-waves in an earthquake

**slabs:** thick, flat sheets of Earth's crust, or plates

### Fluency Tip

Try to read smoothly and expressively, just as a storyteller or news reporter would.

### After You Read

How far do you think the P-waves of an earthquake can travel? Explain.

____________________________________________

____________________________________________

____________________________________________

# SOLVE on Your Own

## Extremes of Nature, *page 32*

### Organize the Information

**Use the table below to organize the information you find on magazine page 32.**

| Arrival of P-Wave | Time Delay | Distance to Epicenter (km) |
|---|---|---|
| Deming, New Mexico | 3 min 19 sec | 1,230 |
| Edmonton, Canada | 3 min 29 sec | 1,250 |
| Minneapolis, Minnesota | 4 min 37 sec | 1,800 |
| Idaho Falls, Idaho | | |
| Salt Lake City, Utah | | |
| Trinidad, Colorado | | |
| Rapid City, South Dakota | | |

### You Do the Math

Use the information in the table to answer these questions. Write your answers in the space provided.

1. Which travels faster, P-waves or S-waves? Explain how you know.

______________________________

______________________________

2. Which stations were at the same distance from the epicenter? How far were they? Explain how you can use the time difference and the graph to find the distance from the epicenter.

______________________________

______________________________

______________________________

3. Did you need to know the distance from the epicenter to prove two sites are at the same distance from the epicenter? Explain.

______________________________

### After You Solve

How could people build earthquake-proof buildings and homes?

______________________________

Application

## The Four-Step Problem-Solving Plan

| Step 1: Read | Step 2: Plan | Step 3: Solve | Step 4: Check |
|---|---|---|---|
| Make sure you understand what the problem is asking. | Decide how you will solve the problem. | Solve the problem using your plan. | Check to make sure your answer is correct. |

**Read the article below. Then answer the questions.**

### Dust From Io's Volcanoes

Earth's volcanoes are not the only ones that give off dust. Volcanoes on Io do so as well. Io is one of the four large moons of Jupiter. It is slightly larger than our own moon. Io has more volcanic activity than any other body in the solar system.

For many years, scientists tried to find the source of a stream of dust detected near Jupiter. The stream was found in 1992 by a spacecraft called *Ulysses*. One possible source of the stream was Jupiter's main ring. Another possible source was comet *Shoemaker–Levy 9*. *Shoemaker–Levy 9* broke up in 1994 and parts of it collided with Jupiter.

However, data collected by the *Galileo* space probe pointed to Io as the source of the dust. *Galileo* carried an instrument that detected amounts of dust that hit the probe. The amount of dust rose and fell in 42- and 10-hour cycles. Io's orbit around Jupiter takes 42 hours. Jupiter itself takes 10 hours to rotate. This evidence suggested that the dust came from Io. The dust particles are influenced by Jupiter's magnetic field and travel as far as 290 million kilometers from Jupiter.

1. How did scientists collect data that suggested that Io was the source of the dust stream?

______________________

______________________

______________________

2. How often will the 42- and 10-hour cycles peak at the same time?

______________________

______________________

______________________

# YOUR TURN

Application

**Read the article below. Then answer the questions.**

## Mars Volcanoes

One of the largest volcanoes in the solar system is Olympus Mons on Mars. This volcano reaches 24 kilometers up into Mars's thin atmosphere and is 175 kilometers across.

Olympus Mons is classified as a shield volcano similar to the Hawaiian volcanoes. One of the Hawaiian volcanoes, Mauna Loa, is the largest volcano on Earth. It is 9 kilometers high and 120 kilometers across.

Olympus Mons is near a region called the Tharsis Dome. The Tharsis Dome is a highland 4,000 kilometers across and 10 kilometers high. Three other large shield volcanoes are found on the Tharsis Dome. They are Ascraeus Mons, Pavonis Mons, and Arsia Mons.

The Tharsis Dome is the largest Martian volcanic region. The second largest is Elysium Planitia. The Elysium Planitia dome is roughly 1,700 kilometers by 2,400 kilometers. It contains smaller volcanoes than the Tharsis Dome.

### Fluency Tip

When reading aloud, change the expression in your voice to reflect whether information is surprising, serious, or descriptive.

1. How many volcanoes the height of Mauna Loa would have to be stacked up to reach the height of Olympus Mons?

   ____________________________

2. What type of volcano are Mauna Loa and Olympus Mons?

   ____________________________

3. What do you think the term "mons" might mean?

   ____________________________

4. Assume that the Elysium Planitia Dome and the Tharsis Dome are rectangular. Which has a greater area?

   ____________________________

   ____________________________

   ____________________________

   ____________________________

# READ on Your Own

## Reading Comprehension Strategy: Previewing/Predicting

**Fluency Tip**

Remember to look up the meanings of unfamiliar words before you read.

## Extremes of Nature, *pages 33–35*

### Before You Read

Recall what you know about volcanoes. What is the difference between a dormant volcano and an extinct one?

### As You Read

**Look through the text features in order to preview "Blowing Its Stack–Mount St. Helens," pages 33–35.** 

Write a prediction for what you think "Blowing Its Stack–Mount St. Helens" will be about. Be sure to elaborate on the prediction.

______________________________________________

______________________________________________

**Now read pages 33–35.** 

Did elaborating on your prediction help you to better understand the text? Explain.

______________________________________________

______________________________________________

### After You Read

What do you think it was like to see the ash cloud coming from Mount St. Helens after the eruption?

______________________________________________

______________________________________________

# SOLVE on Your Own

## Extremes of Nature, *page 36*

### Organize the Information

**Use the list below to organize the information you find in the Math Project on magazine page 36.**

| Angle | Distance |
|---|---|
| 15° | |
| 30° | |
| 40° | |
| 45° | |
| 50° | |
| 60° | |
| 75° | |

Using graphic organizers can help you keep track of numeric information.

### Math Project

Use the information in the list above to answer these questions. Write your answers in the space provided.

1. How can you find the distance that the boulder travels for each angle?

_______________________________________________

2. How can you figure out the longest possible distance?

_______________________________________________

3. What distances from the volcano would be safe from falling boulders?

_______________________________________________

### After You Solve

How could you express the same information in a more visual way?

_______________________________________________

# Put It Together

## Introducing Arithmetic Sequences as Linear Functions

You have learned about linear functions and their graphs. Now you will make connections between arithmetic sequences and linear functions. An arithmetic sequence is a sequence of numbers that have a common difference.

1, 2, 3, 4, 5, 6, 7, ...each term is 1 more than the preceding term

5, 10, 15, 20, 25, 30,...each term is 5 more than the preceding term

You can easily find additional terms in a sequence.
First, find the difference of two consecutive terms.
Then add this common difference to a term to find the next consecutive term.
What are the next three terms in this sequence? 34, 45, 56, 67, ________, ________, ________

Find the common difference: 67 − 56 = 11. Add 11 to terms to get 78, 89, and 100.

It is also easy to find missing terms with only a starting and ending number in a sequence.

62, ________, ________, ________, 94 Find the difference: 94 − 62 = 32.

Count the number of missing terms. Three terms are missing. The common difference was added four times (1 more than the number of missing terms). Divide 32 by 4 to get the common difference, 8. The missing terms are 70, 78, and 86.

## Practicing Arithmetic Sequences and Linear Functions

**Find the missing numbers in each sequence.**

1. 12, 24, 36, 48, ________, ________, ________
2. 7, 14, 21, 28, ________, ________, ________
3. 15, ________, ________, ________, ________, 90
4. ________, ________, ⁻9, ⁻3, ________, ________,

## Thinking About Arithmetic Sequences and Linear Functions

Because consecutive terms of an arithmetic sequence have a common difference, the sequence can be expressed as a linear function. Remember that for graphing purposes, we express $f(x)$ as the variable $y$. That is the wording used here.

Start with the arithmetic sequence 6, 14, 22, 30, _________, _________, . . .

Make a table where the $x$-value is the number of the term and the $y$-value is the term.

| $x$ | $y$ | Now think how you would write the equation of a line. |
|---|---|---|
| 1 | 6 | What is the slope of the line? $\frac{(14-6)}{(2-1)} = 8$ |
| 2 | 14 | Substitute the slope into the equation $y = mx + b$: $y = 8x + b$. |
| 3 | 22 | Substitute any point $(x, y)$ from the table. |
| 4 | 30 | Using (2, 14) $14 = 8(2) + b$ Solve for $b$: $b = -2$ |
| The equation for this sequence is $y = 8x - 2$. | | |

What is the equation for the arithmetic sequence 15, 13, 11, 9, 7, _________, _________?

1. What is the common difference for the terms of the sequence? _______________
2. What is the first term of the sequence? _______________
3. How would you write the first term as a coordinate for a graph? _______________
4. What would be the coordinate of the second term? _______________
5. What is the slope between these first and second points? _______________
6. How does the slope of the line compare with the common difference of the arithmetic sequence? _______________
7. What is the equation of the line that represents the arithmetic sequence? _______________

## Show That You Know

**Read the information below. Use what you know about arithmetic sequences and linear functions to answer the questions. Use the space provided to show your work.**

Alexander heard that you could tell how far away a lightning storm is by counting the number of seconds from the time you see the lightning to the time you hear the thunder. Sound travels through air at "the speed of sound." How fast is that? A reasonable number to use is 1,200 feet per second. How many feet are there in one mile?

There are 5,280 feet in one mile.

$(5{,}280\ \frac{\text{feet}}{\text{mile}}) \div (1{,}200\ \frac{\text{feet}}{\text{second}}) = \frac{5{,}280}{1{,}200}(\frac{\text{seconds}}{\text{mile}})$

A good estimate is that sound travels 1 mile in 5 seconds. If you see a flash of lightning and count 10 seconds before you hear the thunder, then the storm is about 2 miles away.

Remember, when you divide fractions, you multiply one by the inverse of the other. That is why the units are seconds per mile.

1. How far away is the storm if Alexander counts 15 seconds after he sees the flash?

2. If the storm is 4 miles away, how many seconds will it take for the sound to reach Alexander?

3. If Alexander counts 3 seconds, about how many feet away is the storm?

## Show That You Know (continued)

4. Complete the table for time and distance.

| *x* (distance in miles) | *y* (time in seconds) |
|---|---|
| 1 | |
| 2 | |
| 3 | |
| 4 | |

5. Choose two points from your table and calculate the slope between the two points.

6. Use the slope, any coordinate from your table, and the equation $y = mx + b$ to find the value of $b$.

7. What is the equation of the line that relates time and distance for the storm?

## Review What You've Learned

8. What have you learned in this Connections lesson about expressing arithmetic sequences as linear functions?

9. What have you learned in this Connections lesson that you did not already know?

10. What have you learned in this lesson that will help you recognize arithmetic sequences in real-life situations?

# Review and Practice

## Skills Review

**Systems of linear equations:**

$2x + y = 12$ and $3x - y = 8$

Convert to slope-intercept form:

$y = -2x + 12$ and $y = 3x - 8$

Plug in values for $x$ in each equation to find corresponding values for $y$.

$y = -2x + 12$

| x | y |
|---|---|
| 0 | 12 |
| 1 | 10 |
| 6 | 0 |

$y = 3x - 8$

| x | y |
|---|---|
| 0 | −8 |
| 1 | −5 |
| 2 | −2 |

**Intersections of lines:**

To solve a system of linear equations means to find the intersection of the lines, if possible.

You can graph the lines to see where they intersect. You would plot the ordered pairs for the lines, and then extend the lines to find the intersection.

**Verbal representations of functions:**

Functions can be described in words.
"The function of $x$ is two times $x$ plus 15."

**Algebraic representations of functions:**

Functions can be described as algebraic equations.
$f(x) = 2x + 15$

**Solving linear equations with algebra:**

Find the $x$ coordinate of the intersection.

$y = -2x + 12$ and $y = 3x - 8$

$-2x + 12 = 3x - 8$

$-2x = 3x - 20$

$-5x = -20$

$x = 4$

**Solving linear equations with algebra:**

Find the $y$ coordinate of the intersection.

Plug the value of $x$ into one of the equations to find the value of $y$ at the intersection.

$y = -2x + 12$

$y = -2(4) + 12$

$y = -8 + 12$ $y = 4$

## Strategy Review

- Graphing linear equations is a way to make an initial estimate of their solution. If the solution found this way is not precise, it can be revised by solving the equations with algebra.
- Tables or charts can help to organize information prior to graphing.
- Making an input/output or $x$, $y$ values table can also help you to recognize patterns.

## Skills and Strategies Practice

**Complete the exercises below.**

**1.** Change this linear equation to slope-intercept form:

$5x - y = 26$ ________________

**2.** The price of almonds is listed in the table below. It can be graphed as a line. Use the information in the table to determine the slope of the line and the $y$-intercept.

| Ounces (x) | Price (y) |
|---|---|
| 0 | 0 |
| 1 | $0.55 |
| 2 | $1.10 |
| 3 | $1.65 |
| 4 | $2.20 |
| 5 | $2.85 |

____________________________________

____________________________________

**3.** What is the algebraic expression of "$f$ of $x$ is seven times $x$ minus two"?

______________

**4.** For the lines $y = -1x + 3$ and $y = 3x + 4$, find the $x$-value at the intersecting point.

______________

**5.** Use the information in the table to the left to write a slope-intercept form of a linear equation.

______________

**6.** Solve this system of linear equations: $y = -1x + 3$ and $y = 3x + 4$.

______________

**Effective studying takes place over a period of time. Spend time studying new material for several days or weeks before a test. Then spend the day before the test reviewing the material. Solving linear equations takes practice, and you want to have plenty of time to go through the steps.**

## Unit Review

**Circle the letter of the correct answer.**

**1.** What is the slope-intercept form of this equation: $y + 13 = 2x$?

A. $y = 2x - 13$
B. $y + 13 = 2x$
C. $y = 13 - 2x$
D. $y = -2x + 13$

**2.** For $y + 13 = 2x$, if $x = 1$, what is the value of $y$?

A. –13 B. 13 C. –11 D. 11

**3.** What is the algebraic expression of "$f$ of $x$ is ten multiplied by $x$ plus thirty-four?"

A. $f(x) = -34 - 10x$
B. $f(x) = 34 - 10x$
C. $f(x) = 10x + 34$
D. $f(x) = 10x - 34$

**4.** For the lines $y = x - 2$ and $y = 2x + 10$, what is the $x$-value at the intersecting point?

A. 4 C. 6
B. –12 D. 12

**5.** What is the solution for the system of linear equations $y = x - 2$ and $y = 2x + 10$?

A. (2, 0) C. (4, 2)
B. (–12, –14) D. (10, –14)

**6.** What is the algebraic expression of "function of $x$ is thirteen times $x$ minus one"?

A. $f(x) = \frac{x}{13} - 1$
B. $f(x) = -13x - 1$
C. $f(x) = 13x - 1$
D. $f(x) = 13x + 1$

**7.** What is the algebraic expression of "$f$ of $x$ is one–third times $x$ minus two?"

A. $f(x) = -\frac{1}{3}x - 2$
B. $f(x) = \frac{1}{3}x + 2$
C. $f(x) = -\frac{1}{3}x - 2$
D. $f(x) = \frac{1}{3}x - 2$

**8.** What is the first step in solving the system of linear equations $y = x + 3$ and $y = -2x + 45$ using algebra?

A. set $y = 1$ in each equation
B. set $x = 0$ in each equation
C. set $x + 3 = -2x + 45$
D. set $-2x + 45 - x + 3 = 1$

**9.** What is the slope-intercept form of this equation: $2y + 12 = 2x$?

A. $y = 6 - x$ C. $y = x - 6$
B. $y = x + 6$ D. $y + 6 = x$

**10.** For $2y + 12 = 2x$, if $x = 0$, what is the value of $y$?

A. –6 B. 6 C. 12 D. –12

**11.** For $x + y = 315$, if $x$ is equal to 300, what is the value of $y$?

A. 315 C. 15
B. 300 D. 16

**12.** For the lines $y = 7x - 7$ and $y = 2x + 8$, what is the $x$-value at the intersecting point?

A. $\frac{15}{4}$ B. $\frac{1}{5}$ C. –3 D. 3

**13.** What is the solution for the system of linear equations $y = 7x - 7$ and $y = 2x + 8$?

A. $(\frac{15}{4}, \frac{31}{2})$ C. $(-3, 2)$
B. $(\frac{1}{5}, 8\frac{2}{5})$ D. $(3, 14)$

**14.** What is the algebraic expression of "function of $x$ is seventeen times $x$, plus two"?

A. $f(x) = 17x + 2$ C. $f(x) = 15x$
B. $f(x) = 17x - 2$ D. $f(x) = 15x - 2$

**15.** What is the slope-intercept form of this equation: $2y + 4x = 16$?

A. $y = 2x - 16$ C. $y = 2x + 8$
B. $y = -2x + 8$ D. $y = 2x - 8$

**16.** For $2y + 4x = 14$, if $y = -1$, what is the value of $x$?

A. 3 B. −3 C. 4 D. −4

**17.** What is the algebraic expression of "fifty times $x$ minus two equals function of $x$"?

A. $f(x) = 50x + 2$ C. $48x = f(x)$
B. $50x - 2 = f(x)$ D. $52x - x = f(x)$

**18.** What is the slope-intercept form of this equation: $y - 16x = 73$?

A. $y = -16x + 73$
B. $y = -16x - 73$
C. $y = 16x + 73$
D. $y = 16x - 73$

**19.** For $y - 16x = 73$, if $x = 1$ what is the value of $y$?

A. 89 C. 85
B. 98 D. 57

**20.** What is the algebraic expression of "function of $x$ is $x$ plus 17"?

A. $f(x) = -x - 17$ C. $f(x) = x + 17$
B. $f(x) = x - 17$ D. $x = x + 17$

**21.** What is the slope-intercept form of this equation: $y - 6x = 144$?

A. $y = -6x + 144$ C. $y = 6x - 144$
B. $y = 6x + 144$ D. $y = -6x - 144$

**22.** What is the slope-intercept form of this equation: $3y - 6x = 18$?

A. $y = 2x + 18$ C. $3y = 2x + 18$
B. $y = 2x + 6$ D. $y = 2x - 6$

**23.** For $3y - 6x = 18$, if $y = 2$, what is the value of $x$?

A. 2 C. 4
B. −2 D. −3

**24.** For the lines $y + 2x = 13$ and $y + x = -9$, what is the $x$-value at the intersecting point?

A. 4 C. 21
B. 22 D. −22

**25.** What is the solution for the system of linear equations $y + 2x = 13$ and $y + x = -9$?

A. $(4, -13)$ C. $(21, -30)$
B. $(22, -31)$ D. $(-21, 30)$

**26.** What is the slope-intercept form of this equation: $2y + 64x = 16$?

A. $y = -32x + 8$ C. $2y = -32x - 8$
B. $2y = -64x + 8$ D. $y = -32x - 8$

# Unit 4 Reflection

## MATH SKILLS

The easiest part about solving linear equations is

Graphing equations is useful because

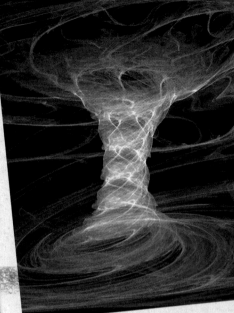

Extremes of Nature

## MATH STRATEGIES & CONNECTIONS

For me, the math strategies that work the best are

I can use linear equations to find intercepts by

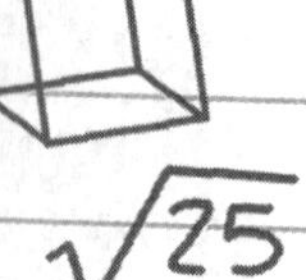


## READING STRATEGIES & COMPREHENSION

The easiest part about previewing is

One way that predicting helps me with reading is

The vocabulary words I had trouble with are

## INDEPENDENT READING

My favorite part of Extremes of Nature is

I read most fluently when

# GLOSSARY UNITS 1–4

## A

**absolute value** (AB-suh-loot VAL-yoo): the distance that a number is from zero on a number line (p. 104)

**additive inverse** (AD-uh-tiv IN-vurs): the opposite of a number (p. 111)

## B

**bar graph** (bahr graf): a way of comparing information using rectangular bars (p. 18)

## C

**circle graph** (SUR-kul graf): a graph shaped like a circle that shows a whole broken into parts (p. 18)

**combination** (kahm-buh-NAY-shun): a group of objects in which order does not matter (p. 8)

**concept map** (KAHN-sept map): a graphic organizer showing a main topic and related ideas (p. 10)

**consistent system** (kun-SIS-tunt SIS-tum): a system of linear equations that has at least one solution (p. 221)

**coordinate grid** (koh-AWR-duh-nit grid): a grid showing ordered pairs (p. 18)

**cross product** (kraws PRAHD-ukt): the products of numbers or expressions diagonally across from each other in a proportion; in $\frac{a}{b} = \frac{c}{d}$ the products of *ad* and *bc* are equal (p. 24)

## D

**data** (DAYT-uh): information gathered from surveys or experiments (p. 79)

**discount** (DIS-kownt): the difference between the original price and the sale price of an item (p. 42)

## E

**equation** (ee-KWAY-zhun): a mathematical sentence with an equal sign (p. 141)

**equivalent equations** (ee-KWIV-uh-lunt ee-KWAY-zhunz): equations with the same solutions (p. 159)

**expression** (ek-SPRESH-un): a mathematical statement (p. 4)

## F

**flowchart** (FLOH-chahrt): a diagram that can be used to show the steps in a process (p. 10)

**function** (FUNGK-shun): a relation that assigns exactly one value in the range (set of all values of *y*) to each value of the domain (set of all values of *x*) (p. 184)

## G

**graph** (graf): a visual display that shows data in different ways (p. 68)

## H

**histogram** (HIS-tuh-gram): a graph that shows how many items occur between two numbers; used to display large amounts of data (p. 79)

## I

**inconsistent system** (in-kun-SIS-tunt SIS-tum): a system of linear equations that does not have a solution (p. 221)

**integers** (IN-tuh-jurz): the set of positive whole numbers, their opposites, and zero (p. 104)

**interest rate** (IN-trist rayt): the percentage of the balance that an account or investment earns in a fixed period of time (p. 42)

**inverse operations** (in-VURS ahp-uh-RAY-shunz): operations that undo one another (p. 141)

## L

**linear equation** (LIN-ee-ur ee-KWAY-zhun): a two-variable expression, usually *x* and *y*, that when graphed forms a straight line (p. 41)

**linear function** (LIN-ee-ur FUNGK-shun): a function that has a constant rate of change and can be modeled by a straight line (p. 184)

## O

**ordered pair** (AWR-durd pehr): a pair of numbers that names one point on a coordinate grid (p. 18)

## P

**pattern** (PAT-urn): objects, designs, or numbers that change in a specific way (p. 6)

**percent** (pur-SENT): a ratio that compares a number to 100; the symbol for percent is % (p. 31)

**percent decrease** (pur-SENT DEE-krees): percent less than an original number (p. 31)

**percent increase** (pur-SENT IN-krees): percent more than an original number (p. 31)

**perimeter** (puh-RIM-uh-tur): the distance around the outside of a shape (p. 16)

**physical model** (FIZ-ih-kul MAHD-ul): a real-life representation of an object (p. 4)

**plot** (plaht): to find and mark the point named by an ordered pair (p. 18)

**proportion** (pruh-PAWR-shun): an equation stating that two ratios are equal (p. 24)

## R

**rate** (rayt): a ratio that compares two quantities measured in different units (p. 68)

**ratio** (RAY-shee-oh): a comparison of two numbers by division (p. 24)

**rational number** (RASH-uh-nul NUM-bur): any number that can be written as a ratio or fraction ($\frac{a}{b}$) where *a* and *b* are integers and *b* is not zero (p. 104)

**rule** (rool): a description of the way a pattern works (p. 6)

## S

**sales tax** (saylz taks): a tax that is a percentage of the price of an item (p. 47)

**scale** (skayl): numbers that are the units used on a bar graph (p. 18)

**scale drawing** (skayl DRAW-ing): an enlarged or reduced drawing of an object that is similar to the actual object (p. 61)

**scale factor** (skayl FAK-tur): the ratio of the dimensions of the image to the dimensions of the original figure (p. 61)

**similar figures** (SIM-uh-lur FIG-yurz): two figures are similar if their corresponding angles have the same measure and the lengths of their corresponding sides are proportional; The symbol ~ means “is a similar to” (p. 61)

**slope** (slohp): a ratio that describes the tilt of a line (p. 68)

**slope-intercept form** (slohp IN-tur-sept fawrm): $y = mx + b$, where *m* is the slope and *b* is the *y*-intercept of the line (p. 191)

**strategy** (STRAT-uh-jee): a plan or way of doing something (p. 4)

**system of linear equations** (SYS-tum uv LIN-ee-ur ee-KWAY-zhunz): two or more linear equations using the same variables (p. 184)

## T

**three-column chart** (three KAHL-um chahrt): a chart that can be used to take notes or organize ideas (p. 10)

**tree diagram** (tree DY-uh-gram): a diagram that shows possible combinations branching off each other (p. 8)

## V

**variable** (VEHR-ee-uh-bul): a letter that stands for a number; the value of an algebraic expression varies, or changes, depending on the value of the letter given to the variable (p. 141)

**Venn diagram** (ven DY-uh-gram): overlapping circles used to compare and contrast ideas (p. 10)

## X

**x-axis** (eks AK-sis): the horizontal axis of the coordinate plane (p. 68)

**x-intercept** (eks IN-tur-sept): the *x*-coordinate of the point where the line crosses the *x*-axis (p. 202)

## Y

***y*-axis** (wy AK-sis): the vertical axis of the coordinate plane (p. 68)

***y*-intercept** (wy IN-tur-sept): the *y*-coordinate of the point where the line crosses the *y*-axis (p. 191)

## STAFF CREDITS

Josh Adams, Amanda Aranowski, Mel Benzinger, Karen Blonigen, Carol Bowling, Sarah Brandel, Kazuko Collins, Nancy Condon, Barb Drewlo, Sue Gulsvig, Daren Hastings, Laura Henrichsen, Ruby Hogen-Chin, Becky Johnson, Julie Johnston, Jody Manderfeld, Carol Nelson, Heather Oakley-Thompson, Carrie O'Connor, Deb Rogstad, Marie Schaefle, Julie Theisen, LeAnn Velde, Mike Vineski, Peggy Vlahos, Charmaine Whitman, Sue Will

## PHOTO AND ILLUSTRATION CREDITS

Cover: background, © Yurok/Shutterstock; foreground, © Tischenko Irina/Shutterstock; bottom, © Blanche Branton/Shutterstock; p.1: background, © Jack Hollingsworth/Stockbyte/Getty Images; top left background, © Yurok/Shutterstock; top left foreground, © Tischenko Irina/Shutterstock; top left bottom, © Blanche Branton/Shutterstock; p. 20: top left background, © Yurok/Shutterstock; top left foreground, © Tischenko Irina/Shutterstock; top left bottom, © Blanche Branton/Shutterstock; bottom, © JuiceDrops; background, © Jack Hollingsworth/Stockbyte/Getty Images; top left, © Tischenko Irina/Shutterstock; p. 23, © Joseph/Shutterstock; p. 76, © David P. Lewis/Shutterstock; p. 78, © Map Resources; p. 98: top right © Tischenko Irina/Shutterstock; bottom, © JuiceDrops; p. 99, background, © Jack Hollingsworth/Stockbyte/Getty Images; top left, © Blanche Branton/Shutterstock; p. 101, © Mike Veitch/Alamy; p. 111, © Laurin Rinder/Shutterstock; p. 122 © William Casey/Shutterstock; p. 130, © David Guyler/Shutterstock; p. 156, © Michael G Smith; p. 167, © Scott Rothstein/Shutterstock; p. 178: top right, © Blanche Branton/Shutterstock; bottom, © JuiceDrops; p. 179: background, © Jack Hollingsworth/Stockbyte/Getty Images; top left, © Yurok/Shutterstock; p. 180, OAR/ERL/National Severe Storms Laboratory (NSSL); p. 181, NOAA Photo Library, NOAA Central Library; OAR/ERL/National Severe Storms Laboratory (NSSL); p. 258: top right, © Yurok/Shutterstock; bottom, © JuiceDrops

All coach characters: KATMO